PUZZLE THEM FIRST!

Motivating Adolescent Readers With Question-Finding

A. Vincent Ciardiello

INTERNATIONAL
Reading Association
800 BARKSDALE ROAD, PO BOX 8139
NEWARK, DE 19714-8139, USA
www.reading.org

The International Reading Association attempts, through its publications, to provide a forum for a wide spectrum of opinions on reading. This policy permits divergent viewpoints without implying the endorsement of the Association.

Executive Editor, Books   Corinne M. Mooney
Developmental Editor   Charlene M. Nichols
Developmental Editor   Tori Mello Bachman
Developmental Editor   Stacey Lynn Sharp
Editorial Production Manager   Shannon T. Fortner
Production Manager   Iona Muscella
Supervisor, Electronic Publishing   Anette Schuetz

Project Editors   Charlene M. Nichols and Amy Messick

Cover   Design: Linda Steere; Photo: © Corbis

Library of Congress Cataloging-in-Publication Data

Ciardiello, A. Vincent, 1941-
  Puzzle them first! : Motivating adolescent readers with question-finding / A. Vincent Ciardiello.
     p. cm.
  Includes bibliographical references and index.
  ISBN-13: 978-0-87207-581-8
  1. Questioning. 2. Critical thinking--Study and teaching. 3. Teaching--Methodology. I. Title.
  LB1027.44.C53 2006
  371.39--dc22

                                                                    2006022723

To my wife, children, and grandchildren

Marie

Debra

Susan

Christopher

Valerie

Brian

Samantha

United in faith
Encouraged by hope
Together with love.

CONTENTS

ABOUT THE AUTHOR

A. Vincent Ciardiello is an associate professor in the Teacher Education Program at Iona College in New Rochelle, New York, USA. As a National Council for Accreditation of Teacher Education program, Iona's Education Department offers bachelor's and master's degrees in teacher education. Vincent teaches courses in social studies methods and literacy and learning in the content areas for adolescent learners.

Vincent earned his Master of Arts from Hunter College of the City University of New York and his doctoral degree in language, literacy, and learning from Fordham University. The focus of his doctoral research was student questioning strategies.

Vincent has taught for 32 years in the New York City public school system. He has taught middle and high school students in fields such as social studies, language arts, mathematics, and foreign language (Italian). He has also trained high school teachers in implementing student questioning strategies in their classrooms.

Vincent is the author of several articles on classroom questioning, critical literacy, text structure comprehension, case-based instruction, cooperative learning, and multicultural education. His articles have appeared in the *Journal of Adolescent & Adult Literacy*, *The Reading Teacher*, *Educational Forum*, *Social Studies and the Young Learner*, *The Clearing House*, and *Magazine of History: Organization of American Historians*.

Vincent and his wife, Marie, have two daughters and three grandchildren. Vincent enjoys ballroom dancing with Marie and watching movie musicals and suspense classics.

PREFACE

There is no agency in the world today that is so seriously affecting the health, education, efficiency and the character of boys and girls as the cigarette habit. Nearly every delinquent is a cigarette smoker.... This great wave of crime is due to the use of cigarettes and nothing else. And Dr. Forbes Winslow says, "Cigarette smoking is one of the chief causes of insanity."

(Alva B. Jones, Superintendent of National Cigarette Law Enforcement League, Letter to President Herbert Hoover, May 25, 1929; U.S. National Archives, Washington, DC)

This book begins with an unusual warning about cigarette smoking. It is not your typical health warning. It associates cigarette smoking and crime. The puzzling warning appeared in a letter written to President Herbert Hoover by an administrator of an organization known as the National Cigarette Law Enforcement League. When I presented this letter as a primary source document in a unit on the 1920s to my 11th graders in American history, they were provoked and truly puzzled. I presented this puzzling document to stimulate the students to generate questions about the "crime wave" among adolescents during what was called the "roaring '20s" in the United States. And I succeeded. My generally reticent students wanted to know the origin of this puzzling document and began asking questions such as, "Do they have given proof that [smoking] cigarettes is the blame or reasons why these waves of crime are happening?" "What does a cigarette have in it to cause someone to commit a crime?" "How many of them do they have to smoke to get insane?"

In this book, I propose a provocative statement that to truly learn something one must be bewildered or puzzled about new knowledge. Advanced learning begins in a state of puzzlement. It is my premise that there is strong educational value in creating cognitive confusion in students' minds so they are driven to ask challenging questions to offset the mental disequilibrium created by the puzzling situation. This premise is based on years of research in the field of student questioning behavior, including my own (Berlyne & Frommer, 1966; Chin, Brown, & Bruce, 2002; Chin & Chia, 2004; Ciardiello, 1990, 1998, 2003; Costa, Caldeira, Gallastegui, & Otero, 2000; J.T. Dillon, 1998; Graesser & McMahen, 1993; Graesser & Olde, 2003; van der Meij, 1998).

There also is educational value in asking open-ended questions that continue to keep one mentally "off-balance." These provocative ideas challenge traditional pedagogical thinking that views learning as a quest to follow fixed and predetermined routes to answers and solutions. One of my high school students, Eduardo (pseudonym), recognized very early in his schooling that he would follow the "uncertain" path to literacy learning. He related to me that he always liked asking questions, beginning from when he was very young. He was always raising his hand in class. He also stated that he thought it was unusual for a student to be able to write questions instead of answer them. Eduardo was filled with questions and especially liked questions that had no answers. He wanted to know about everything, even though there were some things he could not know readily. He still wanted to ask questions that had no answers.

Eduardo's musings became my inspiration. Can students learn from just asking questions—even ones that may never have answers? This kind of thinking goes against the grain of traditional education, which calls for answers, finality, and solutions—not more questions. But how do teachers get adolescent students to begin to ask unanswerable questions? It is difficult enough to get adolescents to ask traditional questions (ones with final answers) in class. Researchers explain that there appears to be a classroom norm or constraint against student questioning (J.T. Dillon, 1988; van der Meij, 1998). My own teaching experiences and research also show that adolescents are quite reluctant to ask questions in class (Ciardiello, 1990, 1998, 2003). Over the years, I have used cognitive-based prompts and procedures to try to offset this inhibition to student questioning. These scaffolds included cue cards with signal words on them and model question types for generating questions (Ciardiello, 1998). With this in mind, let me begin with my own journey in education that started with questions—some that had answers and some that did not.

My Journey: Who Am I?

I am the middle child in a family of five and was born in the Bronx, New York, USA. I attended public schools in New York City and later attended the City University and obtained a Bachelor of Arts in history. I continued my education, obtaining a master's degree in social science education and a PhD in language, literacy, and learning from Hunter College and Fordham University, respectively. After my graduation from college, I started a career in public school teaching that continued for 30 years. During these three decades, I taught adolescents in middle school and high school in the Bronx.

Why Did I Become a Teacher?

This is one of those questions that has many possible answers. Yes, I liked attending school as a child. But I enjoyed playtime much more. Did I like to read? Yes, but not school books. Did I like being with children? Yes, but is that enough reason to become a teacher? Did my family encourage or support my goals? Not really. No one in my immediate or extended family was a teacher—or, for that matter, ever attended college. Was it a love of learning? Perhaps. I was always curious about current events. I enjoyed watching the evening news with my father on a 10-inch, black-and-white television. Still, if I had had my way, I would have preferred watching the cartoon characters Tom and Jerry rather than news anchors Huntley and Brinkley. So, why did I become a teacher? Was teaching a calling? Now, this is one of those unanswerable questions for me, but it is still worth asking as I continue to teach preservice and inservice teachers.

Why Did I Write This Book?

When I attended high school many years ago, I didn't ask questions in class. Nor were my classroom teachers very encouraging. Asking questions was their business. Many years later, the situation has not changed that much. As Eduardo (referenced earlier) remarked, he, too, was not encouraged to ask questions in class.

During my own preservice and inservice teacher training, none of my mentors ever provided staff development in the area of student questioning techniques. All of the training was in teacher questioning techniques. They mentioned how important teacher questioning was and they provided training in this area. After more than 20 years of teaching adolescents at the middle school level, I decided to get a doctoral degree in the area of language, literacy, and learning. I selected teacher questioning as my dissertation topic. As I progressed in my studies, I began to realize that teacher questioning was only one part of the role of inquiry in the classroom. At this point, I began to focus on the neglected other part, student questioning. But the field of student questioning was virgin territory in the literature. It was then that I decided to train myself in the protocols of student questioning. I read every study available in the field and decided that perhaps I could add to the literature through my own doctoral dissertation study. At this point in my educational career, I became a supervisor of social studies teachers in a high school in the South Bronx. My new position provided me with the opportunity to field-test my ideas and do research on student questioning. My schedule included teaching a few classes and also training inservice teachers in effective teaching practices. Student questioning would be one of those effective teaching practices. My research in this field led to a PhD and the publication of articles in education journals.

As I mentioned, I continue to train preservice and inservice teachers in student questioning as an associate professor of teacher education. I decided to write this book to share my knowledge and experience in order to help preservice and inservice teachers learn a new way of conceptualizing and applying student questioning behaviors in the field of literacy instruction across the curriculum. I developed a strategy for adolescent literacy that breaks down the conventions of passive student questioning behavior and reduces the social constraints of student engagement in classrooms. As indicated earlier, this questioning strategy was inspired by an adolescent student's active and welcoming search for self-discovery questions. I call the strategy question-finding (Ciardiello, 2003).

What Is Question-Finding?

Question-finding is a specific manifestation of student questioning behavior. It is student questioning generated by discrepant materials and anomalous situations that create a state of puzzlement in students. There are other generators of student questioning that are not induced primarily by perplexing events. Questions can be generated through what Schank (1979) characterizes as "absolutely interesting things" in life such as disease, death, sex, romance, and power (p. 280). Of course, these innately interesting events can be perplexing to students. But they are not experiences central to the curriculum of academic learning.

Question-finding allows students to probe more deeply into the multiple and ambiguous meanings of text. Students are instructed in a process of search behavior to uncover questions within the layers of text. It is a novel way of conceptualizing questioning in terms of knowledge construction from puzzling or anomalous data. It helps students find reflective questions. The purpose of this book is to develop insights into the process of question-finding.

My Research on Question-Finding

For most of my teaching career with adolescents, I have used inquiry learning in my classrooms. I have taught adolescent students how to generate questions from counterintuitive topics in social studies. In addition, I have taught secondary school teachers how to encourage their students to generate questions from discrepant materials and resources, which became the basis of my dissertation. Currently, as an associate professor of education, I train preservice and inservice teachers in using the strategy of question-finding. Preservice teachers in my course are required in their field experience assignments to tutor and, wherever possible, to teach the strategy to their classes.

I did my research in an inner-city vocational high school in which the reading scores of the students were well below average. The high school juniors who made up the sample averaged 43.2% as a national percentile, five percentiles below the mean. Nearly all the students in the high school were African American and Hispanic. In this vocational school, the students took a core of academic subjects plus subjects in their majors in business, cosmetology, or health services.

My research supports other studies that indicate that all students can be taught to ask both low- and high-level cognitive questions after a relatively brief period of formal instruction (Allison & Shrigley, 1982; Davey & McBride, 1986; King &

Rosenshine, 1993; Risko & Feldman, 1986). I used a similar time frame (two weeks) to teach my students using direct instruction and inquiry methods. The studies just cited agree that students do not ask higher levels of questions without some period of direct instruction. The results of my study also indicated that students from an inner-city high school can be taught to ask different cognitive levels of questions. Indeed, they generated more questions and at different levels of cognition than they were required to do on the final assessment. More recently, an empirical investigation by Taboada and Guthrie (2006) confirmed that younger students (i.e., third and fourth graders) with low-level content knowledge (as well as those with high-level content knowledge) receive the cognitive benefits (e.g., improvement in reading comprehension) of instruction in generating questions.

I have also learned that documents and artifacts that create puzzlement through the use of discrepant or counterintuitive information can stimulate students to generate questions. (Throughout this book, the terms *discrepant* and *counterintuitive* are often used interchangeably.) Discrepant or counterintuitive information is any data that appear surprising, unexpected, or against the norm. For example, when my students read a discrepant letter written by three teenage girls concerning the induction of Elvis Presley into the U.S. Army (see Figure 4 in chapter 1, page 15), they were mentally thrown off balance. In follow-up interviews, some students expressed bewilderment or refused to believe that the letter was real. They called it "weird" that young girls would write this and even weirder that the presidential library or National Archives would have saved the letter. This state of puzzlement stimulated students to generate questions. The generation of questions consisted of the use of both cognitive and metacognitive skills as the students not only created different levels of questions, but also reflected on the nature of their own thinking through their questions.

How Can Question–Finding Improve Adolescent Literacy?

This book attempts to address some of the concerns of the Adolescent Literacy Commission of the International Reading Association (IRA; Moore, Bean, Birdyshaw, & Rycik, 1999). A major concern is the development of advanced literacy skills, which include student self-questioning. Indeed, the commission report provides an explicit model of a self-questioning strategy demonstrated by a fictional seventh-grade language arts teacher, Mrs. Mangrum. Using the adolescent novel *Roll of Thunder, Hear My Cry* (Taylor, 1976), Mrs. Mangrum modeled high-level queries such as, "I wonder why Cassie didn't complain to her teacher about the school bus driver running them off the road?" (Moore et al., p. 104). Then the teacher provided written guides for student self-questioning, and soon the students were exploring and experimenting with the strategy on their own. This kind of explicit instruction in self-questioning training is similar to what I did with my high school students in social studies (Ciardiello, 1998). Both Mrs. Mangrum and I provided scaffolded experiences in self-questioning in which we both gradually released the responsibility for the implementation of the strategy to the learners themselves. As the commission recommends, adolescents deserve instruction in learning strategies that build on the skill and desire to read increasingly complex material. Question-finding satisfies this desire and need. Question-finding also addresses the Adolescent Literacy Commission's recommendation that young people deserve new perspectives on what it means to know a subject. Content area experts themselves use this process when they find new evidence to challenge their initial assumptions.

Other literacy organizations in addition to IRA have recommended the strategy of generating questions to assist adolescent literacy learning. The National Reading Panel (National Institute of Child Health and Human Development [NICHD], 2000) and the Alliance for Excellent Education (Kamil, 2003) both selected generating questions as one of eight major strategies that promotes literacy comprehension. Indeed, the National Reading Panel stated that the "strongest scientific evidence was found for the effectiveness of asking readers to generate questions during reading" (pp. 44–45). Much of the research cited to support generating questions emanates from the highly regarded meta-analysis by Rosenshine, Meister, and Chapman (1996). This analysis of 30 experimentally based studies on generating questions in different subject areas and across grade levels (which ranged from third grade to college) revealed that the effects of this strategy on literacy (comprehension) are consistent over subjects and grade levels. Indeed, generating questions is an extremely flexible and beneficial strategy because it is easily adaptable to a variety of curricula already in place and for all age groups (Meltzer, Smith, & Clark, 2001; Pressley, Duke, & Boling, 2004).

The crisis in adolescent literacy as envisioned by the IRA Adolescent Literacy Commission is the kind of counterintuitive event that in itself stimulates the process of question-finding. In the traditional sense, educators do not expect literacy instruction to address the academic literacy problems of adolescents in middle and high schools. Traditional educational thinking views literacy instruction as only suitable for younger children. Educators typically believe that middle and high school teachers are in the business of teaching content, and that advanced literacy skills come with the acquisition of content knowledge. Content area literacy educators challenge this idea and believe that advanced literacy skills need to be taught directly as part of subject knowledge (Vacca & Alvermann, 1998). Thus, this counterintuitive situation prompts the following questions:

- What benefits could adolescents get from literacy instruction?
- Does literacy instruction in the content area draw away from valuable class time?
- How can content area teachers be trained to teach advanced literacy skills?

The question-finding strategy promotes continued literacy development beyond elementary school. Preadolescents in the upper elementary grades can benefit from instruction in question-finding. Indeed, research indicates that preadolescents also have difficulty reading and interpreting content area texts and need instructional strategies to help them become more engaged in their own learning (Strickland & Alvermann, 2004). Question-finding can help preadolescents and adolescents deal more intelligently with advanced content knowledge in different subject areas. Question-finding offers this opportunity by providing an excursion into what Freire (1994) calls the "deep web of events to get at a true critical explanation of the why of things" (p. 119).

Question-finding also addresses the changing motivational and affective needs of adolescents. Adolescence is a time of change in which young people tend to lose interest in academic subjects. Indeed, this is a period of loss for the wonder of formal learning that characterizes the intellectual state of young children. A high school biology teacher recognized this dilemma when he expressed that one of his main educational objectives was to "strive to stimulate kids' sense of wonder and curiosity" (as cited in D.R. Dillon, 2000, p. 25). On the other hand, adolescence is also a time of growth in the capacity to consider multiple perspectives on a topic and the ability to adjust to the ambiguity of text (Eccles & Roeser, 2003). Question-finding requires that students be able to detect anomalies and deal with ambiguities. Last, question-finding provides literacy opportunities for adolescents to continue their growth into becoming independent readers and inquirers. Indeed, it satisfies the desires of adolescents to investigate self-selected questions.

Organization of the Book

This book is organized around the process of question-finding. It consists of five chapters that address different literacy and inquiry dimensions of question-finding noted in the graphic overview on the following page.

Chapter 1 introduces the topic of question-finding and the cognitive and metacognitive interventions that are needed for its successful execution. Chapter 2 highlights the motivational and affective dimension of question-finding. Motivation is the engine that drives the question-finding mechanism. Chapter 3 focuses on the critical literacy dimensions of question-finding. This chapter is sequential because the motivation to challenge or interrogate texts engenders the formation of critical

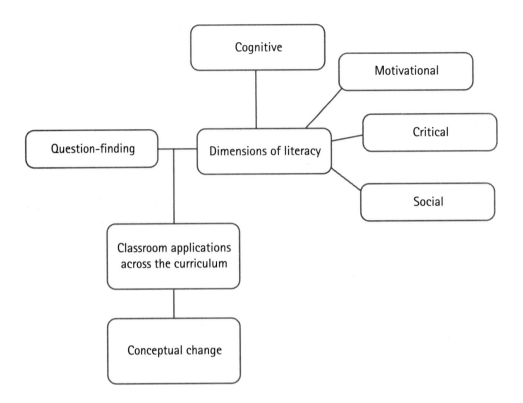

questing skills. Chapter 4 highlights the social literacy dimensions of question-finding, which includes the sociocognitive, sociocultural, and sociolinguistic aspects of social literacy. In several respects, social literacy is an allied dimension of critical literacy. Both of these dimensions challenge the traditional notion that text has an interior life of its own and is not influenced by cultural and social factors. By itself, however, social literacy has an impact on question-finding to such an extent that it warrants its own exploration and investigation. Chapter 5, which focuses on conceptual change, culminates the inquiry process of question-finding; it is through students' self-selected questions that they begin to review and alter their initial misconceptions on a topic.

In this book, question-finding is demonstrated across the curriculum. Specifically, the focus is on its implications and practices in the core subjects of the adolescent education curriculum, including language arts, social studies, mathematics, science, and physical education. I chose to focus on these areas because they are the most universal in the curriculum and are studied every day in school. Further, most research on student questioning for adolescents has been done in these areas.

A list of major concepts and specialized terms appears at the beginning of each chapter; these terms appear in boldface on first mention in each chapter. In addition, within each chapter there are stopping points to pause and ponder the relationship between question-finding and the targeted literacy dimension. Some of these stopping points are tied to the content surrounding them and some are more general in nature; all of them are intended to give readers an opportunity to pause and ponder. At the end of each chapter, there are activities for pondering and practicing the process of question-finding as it relates to each literacy dimension. These detailed reflections and activities also serve to reinforce the concept and extend the application of question-finding across the curriculum. They are important resources to enhance the professional development of content area teachers in implementing a novel approach to academic literacy and learning.

This book uses multimedia resources including digital artifacts, personal family photographs and stories, students' letters, classroom vignettes, literary excerpts, newspaper articles and editorials, humorous anecdotes, and political cartoons. Also included are short bibliographies for further reading about various aspects of the question-finding process.

The appendixes contain a number of useful resources to aid in developing and executing the question-finding strategy. Appendix A consists of an annotated list of materials and resources that foster question-finding by genre, including autobiographies, children's literature, young adult novels, photography, and electronic books. Appendix B consists of a template or conceptual guide that is based on question-finding procedures and a sample lesson plan that incorporates the template and demonstrates the strategy. Appendix C includes everyday motivational sources for question-finding, and Appendix D includes quotations from noted scholars and educators on major concepts related to the question-finding process.

Last, a glossary of the important concepts and specialized terms from each chapter appears at the end of the book.

This preface attempts to place in the foreground the multidimensional nature of the question-finding process. In the following chapters, each of the varied dimensions of question-finding is presented across the adolescent curriculum. To assist content area teachers with this novel experience, I suggest focus units that contain varied resources and engaging materials. It is my hope that teachers find the question-finding experience not only provocative but also practical in its classroom applications.

Acknowledgments

I am deeply grateful for the assistance of CELTIC, the Center for the Enhancement of Learning and Teaching, at Iona College. Coordinator Diana Breen and her staff, including Dsarieme Uwaifo and Rochelle Milke, have been most helpful with computer-assisted instruction related to graphics and photographs. I am also indebted to Ed Helmrich and the interlibrary loan staff at Iona who diligently satisfied my numerous requests for journals and books. I offer a special thanks to my editors at the International Reading Association—Matthew W. Baker, former editorial director of the books program, as well as Charlene M. Nichols and Corinne Mooney of the books program—for their wise counsel and eager support of the manuscript through its various stages of development. Last, I wish to thank my most enthusiastic supporter and diligent proofreader, my lovely wife, Marie.

"How do you expect me to learn anything when you're the one who keeps asking all the questions?"

CHAPTER 1

The Cognitive–Based Literacy Dimension of Question–Finding

IMPORTANT CONCEPTS AND SPECIALIZED TERMS

anomalous event
cognitive-based literacy
conceptual conflict
convergent thinking
counterintuitive
discrepant event
divergent thinking

epistemic curiosity
interrogative mood
precognitive state of doubt
procedural prompts
puzzlement
puzzlement questions
  (awareness type)

puzzlement questions
  (explanation type)
question-finding
rival hypotheses
second-guessing
wonderment questions

I have been trying to teach without books. There was one heady moment when I was able to excite the class by an idea: I had put on the blackboard Browning's "A man's reach should exceed his grasp, or what's a heaven for?" and we got involved in a spirited discussion of aspiration vs. reality. Is it wise, I asked, to aim higher than one's capacity? Does it not doom one to failure? No, no, some said, that's ambition and progress! No, no, others cried, that's frustration and defeat! What about hope? What about despair? You've got to be practical!—You've got to have a dream! They said this in their own words, you understand, startled into discovery.

(Kaufman, 1964, p. 55)

This quote from Syl, a fictional high school language arts teacher in the popular novel *Up the Down Staircase*, provides a relevant introduction to **question-finding**. The English teacher tried something **counterintuitive**—to teach without books and to get her students excited about an idea. Notice how the teacher set up a cognitive-constructivist learning situation in which her students generated their own authentic questions and responses. Notice also how her students were motivated to discuss an idea and were startled into discovery learning.

Another fictional language arts teacher, represented in IRA's Adolescent Literacy Commission report (Moore et al., 1999) but this time working in a middle school, also used a **cognitive-based literacy** approach to generating questions and inquiry learning. (See Table 1 for resources on cognitive-based literacy.) Mrs. Mangrum (the teacher first introduced in the Preface) modeled how to generate questions from *Roll of Thunder, Hear My Cry* (Taylor, 1976), a young adult novel that her middle school students were reading as a class project. She used a cognitive-based and constructivist literacy approach involving direct and explicit instruction to assist her students in self-questioning. For example, she modeled the following query: "I wonder why Cassie didn't complain to her teacher about the school bus driver running them off the road?" (Moore et al., 1999, p. 104). In her explicit modeling, Mrs. Mangrum was concerned with her individual students' acts of constructing meaning. The individual students themselves would construct the new knowledge, with the guidance of their teacher. The Adolescent Literacy Commission of the IRA praised her efforts (Moore et al.).

Neither teacher followed a traditional pattern of literacy instruction in which students find answers to questions that are essentially "planted" in the textbooks. There is no mystery as to where the answers are; it is just a matter of locating them (M.C. Wells, 1996). There are ways to provide mystery and discovery in

TABLE 1. Resources on Cognitive-Based Literacy

Carrver, S.M. (1995). Cognitive apprenticeships: Putting theory into practice on a large scale. In C.N. Hedley, P. Antonacci, & M. Rabinowitz (Eds.), *Thinking and literacy: The mind at work* (pp. 203–228). Hillsdale, NJ: Erlbaum.

Cobb, P. (2005). Where is the mind? A coordinator of sociocultural and cognitive constructivist perspectives. In C.T. Fosnot (Ed.), *Constructivism: Theory, perspectives, and practices* (2nd ed., pp. 39–57). New York: Teachers College Press.

Dole, J.A., & Sinatra, G.M. (1998). Reconceptualizing change in the cognitive construction of knowledge. *Educational Psychologist*, 33(2/3), 109–128.

Hayes, J.R. (1992). A psychological perspective applied to literacy studies. In R. Beach, J.L. Green, M.L. Kamil, & T. Shanahan (Eds.), *Multidisciplinary perspectives on literacy research* (pp. 125–139). Urbana, IL: National Conference on Research in English & National Council of Teachers of English.

Herber, H.L. (1978). *Teaching reading in the content areas* (2nd ed.). Englewood Cliffs, NJ: Prentice Hall.

Manzo, A.V., Manzo, U.C., & Estes, T.H. (2001). *Content area literacy: Interactive teaching for active learning* (3rd ed.). New York: John Wiley.

Palincsar, A.S., & Brown, A.L. (1984). Reciprocal teaching of comprehension-fostering and comprehension-monitoring activities. *Cognition & Instruction*, 2, 117–175.

Smith, F. (1971). *Understanding reading: A psycholinguistic analysis of reading and learning to read.* New York: Holt, Rinehart and Winston.

Stauffer, R. (1976). *Teaching reading as a thinking process.* New York: Harper & Row.

classroom instruction that involve not just finding prefabricated answers but finding authentic questions to ask. In this chapter, I hope to show **how** the question-finding strategy can help startle your students into a mode of generating questions.

The Question-Finding Strategy

Question-finding is a strategy in which a **discrepant** or **anomalous event** is presented to the student by the teacher in order to arouse curiosity or wonder to stimulate inquiry. (In this book, I use the terms *anomalous* and *discrepant* interchangeably, because they both refer to events that promote **puzzlement**.) The purpose of the strategy is to create a state of puzzlement by presenting information that conflicts with the student's prior knowledge and experiences. The student is prompted to search for questions that can help guide him or her in the quest to resolve the discrepancy. I call this process question-finding because these guide questions are often below the surface or "hidden" (figuratively speaking) within the discrepant event. Questions are naturally embedded within anomalies or discrepant events (Schank, 1988). These emerging questions need to be prompted and directed to the surface. "Hidden" questions are genuine information-seeking questions that probe for meanings beneath the surface of a discrepant event (van der Meij, 1998). For example, an unexpected event occurred during World War I in December 1914, when the soldiers of the opposing Allied powers (i.e., Great Britain, France, Russia, and the United States) and Central powers (i.e., Germany, Austria-Hungary, the Ottoman Empire, and Bulgaria) surprisingly stopped fighting on Christmas Eve (without the permission of their officers), sang carols together, played volleyball, and then began fighting again the day after Christmas. One "hidden" question beneath this discrepant event is, Why did both armies suddenly stop fighting, begin celebrating a holiday together, and then resume combat? The event prompts the learner to ask why the enemies acted in this strange way, thereby prompting the learner to try to explain the reasons for the discrepancy. If the student inquirer is successful, then the inquiry usually ends.

But that is not the only inquiry pathway that can be taken. The student can take a more open-ended stance and search for questions that lead to alternate responses that sustain the inquiry. In another example (noted below), my students traveled both inquiry paths: **convergent thinking** and **divergent thinking** routes. Convergent thinking routes lead to narrow or solution-oriented responses. Divergent thinking routes lead to open-ended or alternative avenues of thinking. When discussing World War II, I used a personal discrepant photograph of my spouse's family "celebrating" Victory in Europe (V-E) Day on their apartment rooftop in New York City on May 8, 1945 (see Figure 1). The army uniforms and "weapons"

FIGURE 1. Personal Discrepant Photo: Celebrating V-E Day on a Rooftop

From Ciardiello, A.V. (2003). "To wander and wonder": Pathways to literacy and inquiry through question-finding. *Journal of Adolescent & Adult Literacy*, 47(3), 229.

that were worn and carried by the people in the photograph, including my future mother-in-law, brother-in-law, and wife, puzzled my students. First, this puzzling photograph stimulated a number of **puzzlement questions (explanation type)** such as, Why were the woman, man, and children dressed in military uniforms on a rooftop? Then, the inquiry broadened to include the following questions: Is this typical behavior for celebrating victory? What do you think the photographer wanted to show us? Can we find out more about the different ways that people celebrated V-E Day? To aid students in their continued search, I recommended the website "New Yorkers Remember V-E Day" (www.newsday.com/community/guide/lihistory/ny-history-ww2ved2,0,4894990.story).

At this site, we found several eyewitness accounts. One of these accounts recorded the testimony of Brooklyn resident Mary Polizzi, who stated, "There were block parties everywhere. And everybody did something to salute the soldiers." Apparently my mother-in-law and her family were saluting the Allied victory in their own particular fashion by dressing up as servicemen. This last response satisfied some of my student inquirers. But others wanted to probe more deeply to answer their own questions. The process of question-finding stimulates authentic critical inquiry behavior, because the seekers strive to respond to their own questions. The below-the-surface questions have to be discovered for oneself and may have no known answers (Getzels, 1979).

PAUSE AND PONDER

Question-finding depends on students' recognition of a gap in their knowledge of a subject created by the introduction of a discrepant stimulus. As a result, question-finding usually works best during or after a unit of study when students have acquired enough knowledge to identify discrepancies in content.

• Can you conceive of any time when this process could work at the beginning of a unit of study?

Theoretical Basis of Question–Finding

Many prominent psychologists have established a link between perplexity and cognitive development. Dewey's (1938) theory of uncertainty, Piaget's (1985) theory of equilibration, Festinger's (1957) theory of cognitive dissonance, and Berlyne's (1960) curiosity theory all stress the counterintuitive benefits of surprise and incongruity as sources of knowledge and attitudinal development. Of the above theories, Berlyne's curiosity theory makes the most direct link between puzzlement and student classroom questioning behavior. See Table 2 for a listing of Berlyne's major works on curiosity. Educators will be particularly interested in his work "Curiosity and Education" (1965).

Question-finding is based on Berlyne's (1960, 1965) curiosity theory. Berlyne worked on his groundbreaking research on curiosity throughout the 1950s, 1960s, and 1970s, and his ideas are still considered preeminent in contemporary times (Loewenstein, 1994). Berlyne's curiosity theory contains two important elements that are interrelated: (1) **conceptual conflict** and (2) **epistemic curiosity**. Discrepant events are discordant and puzzling. They derive from what Berlyne (1965) calls conceptual conflict (this term and *cognitive conflict* are often used interchangeably). By the term *conflict*, Berlyne refers not to a struggle between forces,

TABLE 2. Resources on Berlyne's Theory of Conceptual Conflict and Epistemic Curiosity

Berlyne, D.E. (1954). A theory of human curiosity. *The British Journal of Psychology, 45,* 180–191.

Berlyne, D.E. (1960). *Conflict, arousal, and curiosity.* New York: McGraw-Hill.

Berlyne, D.E. (1965). Curiosity and education. In J.D. Krumboltz (Ed.), *Learning and the educational process* (pp. 67–89). Chicago: Rand-McNally.

Berlyne, D.E. (1965). *Structure and direction in thinking.* New York: Wiley.

Berlyne, D.E. (1966). Curiosity and exploration. *Science, 153,* 25–33.

Berlyne, D.E. (1970). Children's reasoning and thinking. In P.H. Mussen (Ed.), *Carmichael's manual of child psychology* (Vol. 1, pp. 939–981). New York: Wiley.

Berlyne, D.E., & Frommer, F. (1966). Some determinants of the incidence and content of children's questions. *Child Development, 37,* 177–189.

Lowenstein, G. (1994). The psychology of curiosity: A review and reinterpretation. *Psychological Bulletin, 116,* 75–98.

but to a contradiction between ideas or events. These include events that are surprising, incongruous, ambiguous, contradictory, and novel. Each of these types of discrepant events leaves the student somewhat puzzled. As mentioned earlier, I use the term *puzzlement* to describe the general state that results from discrepant events and behavior.

Conceptual conflict creates the motivational state of epistemic curiosity. The word *epistemic* refers to a type of behavior in which a student seeks to acquire knowledge. The goal of epistemic curiosity behavior is to acquire new knowledge that will satisfy the student's inquisitiveness about a topic or issue. The student's mind is aroused by discrepant behavior or events. Unusual events perplex the student who searches for information that will attempt to resolve the puzzling situation. The puzzling situation creates the conditions of search behavior for new knowledge. Through the arousal created by discrepant or anomalous conditions, the student is mentally thrown off-balance due to the gap between her or his expectations and the current situation. To restore a sense of equilibrium, the student searches for new knowledge that will reduce these unsettling effects.

Researchers see a major link between discrepant events and questioning behavior (Berlyne & Frommer, 1966; Ciardiello, 1990; J.T. Dillon, 1998; Graesser & McMahen, 1993; Graesser & Olde, 2003; Schank, 1988; van der Meij, 1998). The discrepant event creates a gap in the student's knowledge structure. The student becomes sensitive to and aware of her or his deficiencies about the subject matter. Then, a state of conceptual conflict develops, and a question begins to gnaw at the student. The student is driven to know the reasons for the violations of her or his expectations. Indeed, students are fascinated by discrepant events (Shrigley, 1987). They induce curiosity and set the context for question-finding.

PAUSE AND PONDER

Discrepant events help to generate question-finding behavior. But not all students view discrepant events as puzzling situations. It is important to know that additional factors are instrumental in stimulating conceptual conflict and epistemic curiosity, including students' levels of content area knowledge, personal experiences, sociocultural backgrounds, and sense impressions. For example, in discussing a lesson on the non-Jewish rescuers of Holocaust children, one of my students did not view the rescuers' heroism as an anomalous event. Indeed, the student viewed the rescuers' efforts as normal acts of kindness or humanity. This student could not find questions to ask.

- Do you experience different levels of student perception when it comes to anomalous learning experiences in your content area?
- What kinds of classroom interventions are needed to account for different levels of students' perceptions?

The Question-Finding Process

The question-finding process consists of two stages. In the first stage, which is highly metacognitive, students develop an awareness of the puzzling situation and begin to sense questions related to the puzzlement. In the second stage, which is highly cognitive, students seek new knowledge in order to resolve the puzzling situation, or to reflect even further on the problem.

The First Stage: Becoming Aware of Perplexing Situations and Sensing Puzzlement Questions

Piaget (1977) explains that a state of perplexity is a necessary mental framework for learning. Question-finding begins with a state of perplexity. In this book, perplexity is conceived in terms of surprise and wonder, not bafflement or confusion (J.T. Dillon, 1998). The teacher selects materials of instruction that contain some type of discrepancy or anomaly that sets up a puzzling situation. These learning materials can be of the print or nonprint type. I have used cartoons, photographs, short literary and expository reading passages, and digital primary sources (see Appendix A for a sampling of such materials and resources). The content of the discrepant source should be generally familiar information that has been covered or that is within the students' bank of background knowledge. This is because a state of puzzlement occurs when the student detects a discrepancy between a known fact and new information (van der Meij, 1998). When perplexing material is presented in such a way that it challenges existing beliefs and expectations, students become more sensitive to the gaps in their present knowledge structures. Dewey (1938) describes this orientation as a **precognitive state of doubt**. The perplexed student is set into an **interrogative mood** and is often eager to question the conflict between his or her thinking and the new information (J.T. Dillon, 1998). Berlyne (1954) describes this condition as the "drive to know" (p. 187). This perplexing condition causes a highly metacognitive state in which the student needs to detect the problem and sense the emerging questions. This stage can be defined as the onset or precondition of questioning behavior (Dillon). It is also a highly motivational stage in that the forces at work arouse curiosity and wonderment. See Figure 2 for a graphic representation of the question-finding process. (See Appendix B for a template based on the graphic. The template can be used to scaffold the question-finding process. One of the preservice teachers whom I taught shows how she used the template in her lesson plan, also presented in Appendix B.)

The preliminary or onset stage of question-finding relates to the items represented in the top rectangles of Figure 2 ("puzzling situation" and "awareness of puzzlement"). I have found that many students need strong teacher scaffolding just to develop an awareness of the discrepant event. It is important to keep in mind that it is not the event or situation itself that creates the puzzlement, it is the gap between the student's prior knowledge and beliefs and the new information. This gap leads to conceptual conflict or a condition of mental disequilibrium. If a student's beliefs, worldviews, or ideas do not conflict with the new knowledge, then the puzzlement condition of question-finding does not occur.

It is this mental gap that needs to be filled. There are certain types of questions that the teacher can scaffold for the students to help fill this gap and extend the inquiry process. I call these types of questions **puzzlement questions (awareness type)**; they are metacognitive questions that students ask to express their awareness or detection of the puzzling situation. See Table 3 for characteristics and samples of puzzlement questions (awareness type). What is especially interesting about these types of questions is that the anomaly itself actually creates the fertile ground for the question (Schank, 1988). One has only to sense or get a feel for the question that is in a state of emergence. Or as Berlyne (1965) states, the question is becoming "astir in the learner" (p. 86).

FIGURE 2. Question-Finding Pathways

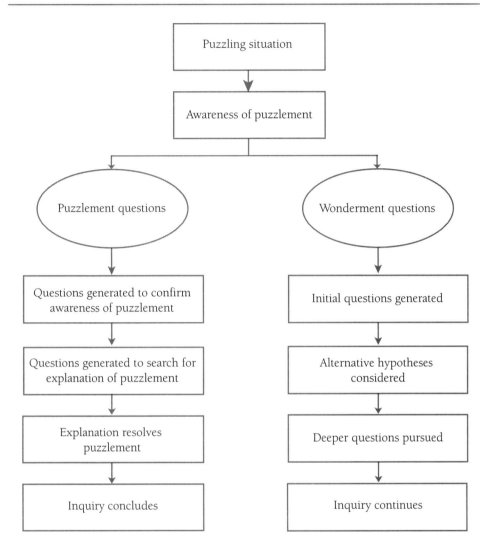

Adapted from Ciardiello, A.V. (2003). "To wander and wonder": Pathways to literacy and inquiry through question-finding. *Journal of Adolescent & Adult Literacy*, 47(3), 231.

The Second Stage: Framing Puzzlement and Wonderment Questions

I have found in my research and practice that many students are able to detect the nature of the puzzling situation but do not know how to put their puzzlement in the form of a clear and compelling question. One of my students expressed that sometimes he really didn't know what questions to write. Other researchers have

TABLE 3. Types, Characteristics, and Samples of Questions Generated by Question-Finding

Types	Characteristics	Question Samples
Puzzlement (awareness type)	Perception of anomalies, recognition of ambiguity, question-sensing, intuitive, metacognitive	Why is the event a surprise? How does the idea conflict with...? How is the event different from what you expected?
Puzzlement (explanation type)	Explanatory, strategic planning, goal oriented, coherence-seeking, convergent thinking	How can you explain? What steps can you take to resolve puzzlement? What rationale can be given for...?
Wonderment	Generative, imaginative, speculative, exploratory, divergent thinking	What are some other ways? What if...? Can you imagine...?

discovered the same problem of student inability to frame questions to ask (Graesser & McMahen, 1993). Specifically, van der Meij and J.T. Dillon (1994) found that "becoming perplexed was not sufficient for question construction. Some students would begin phrasing a question and then stop suddenly before asking it. They were experiencing perplexity but couldn't put it into the proper words" (p. 278). Students need to be trained in the linguistic format of these question types. (See Table 4 for cue cards for question types.) They do not ask higher order thinking questions spontaneously. Indeed, "leaving questioning to chance is tantamount to leaving students' puzzlement undetected and this stifles further inquiry" (Alvermann, 2004, p. 232).

During the second stage, the question-finding process takes two necessary but alternate paths (see Figure 2, page 9). One path is narrow, leading to an explanation or resolution of the puzzle. Here students seek to find puzzlement questions (explanation type) that are embedded within the discrepant sources. These question types are convergent in nature, because they seek to elicit narrowly defined or focused objectives, namely, the explanation and resolution of the puzzling situation. For example, the student might ask, "Why is the subject acting in such a strange or puzzling way?" The student's—or question-finder's—objective is to explain away or resolve the anomaly or discrepancy. Here the teacher will demonstrate (using cue cards) how to construct puzzlement questions (explanation type). (See Table 4.)

Students can also follow a more open-ended path that is only limited by their imagination. Here the question-finder recognizes that there are questions to be found

TABLE 4. Procedural Prompts: Cue Cards for Question Types

Puzzlement Questions (awareness type)
Signal words/short question stems: why, how, in what ways
Cognitive operations: perceiving anomalies, recognizing ambiguity, developing awareness

Examples
Perceiving anomalies: In what ways does the scientific explanation of evolution conflict with my own beliefs?
Recognizing ambiguity: Why did the women's organization vote against the equal rights amendment?
Developing awareness: How does multiplication sometimes make the product smaller?

Puzzlement Questions (explanation type)
Signal words/short question stems: why, how, in what ways
Cognitive operations: explaining, seeking coherence, strategic planning (convergent thinking)

Examples
Explaining: Can you explain why the president holds two contradictory opinions about the hostage crisis?
Seeking coherence: What rationale can be given for teaching intelligent design in science class?
Strategic planning: How can I teach the implications of the whole-number bias to my mathematics class?

Wonderment Questions
Signal words/short question stems: imagine, suppose, predict, if...then..., how might..., can you create..., what are some possible consequences...?
Cognitive operations: hypothesizing, inferring, imagining, divergent thinking

Examples
Hypothesizing: How might life have been different without penicillin?
Inferring: What are some possible consequences of the rise of teen pregnancy?
Imagining: Can you imagine the possibilities of a world without violence?

Adapted from Ciardiello, A.V. (1998). Did you ask a good question today? Alternative cognitive and metacognitive strategies. *Journal of Adolescent & Adult Literacy*, 42(3), 214.

embedded within discrepant sources that cannot be explained or justified. These are **wonderment questions** that are divergent in nature and lead to alternative avenues of discovery (Opdal, 2001). These questions do not seek to resolve puzzlement but to generate **rival hypotheses** (Flower, Long, & Higgins, 2000). The thinking process is one of generating alternative questions. The student asks questions that begin with stems that indicate what Lindfors (1999) calls "tentativeness markers," or words that begin with *maybe, what if..., suppose, imagine.* (See Table 4.) These types of questions stimulate additional questions, or are self-propagating. As one of my students realized, there will always be questions, ones that have no answers.

PAUSE AND PONDER

One of my high school students remarked during a question-finding session that she never knew that there were different types and levels of questions such as puzzlement and wonderment questions.

- Are your own students aware of the different cognitive types of classroom questions?
- Do you feel it is important for students to know the difference between question types in your subject area?

The Sequence of the Question-Finding Process

Question-finding is a sequential and progressive process. It begins with a puzzling situation that conflicts with students' expectations and leads to alternative paths of inquiry. The following example shows the question-finding process I used with my 11th-grade American history class while discussing a political cartoon entitled "Steady Diet" (see Figure 3). By using this process, teachers can help students find and frame puzzlement and wonderment questions.

- Inspect the document (cartoon) closely for a puzzling situation.
- Look for a mismatch between any elements in the document. Check for any incongruity between the message in the document and the title.
- Notice whether there is a mismatch between your expectations of what you think the meaning of the source (cartoon) is and the author's (cartoonist's) interpretation.
- Try to sense the emerging question. Think of what you would ask yourself or someone else to try to identify and describe the discrepancy (puzzlement question—awareness type).
- Create a mental image of your discovered question. Write it down freely without concern for proper structure.
- Refer to the **procedural prompts** and facilitators (see Table 4, page 11) to frame your puzzlement question (explanation type) properly.
- Frame the appropriate puzzlement question (explanation type) based on the cues.
- Answer your puzzlement question (explanation type).

FIGURE 3. Political Cartoon: "Steady Diet"

Steady Diet

51 DPA SERIES: A CARTOON VIEW OF DOMESTIC ISSUES — Engelhardt in the St. Louis Post-Dispatch. June 13, 1968

DOCUMENTARY PHOTO AID!
Box 956, Mount Dora, Florida 327

- Consider alternate ways of looking at this situation. Create a different mental image and try to go deeper into the problematic situation by finding penetrating and generative wonderment questions.
- Use the prompts (cue cards) for constructing wonderment questions. Write one wonderment question. (See Table 4.)
- Think of other questions that stem from your original wonderment questions.
- Follow the same procedure for writing additional questions.
- Speculate on possible answers.

Some of my 11th-grade students found and framed puzzlement (explanation) and wonderment questions related to "Steady Diet" after they received instruction in question-finding strategies (see Table 5).

I also aroused in students a state of perplexity when I used a print document (i.e., a letter) concerning adolescents' reactions to the induction of Elvis Presley into the army in March 1958 (see Figure 4). In general, my students were confounded by the seriousness of the teenagers' protests to President Eisenhower. They reacted to this discrepant document with many stimulating puzzlement (explanation type) and wonderment questions (see Table 6). One student summarized his thinking when he stated, "If you have a different opinion from the person who wrote it, you want to know why they thought that way—the way they reacted. Everybody has their own opinion on everything."

TABLE 5. Examples of Question-Finding: A Perplexing Political Cartoon

Puzzlement questions (explanation type)
Why is someone holding a tray with weapons from the television?
Why is this document called "Steady Diet"?
Why are these children watching a bomb, with guns on a plate, coming out of the television?
Why is the rope hanging down from the television?

Wonderment questions
How can we change this diet to a peaceful one?
Can you imagine television without violence?
Where were the kids' parents while they were watching television?
What would be a good steady diet?

Adapted from Ciardiello, A.V. (2003). "To wander and wonder": Pathways to literacy and inquiry through question-finding. *Journal of Adolescent & Adult Literacy*, 47(3), 233.

Detail letter from Elvis Presley fans to President Dwight Eisenhower. Dwight Eisenhower Library, U.S. National Archives, Washington, DC. Public domain.

Guidelines for Implementing Question-Finding in the Classroom

The preplanning stage of question-finding involves an awareness and execution of several important factors. Following are some guidelines for planning and implementing the question-finding strategy in the classroom.

Be aware of limitations of students' questioning abilities. Teachers should know the inadequacies of adolescents in asking spontaneously generated questions in

TABLE 6. Examples of Question-Finding: A Discrepant Letter

Puzzlement questions (explanation type)
Why do they (the government) want to send Elvis Presley into the army? Was there a war going on at the time?
Why are these people writing to President Eisenhower?
Why don't Elvis Presley fans or lovers want Elvis to get a government issue (GI) haircut?
Do all Presley fans feel the same way as these three fans who wrote the letter?

Wonderment questions
Do you think Elvis would lose all his fans without his hair?
Do you think the girls have the right to tell the president his business?
Do you think a star should be treated differently?
Do you really think the president would take your letter seriously?

Adapted from Ciardiello, A.V. (2003). "To wander and wonder": Pathways to literacy and inquiry through question-finding. *Journal of Adolescent & Adult Literacy, 47*(3), 235.

class. Indeed, research shows that even in a positive and encouraging environment, teachers need to model and scaffold questions for students to generate (Chin, Brown, & Bruce, 2002; Ciardiello, 1998; Olsher & Dreyfus, 1999).

Be aware of the challenging nature of detecting puzzlement. Many adolescents will have trouble identifying discrepant or anomalous events in text (Chin, 2001; Graesser & McMahen, 1993). Often this is due to both knowledge deficits and shallow processing of information. Many students need assistance monitoring their comprehension. The teacher can help by providing scaffolds to help adolescents construct puzzlement questions (awareness type) such as the following:

- Is there anything unusual about the events in this reading?
- How did the happenings in this reading differ from what I was led to believe?
- How did the subject act contrary to my expectations?

Be knowledgeable of adolescents' needs and curriculum topics. Adolescence is a time of biological changes. Teenagers are often bewildered by the many changes in their own bodies. If handled discreetly, these changes can become a focal point for question-finding. Oliver and Lalik (2004a) capitalized on this knowledge to create a unit in physical education on adolescent girls' body image and cultural domination. Students practiced their critical inquiry skills and raised many high-level questions on this motivational topic. See chapter 3 for a focus unit on this topic in which the question-finding strategy was applied.

Teachers should review their courses of study and look for topics that contain items for discussion that are either discrepant, speculative, novel, ambiguous, surprising, personally relevant, or consisting of multiple points of view. For example, in the field of science, topics could include photosynthesis, genetic engineering, stem cell research, alternative use of fossil fuels, and evolution. Topics that are too abstract or esoteric, such as comparing electrons and neutrons in chemistry or examining the process of molecular intracellular division in biology, do not generally lend themselves to question generating by adolescents (Olsher & Dreyfus, 1999). Teachers need to work with everyday objects and experiences and tap students' prior knowledge. They can use photographs and personal events in students' lives. They also can consider topics that have high-interest qualities—that is, ones about which students have experience or prior knowledge such as topics associated with social and emotional learning.

Immerse students in the topic. Students need sufficient background knowledge to enable them to detect anomalies and develop an awareness of puzzling learning experiences. Shepardson and Moje (1999) found that fourth-grade preadolescents were more likely to react to anomalous data in a unit on electric currents when they had established well-developed frameworks on the topic. Students' prior knowledge enabled them to detect anomalies as threats to their original preconceptions.

Students also need sufficient domain-specific knowledge to be able to generate questions from anomalous data and emergent puzzlement conditions. In a research study with middle school students in the science classroom, students raised more questions and those of a higher quality on the topic of endangered species, and fewer on the topic of fossil fuels. The researchers believed that the former topic raised higher level wonderment questions because the information was within students' funds of background knowledge (Scardamalia & Bereiter, 1992). Language arts and social studies educators have also recognized the importance of topic immersion on student questioning behavior (Busching & Slesinger, 2002; Ciardiello, 1998). (See Appendix B for the lesson plan that demonstrates how to use the question-finding strategy to inquire about discrepant social living conditions during the U.S. Great Depression.)

Organize question-driven classroom conditions. Organize the room in ways that facilitate questions so it is question driven (Shodell, 1995). Set up bulletin boards and visuals that provide prompts and signal words to scaffold question-finding (see Table 4, page 11).

Provide a reward system for the most effective questions generated on a given topic or unit. In my classes, I provided pins with the inscribed words, "I asked a great question today!"

Provide flexible seating arrangements and tolerance of social talk. Question-finding, or any kind of search behavior, requires a learning environment that supports flexibility and student interaction. A classroom setting with a fixed-row desk arrangement and quiet children does not work. In her research with a physical education class, Oliver (Oliver & Lalik, 2004a) allowed high school students to generate questions as part of the construction of an interview questionnaire on the topic of girls' bodies in an atmosphere in which social talk and academic talk (specific to the task) were overlapping and interchangeable. Oliver believed that social talk actually supported academic learning because the issues of the body were personal, social, and academic. Joseph Ruhl, a high school biology teacher, also permitted his students to intertwine their social and academic conversations in class (D.R. Dillon, O'Brien, & Volkmann, 2001).

Stress the inquiry nature of the task. The learning procedure should center on students formulating problems. The focus needs to be one in which students discover problems rather than solve problems. Using surprising and discrepant episodes creates the proper learning environment for creative teaching and discovery learning to occur (Massialas & Zevin, 1983). Routine tasks such as completing work sheets or lab reports are not suitable for question-finding.

Organize an open-ended learning environment. Related to the above idea, the classroom learning environment needs to be one in which there is an openness of investigation and a climate of inquiry and of sharing ideas. Students need to know and feel that it is all right to express ideas that might be undeveloped or even controversial. Indeed, Elkins and Luke (1999) tell us that "adolescents need to be taught how to second guess, analyze, weigh, and critique texts" (p. 215). **Second-guessing** is the kind of cognitive practice that facilitates question-finding. In addition, the learning environment should be one in which getting correct answers does not dominate instruction.

Greenleaf, Schoenbach, Csiko, and Mueller (2001) worked with adolescents in an academic literacy program and created a classroom milieu where the unstated motto was "It's cool to be confused" (p. 96). This idea of uncertainty and open questioning is counter to what most adolescents experience in many content area classrooms. For example, Rosa, a ninth-grade student in an academic literacy class, stated that most times she just reads the text and "answers the red square questions" at the end of the chapter (p. 101). Tina related a similar experience in her biology class where she and other members in her group worked on their study guides in biology. She stated, "Yeah (we compare answers), and then we'll find out what the right answer is. One time we had to get (done) two or three labs in one day.... We just look up specifically what we have to do and then just hand it in" (D.R. Dillon et al., 2001, p. 62). Getting the right answer or completing the work quickly is not the right learning atmosphere for question-finding.

Be aware of time constraints. Every content area teacher has time pressures, especially when it comes to covering the requirements of the curriculum. Often teachers do not have the classroom time for the deep processing of text that question-finding requires. Teachers need to be selective about the choice of topics for question-finding. As indicated above, some topics lend themselves to greater student engagement and inquiry and are worth the investment of time. Teachers need to select those areas that are most worthy of students' deep engagement. In my social studies classes, I was able to spend more time on developing student questioning in teaching a unit on the U.S. civil rights movement than I was for other topics in American history. This particular topic included many rich stories and events that are so counterintuitive that they generated many puzzlement (explanation type) and wonderment questions. Indeed, the unusual and inspiring role of adolescent activists (e.g., 15-year-old Claudette Colvin) in the civil rights movement created puzzlement and wonderment and promoted active student questioning.

Teachers should plan for developing question-finding skills in homework and other outside class projects. Students can keep reflection journals in which they record meaningful questions about topics. Out-of-class activities can provide optimum time to practice these demanding skills. Scardamalia and Bereiter (1992) found that middle grade students in science asked very few questions in class about the topic of the boiling point, but when given a homework assignment on the same topic, they asked more questions and at higher levels of cognition.

PAUSE AND PONDER

Psychologists (Ames & Ames, 1989; Byrnes, 2003; Eccles & Roeser, 2003) tell us that adolescence is a time when students are ready developmentally for critical thinking competencies that are essential for question-finding. These competencies include the increased ability to maintain different representations of knowledge simultaneously and an appreciation of the relativity and uncertainty of knowledge. Yet my own experience in teaching middle school and high school students revealed to me that there were structural barriers to this type of teaching, including large class size and standardized high-stakes testing review.

• Do you experience similar structural barriers to the implementation of question-finding in your classroom?

• Is there any way to adapt your instruction to provide for the changing intellectual needs of adolescents including the critical thinking attributes of question-finding?

Summary

This chapter focused on the cognitive-based literacy dimension of question-finding. It showed how question-finding derived from Berlyne's theoretical notions of conceptual conflict and epistemic curiosity. It also showed that question-finding is an information-processing procedure that incorporates cognitive strategy instruction and guided inquiry learning. This process included the use of scaffolds, procedural prompts, and guidelines for implementation. In the next chapter, we will examine how cognitive-based literacy affects the development of the motivational dimension of question-finding.

PONDER AND PRACTICE

1. Personal photographs and family stories are excellent human resources for question-finding. These artifacts often contain interesting discrepant details. As indicated in this chapter, I used personal stories and family photographs to illustrate how these materials can stimulate question-finding. In my teacher education classes, students have searched for personal discrepant stories and/or photographs. One of the preservice teachers whom I taught brought in a photograph of a wedding celebration featuring the smiling faces of all members of the immediate family except her grandmother. The grandmother wore a common black dress, often worn in memory of her long deceased husband, along with a sad expression on her face. The student felt that it was discrepant for the grandmother to wear "mourning" clothes during a happy occasion. This prompted very interesting questions.

  • Do you have any discrepant personal artifacts that could prompt question-finding? Practice your question-finding skills using the family photographs that I provide that display discrepant situations (see Appendix C).

2. Refer to the question-finding process discussed in this chapter. Use this process to help find questions related to the historical meeting as presented below between President Nixon and Elvis Presley. (According to the Library of Congress, this letter and an accompanying photograph of the meeting are the most requested documents from its duplicating service.)

    On December 21, 1970, Elvis Presley visited President Richard M. Nixon at the White House. Presley had written a six-page letter requesting the visit, suggesting to the president that he (Presley) be made a "Federal Agent-at Large in the Bureau of Narcotics and Dangerous Drugs." The following excerpt includes selections from this letter.

Dear Mr. President:

I talked to Vice President Agnew in Palm Springs three weeks ago and expressed my concern for our country. The drug culture, the hippie elements, the SDS (Students for a Democratic Society), Black Panthers, etc. do not consider me as their enemy or as they call it the establishment. Sir, I can and will be of any service that I can to help the country out. So I wish not to be given a title or an appointed position. I can and will do more good if I were made a Federal Agent at Large and I will help out by doing it through my communications with people of all ages. First and foremost, I am an entertainer, but all I need is the Federal credentials....

Sir, I am staying at the Washington Hotel.... I am registered under the name of Jon Burrows. I will be here for as long as it takes to get the credentials of a Federal Agent. I have done an in-depth study of drug abuse and Communist Brainwashing techniques and I am right in the middle of the whole thing where I can and will do the most good.... I am glad to help as long as it is kept very private. I am sending you the short autobiography about myself so you can better understand this approach. I would love to meet you just to say hello if you're not too busy.

Respectfully
Elvis Presley

Note: Selections from handwritten letter of Elvis Presley to President Richard Nixon. Nixon Presidential Materials holdings, U.S. National Archives, Washington, DC.

- How would you use this discrepant source to teach the strategy of question-finding?
- What additional background knowledge may be necessary in order for students to become aware of the discrepancy in this situation?
- How would you scaffold puzzlement questions (awareness type) related to this source? Puzzlement questions (explanation type)? Wonderment questions?
- What research questions can guide students to follow-up on this discrepant request made by Elvis? For example, ask students how they think President Nixon reacted to this unusual request.

3. Children's personal letters also provide a rich resource for question-finding. This is the case especially with regard to children's letters to historical figures, as demonstrated by the illustrative example of the teens' letter to President Eisenhower (see Figure 4, page 15) and the following excerpt from an adolescent's letter to President Reagan. In 1984, Andy Smith, a seventh grader, wrote to President Ronald Reagan about a problem that plagues adolescents everywhere, a messy room. Andy wrote, "Today my mother declared my bedroom a disaster area. I would like to request federal funds to hire a crew to clean up my room." The president wrote back: "Dear Andy, your application for disaster relief has been duly noted but I must point out one technical problem: the authority declaring the

disaster is supposed to make the request. In this case, your mother" (letter to President Reagan. U.S. National Archives, Washington, DC).

Historian Robert Cohen (2002) has collected and edited a number of letters from children to First Lady Eleanor Roosevelt. Below is an example of a "Dear Mrs. Roosevelt" letter.

Nov. 6, 1936

Dear Mrs. Roosevelt,

I am writing to you for some of your old soiled dresses if you have any. As I am a poor girl who has to stay out of school. On account of dresses & slips and a coat. I am in the seventh grade but I have to stay out of school because I have no books or clothes to ware. I am in need of dresses & slips and a coat very bad. If you have any soiled clothes that you don't want to ware I would be very glad to get them. But please do not let the newspaper reporters get hold of this in any way and I will keep it from getting out here so there will be no one else to get hold of it. But do not let my name get out in the paper. I am thirteen years old.

Yours Truly,
Miss L.H.

Note: From *Dear Mrs. Roosevelt: Letters from children of the Great Depression* by Robert Cohen. © 2002 by the University of North Carolina Press. Used by permission of the publisher.

- Which items in these letters are counterintuitive?

- How would you use these documents to provoke question-finding?

4. Incongruous images that present diametrically opposed views or statements within the same frame can be a rich source of question-finding. Examine the following photographs.

(Left) Rothstein, A. (1937). World's highest standard of living...There's no way like the American way. Birmingham, AL. Farm Security Administration/Office of Ware Information Collection, U.S. Library of Congress, Washington, DC. LC-USF3301-002393-M2. Public domain.

(Right) Westgard, A.L. (1912). Covered wagon with jackrabbit mules encounters an automobile on the trail near Big Springs, Nebraska. U.S. National Archives, Washington, DC. Public domain.

- What questions come to mind from these conflicting images? Use the question-finding procedure as a guide for generating questions.

Schank (1988) has recommended that teachers actually create their own anomalous artifacts to stimulate student questioning.

- Can you create your own "incongruous images" in your subject area?

- Try cutting and pasting incompatible images on the same frame as reflected in the above photographs.

CHAPTER 2

Question-Finding and Motivation

IMPORTANT CONCEPTS AND SPECIALIZED TERMS

academic motivation	immersion model of inquiry	self-efficacy
adolescent literacy	intrinsic motivation	self-regulation
affective/cognitive synthesis	motivation domain/synthesis	sensation-seeking
augmented activation activity	motivational construct	situational interest
catch facets	refutational discussion	social construction of
curiosity	refutational text	knowledge
hold facets	self-determination	

Can a picture of a tube of toothpaste stimulate question-finding?

This question guided a preservice teacher whom I was teaching in her field-experience assignment. The assignment involved tutoring an eighth-grade student in the strategy of question-finding using an example of an unusual photograph. The photograph shows a Claes Oldenburg sculpture with a very large tube of toothpaste turned upside down resting on a lawn. The title of the photo is "Defying Gravity." The photo is puzzling because it shows the soft toothpaste holding up the tube. Nevertheless, there were some obvious questions and potential answers about the photo. One question was why the artist chose to show the toothpaste upside down. There was a partial answer in the title, but the teacher and the student still wondered why the artist chose to depict this item in such an unusual way. Another question was what the artist was trying to make a person think when viewing the sculpture. The teacher and the student enjoyed analyzing the photo, and the experience helped to introduce the process of question-finding.

This reflection reveals how a preservice teacher collaborated with an eighth-grade student on an inquiry project involving the strategy of question-finding. It reveals the motivational nature of collaboration in the process of learning. The selection of the unusual photograph captured the attention of the student immediately, and the content of the photograph challenged the common sense nature of the student's experience with the object (toothpaste tube). Because of the puzzlement created by the photograph, the teacher and student began to think about why the sculptor chose to do this. This state of **curiosity** prompted the teacher and the student to raise questions to try to resolve the contradictions in the situation. Literacy researchers have described this curiosity as an important aspect in reading motivation for adolescents. Indeed, Moss and Hendershot (2002) describe this motivating quest as "the need to know" (p. 12). This "need to know" was articulated by a young adolescent, who after having looked at the back cover of *Buried in Ice* (Beattle & Geiger, 1992) stated, "I saw a picture of a dead man. I wondered why he didn't decay and what the big bump was" (Moss & Hendershot, 2002, p. 12). Berlyne (1965) calls this "need to know" a key index of curiosity, which is an important feature of motivation.

In this chapter, I explain how motivation is an important factor in adolescent development and literacy. Then, I describe the relationship between motivation and question-finding. Finally, I present classroom applications of how question-finding can motivate adolescents to learn in different content areas.

Motivational Constructs and Adolescent Development

The **motivational construct** of curiosity is not the only important psychological need of adolescent development. The psychological needs of adolescents also are explained through the construct of **self-regulation**. This construct suggests that individuals need to monitor, control, and direct their actions and decisions. It is a characteristic of thinking about one's own thinking processes. Because adolescence is a period of higher intellectual challenges and greater decision-making responsibilities than childhood, it is important for teens to develop these metacognitive skills. Another important motivational construct is that of **self-efficacy**. This important construct helps to build student confidence and competence in instructional pursuits (Schunk & Zimmerman, 1997).

Adolescence also opens up new avenues of competencies, interests, and curiosities. In terms of competencies, adolescence is a period of maturing reasoning powers, characterized by the ability to tolerate ambiguity and weigh evidence for the claims of opposing views (Wigfield & Tonks, 2002). Unfortunately, the adolescent curriculum becomes more formalized and standardized at a time when developmentally, adolescents are ready for in-depth, open-ended questions involving value or moral dilemmas. Indeed, as adolescents search for adult identity, the opportunity to express such value questions allows them to develop a closer identification with and motivation for the content matter under study (Ames & Ames, 1989). Adolescence is also a time of greater preoccupation with body image, autonomy, social relationships, and controversial issues. This greater preoccupation with personal needs and physical space provides opportunities for classroom motivation.

As indicated in chapter 1, I have used letters from adolescents to historical figures (e.g., U.S. presidents and first ladies) concerning personal needs and interests as prompts to motivation (and also question-finding). Motivational constructs such as curiosity, self-efficacy, and self-regulation do not operate in isolation. They have an impact on one another. Furthermore, these constructs are also mediated by social and environmental contexts. Indeed, it is within these social contexts that these motivational constructs affect **adolescent literacy**.

PAUSE AND PONDER

One year after the Columbine high school massacre, *USA Weekend* (April 16, 2000) featured a high-interest photo on its cover that showed an adolescent writing a punishment assignment on the chalkboard with the following repeated words:

Please don't let me get hurt in school today
Please don't let me get hurt in school today...

The theme of the special issue was, "Do our kids feel safe? One year after Columbine, thought-provoking answers from students across America."
   I have used this disturbing counterintuitive source to motivate discussion and generate question-finding behavior with preservice teachers.

• Do you feel this topic and source are appropriate for middle school students? High school students? Why or why not?

In the following section, I examine how each of the motivational constructs discussed in this section have implications for adolescent literacy learning. I also show how the appropriate literacy environment can satisfy adolescent motivational needs related to literacy.

Motivation and Adolescent Literacy

The Adolescent Literacy Commission of the International Reading Association has stated emphatically that schools "need teachers who act on adolescents' interests and design meaningful projects addressing motivational needs" (Moore et al., 1999, p. 6). I agree with the findings of the commission. Classrooms that encourage student "voice and choice" can affect positively adolescents' need for autonomy and self-determination (D.R. Dillon & O'Brien, 2002). Providing opportunities for students to select personally meaningful topics and engaging materials supports adolescents' expression of identity formation (Bean, 2002; Ivey & Broaddus, 2001).

Structuring classroom environments that foster direct cognitive strategy instruction with its characteristics of modeling, directed practice, independent practice, and feedback helps adolescents to develop confidence in their new abilities to successfully complete academic tasks. As indicated earlier, this strengthens the motivational attribute of self-efficacy. I have worked with academically challenged high school students in the development of higher level student questioning behavior using direct cognitive strategy instruction (Ciardiello, 1998). I have also worked with adolescent students to develop their metacognitive and executive control skills as they engaged in generating questions (Ciardiello, 1993). This type of instruction fosters the motivational constructs of self-regulation and competence building. It addresses the Adolescent Literacy Commission's recommendation that adolescents need to develop "advanced levels of literacy" such as thinking divergently and imaginatively, synthesizing ideas from multiple sources, and dealing with ambiguities and contradictory information. Indeed, these higher expressions of thinking will be needed to "feed their [adolescents'] imaginations so they can create the world of the future" (Moore et al., 1999, p. 99). (See Table 7 for resources on motivation and literacy.)

A number of educational philosophers, psychologists, and teacher education researchers have made strong connections between the constructs of motivation and interest (Berlyne, 1965; Brophy, 2004; Dewey, 1913; Guthrie, 2001; James, 1900). Indeed, Dewey (1913) described genuine interest in a topic as identification, absorption, and maintenance in a self-selected activity. Contemporary motivational researchers call this type of motivation "individual interest" (Hidi & Harackiewicz, 2000). In contrast, there is a type of interest that is more amenable to teacher control and external interventions. It is known as **situational interest**. Situational interest is a type of engagement in which the environment triggers and sustains learning (Hidi & Harackiewicz). Materials, topics, and strategies that arouse curiosity, novelty, ambiguity, universal interest, and personal relevance characterize the learning environment. Situational interest stimulates topic engagement that fosters the emergence of **intrinsic motivation** (Guthrie & Wigfield, 2000). Therefore, teachers should consider artifacts and events that arouse situational interest when planning instructional tasks for students (Freeman, McPhail, & Berndt, 2002).

Teachers do not have to limit themselves to classroom experiences to stimulate situational interest. I have arranged school neighborhood field trips to search out counterintuitive and discrepant street signs (e.g., a sign had two one-way arrows going in opposite directions) and incongruous house and yard features (e.g., house built on a huge stone boulder). See Figure 5 on page 30 for a sample guide that I used with preservice teachers whom I was teaching so they could record discrepant artifacts on a neighborhood tour.

TABLE 7. Resources on Motivation and Literacy

Ainley, H., Hidi, S., & Berndorff, D. (2002). Interest, learning and the psychological processes that mediate their relationship. *Journal of Educational Psychology*, *94*(3), 545–561.

Boyd, F.B. (2002). Motivation to continue: Enhancing literacy learning for struggling readers and writers. *Reading & Writing Quarterly*, *18*, 257–277.

Guthrie, J.T., & Davis, M.H. (2003). Motivating struggling readers in middle school through an engagement model of classroom practice. *Reading & Writing Quarterly*, *19*, 59–85.

Guthrie, J.T., Wigfield, A., & Perencevich, K.C. (2004). *Motivating reading comprehension: Concept-oriented reading instruction*. Mahwah, NJ: Erlbaum.

Hidi, S., & Anderson, V. (1992). Situational interest and its impact on reading and expository writing. In K.A. Renninger, S. Hidi, & A. Krapp (Eds.), *The role of interest in learning and development* (pp. 215–238). Hillsdale, NJ: Erlbaum.

Oldfather, P. (2002). Learning from students about overcoming motivation problems in literacy learning: A cross-study analysis and synthesis. *Reading & Writing Quarterly*, *18*, 343–352.

Oldfather, P. (2002). Students' experiences when not initially motivated for literacy learning. *Reading & Writing Quarterly*, *18*, 231–256.

Wigfield, A., Guthrie, J.T., Tonks, S., & Perencevich, K.C. (2004). Children's motivation for reading: Domain specificity and instructional influence. *Journal of Educational Research*, *97*, 299–309.

In an example from the National Research Council (NRC, 2000), Ms. Idoni, a 10th-grade biology teacher, also saw the motivational benefits of a field trip to arouse situational interest in her discipline. She took her students to a local lake because she wanted them to study an aspect of the environment that they found interesting, and to allow the experience to help them decide what questions to pursue for a science project. She asked the students to simply walk around the lake and to think about questions that they might be interested in answering. They were to record their observations in their journals. Students generated questions such as, "Is the lake water safe to drink?" "What kinds of plants and animals live in the lake?" "How have humans changed the lake?" (p. 67). Instead of having preformulated teacher questions drive the research, Ms. Idoni allowed the experience of the field trip itself to generate students' own research questions for the unit of study.

PAUSE AND PONDER

Dewey, a philosopher and educational reformer, was one of the first educators to see the connection between interest and curiosity as motivational constructs. He associated interest with student questioning, saying, "no one has ever explained why children are so full of questions outside of the school, and the conspicuous absence of display of curiosity about the subject matter of school lessons" (Dewey, 1916, p. 86).

- Do you agree with Dewey's point?
- Can you offer any explanation that might satisfy Dewey's concern?

Adolescent psychologists propose that many teenagers have a biological and psychological need for **sensation-seeking** experiences (Anderman, Noar, Zimmerman, & Donohew, 2005). In an academic context, this means they have an inner desire for school tasks that are novel, intriguing, unusual, and ambiguous. This personality factor has strong implications for **academic motivation**, because adolescents do not engage in academic tasks that they consider boring. Teachers need to create more interesting learning environments. Indeed, classrooms in which adolescents can perceive the sensation-seeking value of instructional tasks trigger situational interest.

Situational interest has strong potential for adolescent literacy because as young students get older they tend to lose academic motivation in almost all school subjects (Hidi & Harackiewicz, 2000). This appears to be the case for preadolescents as well as adolescents. Indeed, students in the upper elementary levels (i.e., grades 4 and 5) also reveal a declining interest in subject matter (Strickland & Alvermann, 2004). Many motivational researchers believe that situational interest can offset this decline in academic motivation (Hidi, Weiss, Berndorff, & Nolan, 1998; Mitchell, 1993; Schraw, Flowerday, & Lehman, 2001). Mitchell (1993) offers the stimulating hypothesis that situational interest consists of both **catch facets** and **hold facets**. The catch facets are the stimuli that catch students' immediate attention such as novel, discrepant, and ambiguous artifacts and stories. The hold facets are the ones that are meaningful to students and keep them continually engaged after the catch facets begin to wear off. Mitchell found that high school students who experienced this sense of meaningful engagement increased their motivation in their algebra and geometry classes, areas of mathematics that often register a decline in academic motivation as children get older.

In science, too, catch and hold facets have been known to motivate and sustain inquiry learning. One of these motivating devices that can be been used is the "dancing raisins" discrepant event experiment (Huber & Moore, 2001). This experiment has been used to teach the topic of buoyancy and density of objects to middle school science classes. In the experiment, a raisin is dropped into a glass of carbonated water. Being slightly denser than the liquid, the raisin initially sinks to the bottom of the glass. Unexpectedly, the raisins do not remain on the bottom but

FIGURE 5. Sample Guide Sheet: Looking for Discrepant Artifacts in Our School Neighborhood

What do you observe that is out of the ordinary from what you expect to be in this place or site?

1. Describe item _____

2. Describe item _____

3. Describe item _____

What makes these things discrepant? Answer by using the following prompt:

It is unexpected that...

_____

_____

_____

_____

_____

What question(s) comes to mind to explain the puzzling artifact? Is there a reasonable answer? What is it?

Think of a puzzlement question (explanation type) that is convergent in nature such as, What is an old stone fence doing in front of a newly remodeled house when one would have expected a new fence to match the newly remodeled house?

Possible answer: The reason why this old fence is in front of this new, remodeled house could be that the owner ran out of money after buying the new house and could not afford a new fence right away. (This is a close-ended question that points to a verifiable answer.)

Puzzlement question:

_____

_____

_____

_____

_____

Now, think of wonderment or open-ended questions that can have multiple answers or are divergent in nature. For example, what if remodeled houses included both new and old features. Would this make for a more interesting neighborhood? What kind of homeowners would prefer this type of dwelling? Should there be housing codes to prevent old houses in new neighborhoods?

Wonderment questions:

_____

_____

_____

_____

_____

begin to bob up to the surface. The bubbles of CO_2 begin to attach themselves to the raisins, creating buoyancy that causes them to bob up. But as the raisins reach the surface, the bubbles on top of them begin to break. Then the raisins roll over, breaking the remaining bubbles and causing the raisins to sink once again. The "dancing raisins" experiment can capture students' interest and be held and sustained by the question-finding activity. For example, the students can ask wonderment questions such as, How can we make raisins dance faster? What other substances (other than carbonated water) can make raisins "dance"? Students can design their own experiments to answer their own self-selected questions.

Flowerday, Schraw, and Stevens (2004) have stipulated that situational interest has both strong cognitive and affective effects on students. Through greater engagement in topics, students manifest deeper processing of text and increased positive attitudes about text. This latter facet is especially important for adolescent literacy because a positive attitude is a strong element in the academic motivation of teens.

Situational interest also has implications for the **social construction of knowledge**. This occurs when the class is engaged in inquiry projects in which both the teacher and the students acknowledge the value of multiple perspectives and share in the construction of knowledge. This kind of learning environment is one in which the teacher displays respect and appreciation of students' opinions and ideas. Oldfather and Dahl (1994) describe this propensity as "honoring students' voices" (p. 143). It is one that promotes inherent motivation for literacy learning. In particular, it is a kind of shared commitment to knowing. Teachers and students become coresearchers on a topic that stimulates interest for both inquirers.

Socially constructed classroom environments support and enhance each individual's natural curiosity or desire to inquire. Oldfather and Thomas (1998) call this intense involvement in a topic through a deeply personal agenda the "continuing impulse to learn" (p. 650). This continuing impulse to learn is related to the motivational concept of "flow," in which the learner is inherently absorbed in an activity for its own sake (Csikszentmihalyi, 1990). It is also related to Berlyne's (1954) ideas of epistemic curiosity.

The Connection Between Question–Finding and Motivation

As indicated earlier, the strategy of question-finding is based on the epistemic curiosity theory of Berlyne (1954). Epistemic curiosity is the motivational condition in which students actively seek conditions to satisfy an inherent "drive to know" (p. 187). Indeed, students often want to acquire the information not necessarily for some external reward, but for the sheer desire to know. This desire to know is self-reinforcing and inherently motivating.

This drive-to-know orientation is further stimulated by ideas and events that conflict with students' prior knowledge and experiences. When students are presented with new information that is discordant with their views, they reach a knowledge state of conceptual conflict (Berlyne, 1965). This discrepant state of affairs encourages students to develop sensitivity to the vulnerable points in their existing knowledge structures, and drives them to remedy the conflicting ideas. In other words, questions begin to gnaw at students. It is this self-questioning that is the foundation of new learning, for every new item of knowledge is the answer to a question and is "most readily ingested when the question is astir within the learner" (p. 86). Berlyne's motivational theory of epistemic curiosity is directly related to student questioning behavior. Conditions that create conceptual conflict stimulate the need to generate questions about the discrepant events.

Presenting novel, challenging, and counterintuitive topics and materials helps to develop situational interest for adolescents and stimulates students' ability to generate questions. The strategy of question-finding utilizes situational interest to stimulate intrinsic motivation in literacy learning (Ciardiello, 2003). Indeed, situational interest addresses not only the cognitive dimension of literacy learning but also the affective dimension. Situational interest tends to remove some of the personal constraints of student questioning. Motivation researchers call this phenomenon the **affective/cognitive synthesis** (Hidi & Harackiewicz, 2000, p. 156). A young adolescent expressed the type of classroom culture that epitomizes this affective/cognitive synthesis:

> One of the things I love in school is that we're trying to learn—not just get the right answer.... You want to get the right answer, but you still learn. You do better because learning is more important than getting the right answer. (Oldfather & Dahl, 1994, p.147)

Earlier I explained the importance of catch and hold facets in creating situational interest. These facets of situational interest also apply to question-finding. The first phase of the question-finding process, which incorporates the introduction of counterintuitive and puzzling stimuli, could be considered the catch facets of situational interest. These stimuli entice and capture the student's attention. But these "catch" stimuli need to be directly related to the topic. If not, they will only seduce the student briefly, and then quickly lose their appeal and relevance (Garner, Brown, Sanders, & Menke, 1992). The conceptual conflict created by the discrepant sources creates the expectancy gap in the learner. The gap between the student's original perceptions and the new perceptions created by the discrepant event propels the "drive to know" (Berlyne, 1954) and "the impulse to learn" (Oldfather & Dahl, 1994). This drive or impulse prompts the student to begin a process of self-questioning that is personal and satisfying. Thus, the initial precipitating event has captured the attention of the learner, who begins to engage in a self-initiated questioning activity. In summary, the motivational constructs of epistemic curiosity and situational interest often work together to stimulate question-finding.

In this book, question-finding is most closely related to the motivational constructs of curiosity and situational interest. But there are other motivational constructs that are also associated with question-finding. The construct of **self-determination** is expressed by students' persistence to generate self-selected questions through the question-finding process (Ryan & Deci, 2000). In addition, as students become skillful in implementing the strategy of question-finding, they develop a competence that instills confidence in their ability to attain a deeper understanding of subject matter. This is related to the motivational construct of self-efficacy. Developing competence in the use of question-finding enhances self-efficacy. Instruction in question-finding empowers students with the cognitive and motivational tools that build confidence and knowledge (Wigfield, Guthrie, Tonks, & Perencevich, 2004).

PAUSE AND PONDER

Some researchers (Berlyne, 1965; Wigfield et al., 2004) claim that the motivation for student questioning is subject specific. One of my students, a high school junior, seemed to support this notion. When I asked him which types of questions he preferred to ask in class, he remarked that he preferred to ask wonderment questions, especially on the topic of astronomy. He said that he could ask many questions about space such as about life in another galaxy or the possibility of water on Jupiter's moons.

- Have you found that motivation for students to generate questions has a lot to do with specific content and subject matter?
- Are there certain topics in your content area curriculum that are more conducive to students generating questions?

Motivation and Question–Finding Across Content Areas

Motivational researchers explain that curiosity and situational interest require a sufficient content knowledge base in order to be effective (Gottfried, Fleming, & Gottfried, 2001; Wigfield et al., 2004). Deeper immersion in the topic offers greater opportunities for curiosity and interest factors to take effect. This means that content area teachers can specifically tailor their course content and instructional strategies to topics that stimulate curiosity and situational interest.

There are two approaches that content area teachers can follow to stimulate curiosity and situational interest. One approach is for teachers to directly create conceptual conflict through the presentation of discrepant learning events (Davis, 2001). For example, a 12th-grade physics teacher followed this approach when he took his class onto the high school football field and set up a "bottle rocket" experiment. This homemade contraption consisted of a two-liter soda bottle containing some water, then turned upside down and connected to a hose from an air compressor. At the appropriate moment, a student was allowed to pull a cord that was attached to the apparatus and the bottle soared into the air. The puzzled students began to generate such questions as, "How did you do that?" and "Would more water in the bottle make it go higher?" (Layman, 1996, p. 21). (See Table 8 for resources on the relationship between discrepant events and student questioning.)

Another approach to creating conceptual conflict is to introduce anomalous data or evidence that directly contradict students' preconceptions and personal beliefs (Davis, 2001). Another 12th-grade physics teacher challenged his students' alternate conceptions on heat sources with this approach. Mr. Carlyon believed that his students had the common misconception that different kinds of fabric such as wool, silk, and cotton generated different degrees of heat. He tested his beliefs by conducting an experiment in which he wrapped three identical thermometers in different pairs of socks each made of one of the types of fabric. From their own personal experiences with clothing, the students predicted that the woolen socks would register the highest temperature. When the results showed that all the socks registered the same temperature, the students were puzzled, and this condition generated several questions from students (Layman, 1996).

In the following sections, I show how the motivational factors of curiosity, situational interest, and self-determination can be used to generate question-finding in different content areas. Teachers can refer to these sample units as models of question-finding.

Motivating Language Arts Instruction Through Question–Finding

The following language arts teachers have used the motivational construct of situational interest to stimulate literacy instruction and student questioning. Their experiences can serve as models to help other teachers replicate in some fashion these endeavors. Seventh-grade language arts teacher Betty Slesinger (Busching & Slesinger, 2002) began a unit of study on social life and race relations during the U.S. Great Depression and realized early that her students had very little background knowledge on the topic. She also became aware that their initial probing questions were shallow and low level due to their limited background knowledge on the topic. For example, the strained relationship between the African Americans and whites presented in the book that they were reading, *Roll of Thunder, Hear My Cry* (Taylor,

TABLE 8. Resources on Discrepant Events as Catalysts for Student
Questioning

Berlyne, D.E., & Frommer, F. (1966). Some determinants of the incidence and content of
children's questions. *Child Development, 37,* 177–189.

Caine, G., Caine, R.N., & McClintic, C. (2002). Guiding the innate constructivist. *Educational
Leadership, 60*(1), 70–73.

Chinn, C., & Brewer, W.F. (1993). The role of anomalous data in knowledge acquisition: A
theoretical framework and implications for science instruction. *Review of Educational
Research, 63*(1), 1–49.

Echevarria, M. (2003). Anomalies as a catalyst for middle school students' knowledge construction
and scientific reasoning during science inquiry. *Journal of Educational Psychology, 95*(2),
357–374.

Graesser, A.C., & McMahen, C.L. (1993). Anomalous information triggers questions when
adults solve quantitative problems and comprehend stories. *Journal of Educational Psychology,
85*(1), 136–151.

Kienholz, K.B. (2002). Conflict and resolution: Catalysts for learning. *Kappa Delta Pi Record,
38*(3), 124–127.

Schank, R. (1988). *The creative attitude: Learning to ask and answer the right questions.* New York:
Macmillan.

Seidman, R.F. (2002). Making historical connections: A historian shows how documents can be
used to teach critical inquiry. *School Library Journal, 48,* 36–37.

Shepardson, D.P., & Moje, E.B. (1999). The role of anomalous data in restructuring fourth
graders' frameworks for understanding electric circuits. *International Journal of Science
Education, 21,* 77–94.

Shrigley, R.L. (1987). Discrepant events: Why they fascinate students. *Science and Education, 24,*
24–25.

Suchman, R. (1966). *Inquiry development program: Developing inquiry.* Chicago: Science Research
Associates.

Van Fossen, P.J., & Shiveley, J.M. (1997). "Hmmm...": Creating inquiry problems in the elementary
social studies classroom. *The Social Studies, 88,* 71–77.

Yell, M.M. (2002). Inquiry with an e-book: A natural strategy for social studies. *Social Education,
66*(3), 184–185.

1976), puzzled the children. Some students asked, "Why would Cassie's white
friend demand that Cassie [an African American] step off the sidewalk to let her pass
when they met in town?" "How could she [white friend] want to be friends with
Cassie but act like that?" (Busching & Slesinger, p. 126). The teacher believed that
by deeply immersing the class in the topic through a mix of fiction and nonfiction,
family histories, poetry, and visuals that the students would develop an adequate
knowledge base to frame higher level research questions. These questions could
relate to the conceptual conflict between the actions of a segregated society and the
democratic ideals of tolerance and equality. The teacher and research collaborator
called this knowledge-based thinking approach an **immersion model of inquiry**.

Ms. Slesinger also engaged the students in developing a personal awareness that social issues are not just somebody else's problems, but are ones that could be faced by all people during times of crisis. Within this framework, her students began to demonstrate the ability to ask higher level thinking questions.

Ms. Slesinger's instruction in language arts is similar to that of the fictional Mrs. Mangrum, the language arts teacher represented in the Adolescent Literacy Commission report (see Preface). Both teachers used the same popular adolescent novel, *Roll of Thunder, Hear My Cry*, as an engaging resource to help students immerse themselves in the unit of study. They also used the young adult novel as a vehicle to instruct students in self-questioning as both comprehension and inquiry strategies. They recognized the motivational impact of relevant young adult children's literature as a source of student questioning.

In another inquiry unit on the Holocaust, Ms. Slesinger used young adult literature again. But this time she selected an ambiguous story of a young hero, *Rose Blanche* (Innocenti & Gallez, 1990), to actually launch the new unit. The story engaged the class and served as an effective catch facet. The students generated a number of spontaneous questions. But the teacher learned again, as with the unit on the U.S. Great Depression, that these initial student questions were low level or superficial. She discovered that many of the students were unable to discuss the topic deeply, because they were critically unaware that barriers of separation existed between European Jews and other Europeans during the Nazi era. She realized again that the class needed to be immersed in the topic to develop a sufficient knowledge base to generate higher level questions. When the students developed a strong factual foundation, their higher level questions grew naturally out of their new knowledge. Through the immersion inquiry method, Ms. Slesinger was able to hold the students' attention to the extent that they could develop mature self-generated questions.

PAUSE AND PONDER

Pulitzer Prize–winning author and language arts high school teacher Frank McCourt (2005) describes his teaching philosophy and pedagogy in the following way:

> It was clear I was not cut out to be the purposeful kind of teacher who brushed aside all questions, requests, complaints, to get on with the well-planned lesson. That would have reminded me of that school in Limerick (Ireland) where the lesson was king and we were nothing. I was dreaming of a school where teachers were guides and mentors, not taskmasters... If a principal had ever said, the class is yours, teacher. Do with it what you like; I would have said to my students, push the chairs. Sit on the floor. Go to sleep. What? I said, Go to sleep. Why? Figure it out for yourself... The bell rings and they're slow off the floor. They leave the room, relaxed and puzzled. Please don't ask me why I'd have such a session. It must be the spirit that moves. (p. 24)

Motivating Physical Education Instruction Through Question-Finding

The motivational constructs of self-determination and curiosity can be used to develop question-finding in physical education. Earlier in this chapter, I mentioned how the construct of self-determination explained the importance of autonomy and relevance as innate needs in a person's life (Ryan & Deci, 2000). These self-determination factors play a significant role in the physical education curriculum, particularly in the study of body knowledge and image (Oliver & Lalik, 2004a). Adolescents, especially girls, show a strong interest in their bodies as they undergo a developmental period of extensive physical change. Indeed, psychologists who work with adolescents tell us that "body image" becomes a primary concern for girls at this age (Jones, Vigfusdottir, & Lee, 2004).

Adolescence is also a time of enhanced self-exploration. To capitalize on this natural inclination, researchers in a physical education project related to gender stereotypes gave students the choice of topic selection (Oliver & Lalik, 2000). The students selected how fashion magazines present stereotypical and harmful body images of teens. As part of their project assignment, the instructors suggested interviewing other students, faculty, and parents related to the topic of girls' body image and cultural norms. The instructors modeled how to construct specific questions for the interview questionnaire in order to guide exploration of how texts construct identities. They also modeled how to raise questions that challenge society's view of normal adolescent identity development, which often stipulates only one authentic adolescent identity. Their questions were posed to resist this notion in favor of one that showed the creation of multiple, subjectively acceptable identities that are in states of flux. Of course, this topic was intrinsically motivating to the students because it was highly relevant to their needs for autonomy and identity development.

Oliver and Lalik (2004b) also discussed with several adolescent girls the issue of beauty pageants as a subtopic of body image awareness. In one girls' high school, a pageant called "the Beauty Walk" was an annual school event. To investigate what other students in the school felt about the event, the researchers and girls devised an interview questionnaire. The researchers modeled and scaffolded good questioning techniques. Then they directed the girls to consider the assumptions embedded in the students' own questions. Some of these assumptions revealed the conceptual conflict between students' personal views on the issue and dominant cultural narratives. Some of the student-generated questions included both puzzlement questions and wonderment questions such as, "How do you think the Beauty Walk makes girls feel about themselves? Why do they have a Beauty Walk for girls and not for boys? Imagine you won/lost the Beauty Walk, describe how it would make you feel about yourself" (p. 559). The process of creating the questionnaire helped the girls to use their own questions to dialogue across their own differences, as well as those of the dominant cultural narratives (Oliver & Lalik). This is a good example of question-finding in action.

PAUSE AND PONDER

> Motivation and disposition are important criteria for question-finding in all content areas. During a discussion on the topic of whether the universe is finite or infinite, a student in Michael Rose's (1989) astronomy tutorial class, which consisted of high school graduates, commented, "This is the kind of question that you'll argue and argue about. It's stupid. No one wins. So why do it?" (pp. 189–190).
>
> • Compare this student's attitude toward unanswerable questions to that of Eduardo's (see Preface). Which type of disposition regarding questions do students in your classes have?

Motivating Science Instruction Through Question-Finding

There is strong evidence in the research literature that motivation is subject and domain specific (Wigfield et al., 2004). The natures of certain academic disciplines lend themselves to particular motivational constructs and vice versa. Some of the earliest empirical evidence for the **motivation/domain synthesis** occurs in the work on epistemic curiosity by Berlyne (1965), who noted, in particular, that the physical, natural, and chemical natures of the different science disciplines relied on the motivational element of surprise, a main feature of epistemic curiosity. Berlyne claimed that whenever scientific evidence challenged the naïve or sense impressions of scientific phenomena, the new evidence surprised people. These surprising events are often discrepant because they violate people's expectations of what should be happening. Suchman (1969) also recognized the affinity of discrepant events and science and created a successful science inquiry-training project for adolescents in the 1960s. Suchman's inquiry methods used discrepant events to stimulate students to generate questions. This inquiry method is also sometimes known as the discovery approach to learning and has become an important instructional strategy in all content areas.

Suchman's (1969) inquiry-training method of using counterintuitive scientific episodes to engender motivational interest is used in science classes today, although in a somewhat different format. High school physics teacher Wayne Williams and a university literacy professor used one such adaptation (Guzzetti, 2001). The teacher and the professor used a motivational strategy called **refutational discussion** as an inquiry procedure. In this procedure, Mr. Williams introduced a **refutational text** related to a teaching episode involving projective motion (e.g., movement and frequency of an electric fan). The counterintuitive idea was introduced to challenge students' naïve conceptions about projective motion. To stimulate interest in the content, the teacher secretly selected a student who would, on cue, supply the scientifically incorrect but logical answer to the counterintuitive question. This student ally was called a "shill." The shill had to convince the class that the unscientific answer was correct.

Refutational discussion created what Berlyne and Frommer (1966) called a motivational state of conceptual conflict. The elements of surprise caused students to become puzzled by their initial answers related to the experiment discussed above. This puzzlement stimulated epistemic curiosity and aroused the students to seek information through self-generated questions.

Experiments and classroom demonstrations can be deliberately planned to stimulate conceptual conflict. Anders and Guzzetti (1996) have labeled this type of demonstration an **augmented activation activity** because it is designed to create surprise and incongruity in students' minds. It is a powerful technique for teaching and learning counterintuitive concepts in science and other content areas and for developing question-finding skills (Guzzetti, Snyder, Glass, & Gamas, 1993).

According to the National Science Education Standards (NRC, 1996), "inquiry into authentic questions generated from student experiences is the central strategy for teaching science" (p. 31). The following classroom example from the NRC (2000) indicates that discrepant situations can literally occur in one's own backyard, or as in the case below, in the schoolyard. These situations can stimulate authentic question-finding on the part of students.

Several students in a middle school science class returned from an outdoor activity and told their teacher about the unusual appearance of three trees growing side by side. They described one tree that lost all its leaves, the middle one had multicolored leaves, and the third had lush, green leaves. They asked, "Why are those three trees different? They used to look the same, didn't they?" (NRC, 2000, p. 6). The teacher indicated that she did not know the answer, but that they would collaboratively investigate the matter in class later in the week. Mrs. Graham realized that even though the topic of plant life would appear later in the curriculum, this was an opportunity to investigate questions that the students themselves had originated and were especially motivated to answer.

Although she was uncertain about where the students' questions would lead, she allowed the students to pursue their investigation under her guidance. The students generated lists of ideas as possible explanations and set up investigations to confirm or reject these hypotheses. As the investigation continued, some ideas were discounted and then the students formulated new questions. Eventually, some students found evidence to answer their initial questions. They shared their research findings with other class members. Mrs. Graham and her students practiced what the National Science Education Standards (NRC, 1996) calls "full inquiry or the asking of a simple student generated question, completing an investigation, answering the question, and presenting the results to others" (p. 123). That is, they demonstrated question-finding in the science classroom.

PAUSE AND PONDER

According to Berlyne (1965), conceptual conflict situations occur from different sources (e.g., incongruity, novelty, surprise, and so forth). Some of these sources are more directly associated with specific content area learning than others. Berlyne claims that the motivational potential of surprise is especially powerful in science lessons involving demonstrations of physical, chemical, or biological phenomenon. He states that surprising scientific events violate one's expectations based on prior knowledge. On the other hand, he states that there is little pedagogical value of surprise in such disciplines as mathematics because students generally have insufficient previous knowledge in this discipline to challenge new knowledge. Thus, Berlyne claims that students in mathematics are less likely to experience the effects of surprise and conceptual conflict.

• Do you agree with Berlyne? Does the motivational element of surprise have an impact on students' ability to generate questions in content areas?

Summary

In this chapter, I focused on question-finding and the motivational dimension of literacy. Specifically, I showed how activities that induce student questioning enhance academic motivation. I also discussed the psychological parameters of motivational literacy including the important constructs of self-efficacy, self-determination, and curiosity. I provided classroom examples showing the impact of question-finding on these constructs. Last, I showed how a question-driven learning environment could stimulate situational interest and induce academic motivation. In the next chapter, I discuss another literacy dimension of question-finding, one that stimulates the development of critical literacy practices.

PONDER AND PRACTICE

1. Using refutational text with adolescents is an instructional strategy that is effective in helping them to generate questions. Refutational text consists of a passage that identifies a misconception and then directly challenges it by explaining the scientifically accepted conception (Anders & Guzzetti, 1996). By juxtaposing the conflicting alternative conceptions and pointing out the error in one of them, refutational text induces conceptual conflict, the stimulant to question-finding. The following is an example of refutational text:

   > Many people believe a bowling ball rolling freely down a level alleyway will slow or stop on its own. This will not happen. If the floor did not produce friction to slow the bowling ball, it would continue to move forward down the alley at a constant speed. Scientists have created frictionless environments in which moving objects do not stop on their own. (Adapted from Shanahan, 2004, p. 84)

   - Science educators have been using refutational text for many years. Can you create refutational text in your content area?
   - How can refutational text induce question-finding in your content specialty?

2. Adolescents need heroes or models to emulate in order to enhance their self-identities. Too often school curricula neglect to focus on young people's accomplishments in different areas of life. One eighth-grade student remarked about the problem with social studies, "We're not taught about younger people (in school) who have made a difference" (Hoose, 2001, p. vi). In his unique book, *We Were There, Too! Young People in American History*, Philip Hoose describes the contributions of young people in American history. I use this book in my social studies methods classes to help students practice the strategy of question-finding.

   - Are there young people who have made contributions in your field of study?
   - If there are, how can their accomplishments stimulate question-finding?

3. Literacy researchers tell us that there are cultural and linguistic ways of knowing that influence the motivation for literacy (Alvermann, 2003; Willis, 2002). This is

particularly important in terms of adolescents' identities that are often shaped by literacies other than traditional school-based ones. Bean had an intergenerational conversation with his adolescent daughters and learned that popular culture seemed to have a greater effect on their literacy development than schoolwork (Bean, Bean, & Bean, 1999). I have also gained some insights on this topic from my daughter, who is a social worker with adolescents. She discovered that popular culture is an effective and motivating factor in adolescent adjustment (S. Ciardiello, 2003). Specifically, she organized a group work program called The Lab where youth in residential settings such as group homes analyzed hip-hop music lyrics during discussion groups. They discussed the themes that were similar to their own lives such as domestic abuse, familial drug addiction, and foster care placement. Studio equipment was available to residents in The Lab so they could create their own music to accompany lyrics they wrote about their life experiences. The Lab became an engaging milieu where the residents felt safe in expressing their feelings and sharing their stories. The program expanded to the creation of a resident magazine called *The Real Deal: Kids Keeping It Real.* This program demonstrates the power of using popular culture to engage adolescents in learning and healing.

- Are you able to include adolescents' linguistic and cultural ways of knowing in your teaching?
- How can knowledge of adolescents' multiple literacies support question-finding?

4. Literacy educator Donna Alvermann (2003) has proposed that adolescents need a re/mediation of literacy instruction. By re/mediation, she does not mean the traditional fix-up strategies to remove so-called literacy deficits. She refers to re/mediation in its expanded sense of "refashioning curricular and instructional conditions so that they incorporate multiple forms of media" (p. 2). These multiple forms include books, magazines, visual images, music lyrics, and the Internet. Alvermann believes that re/mediation can be an effective literacy orientation in all content areas and is highly engaging to adolescents who already possess a rich background of experience in working with texts that go beyond print.

- Can you think of ways to re/mediate instruction in your discipline?
- How can re/mediation induce students to generate questions in your field?

5. Can music be used to develop literacy learning in content area instruction? Former middle school science teacher and current teacher educator Carol Lloyd (2003)

used music lyrics from the 1970 Cat Stevens song, "Where Do the Children Play?" as a motivational tool to explore the issue of the human and environmental costs of progress in an elective science class called "Ecology and Botany." Alvermann (2003) praised the motivational technique as an aid to student questioning. She claimed that an important result of this integrated science and music lesson was that the "students became more aware of a society's decision-making powers (with regard to problems) in their own environment and began asking the kinds of questions that informed citizens need to have answered" (p. 8).

- Do you see the value of using music in teaching literacy and learning in your discipline?
- Do you believe that music lyrics can stimulate students to ask questions in your classes?

CHAPTER 3

Question–Finding and Critical Literacy

```
IMPORTANT CONCEPTS AND SPECIALIZED TERMS

competing narratives          critical questions              recognizing social barriers and
critical awareness            cultural constructions              crossing borders of
critical literacy             examining multiple                  separation
critical literacy practices       perspectives                regaining one's identity
critical literacy proficiencies   finding one's authentic voice   resistant reading
critical orientation to literacy  internalized oppression         tentative exploratory behavior
```

Teacher: Our class has been examining different types of puzzling materials on the Great Depression in the United States. Some are controversial or contain different opinions on a topic. Do these contradictory documents have an effect on your ability to find questions to ask?

I asked this question of my 11th-grade social studies class. In response to this question, one of my students expressed puzzlement. He described the learning experience of using contradictory sources of information as creating a feeling of going against yourself in your thinking. As previously mentioned, Berlyne (1960) called this type of puzzlement conceptual conflict. In the unit of study in 11th-grade American history, this conflict was created by the competing ideas or opinions related to the topic of the U.S. Great Depression. This type of puzzlement is different from that presented in chapters 1 and 2. In these chapters, the sources that stimulated the puzzlement contained an internal dissonance or self-contradiction. These materials created a conflict between the reader's expectations about the topic and the discrepant source of new information. In this chapter, multiple discrepant sources are presented as **competing narratives**, or divergent perspectives of the same event. Some of the conflicting narratives and incongruous messages in these units of study are ideological in nature. Incongruous materials reveal the problematic and tentative nature of visual and written text. Often these narratives try to position the reader.

Helping students become more aware of the ideological and nonneutral nature of text can help develop their critical literacy skills. For the purposes of this book, **critical literacy** is defined in terms of self-questioning and conceptual inquiry. Specifically, it is communication acts and habits of thought that question official knowledge by going beneath dominant myths and official pronouncements to understand the deep meaning, social context, and ideology of literate events. Critical literacy seeks to provoke conceptual inquiry into self, society, and the very nature of disciplines or content areas under study (Shor, 1987, 1992). **Critical literacy practices** empower students to go beneath surface impressions to become active questioners of the social reality of text (Freire, 1994). (See Table 9 for resources on critical literacy.)

In this chapter, I show how question-finding can help students to develop a **critical orientation to literacy**. This critical orientation calls for a different type of questioning behavior. It calls for the development of **critical questions** that interrogate the ideological meanings of text.

Models of Critical Literacy

Herbeck and Beier (2003) explain that teachers need models of critical literacy in order to incorporate critical literacy perspectives into their teaching. In this chapter, I describe units of study in different content areas as models of critical literacy. These models can help illustrate for teachers how students can be taught to develop critical perspectives toward different types of textual materials. The models consist of the following guidelines: criteria for topic selection, designation of critical literacy practices, and development of **critical literacy proficiencies**. With some adaptation depending on the content area, these teaching units can be used to show how question-finding skills can be used to develop in students a critical orientation to literacy.

Criteria for Topic Selection

Not all topics in every teacher's curriculum will lend themselves to critical literacy and question-finding. Teachers need to select a topic that contains competing ideological narratives and conflicting events in their content area. Also, teachers need to select a unit of study that is motivational so students are eager to pursue their own critical questions (refer to examples of motivational units in chapter 2). Teachers should provide sufficient time and resources for students to immerse themselves in the topic. Do not present introductory and fixed unit guide questions; let the questions emerge as students acquire greater background knowledge on the topic. Select a topic that is relevant to critical literacy concerns and generally deals with social and cultural issues. Topics also should lend themselves to a critical exploration of the literacy practices and proficiencies described in the next section.

TABLE 9. Resources on Critical Literacy

Bean, T.W., & Moni, K. (2003). Developing students' critical literacy: Exploring identity construction in young adult fiction. *Journal of Adolescent & Adult Literacy*, 46, 638–648.

Berry, K.S. (2000). *The dramatic arts and cultural studies: Acting against the grain*. New York: Falmer.

Cadeiro-Kaplan, K. (2002). Literacy ideologues: Critically engaging the language arts curriculum. *Language Arts*, 79, 372–381.

Cairney, T.H. (1995). *Pathways to literacy*. London: Cassell.

Comber, B. (1994). Critical literacy: An introduction to Australian debates and perspectives. *Journal of Curriculum Studies*, 26, 655–668.

Freebody, P., & Luke, A. (1990). Literacies' programs: Debates and demands in cultural context. *Prospect: The Journal of Adult Migrant Education Programs*, 5. Retrieved August 13, 2003, from http://www.discover.tased.edu.au/english/critlit.htm

Freire, P. (1970). *Pedagogy of the oppressed*. New York: Continuum.

Freire, P., & Macedo, D. (1987). *Literacy: Reading the word and the world*. Westport, CT: Bergin & Garvey.

Gee, J.P. (2000–2001). Identity as an analytic lens for research in education. In W.G. Segato (Ed.), *Review of research in education* (pp. 99–125). Washington DC: American Educational Research Association.

Giroux, H. (1991). Beyond the ethics of flag waving: Schooling and citizenship for a critical democracy. *The Clearing House*, 64, 305–308.

Leistyna, P., Woodrum, A., & Sherblom, S. (Eds.). (1996). *Breaking free: The transformative power of critical pedagogy*. Cambridge, MA: Harvard Educational Review.

Leland, C., Harste, J., Ociepka, M., Lewison, M., & Vasquez, V. (1999). Exploring critical literacy: You can hear a pin drop. *Language Arts*, 77, 70–77.

Luke, A., & Freebody, P. (1997). Shaping the social practices of reading. In S. Muspratt, A. Luke, & P. Freebody (Eds.), *Constructing critical literacies: Teaching and learning textual practice* (pp.185–225). Cresskill, NJ: Hampton.

Powell, R., Cantrell, S.C., & Adams, S. (2001). Saving Black Mountain: The promise of critical literacy in a multicultural democracy. *The Reading Teacher*, 54, 772–781.

Semali, L.M. (2000). *Literacy in multimedia America: Integrating media education across the curriculum*. New York: Falmer.

Shannon, P. (2001). My mind is going through them changes. *The Reading Teacher*, 54, 586–589.

Simpson, A. (1996). Critical questions: Whose questions? *The Reading Teacher*, 50, 118–127.

Vasquez, V. (2003). *Getting beyond "I like the book": Creating space for critical literacy in K–6 classrooms*. Newark, DE: International Reading Association.

Critical Literacy Practices and Proficiencies

Critical literacy practices are literacy activities that help enlighten the reader about the ulterior designs and multiple meanings of text (Luke & Freebody, 1997). In this section, I introduce four practices that all teachers can use to help develop a critical orientation in their subject areas: (1) **examining multiple perspectives**, (2) **finding one's authentic voice**, (3) **recognizing social barriers and crossing borders of separation**, and (4) **regaining one's identity** (see Figure 6). I also show how these critical literacy practices can be integrated into selected units of study in different content areas. In order to engage effectively in these critical literacy practices, it is first necessary to develop certain critical proficiencies.

Teachers need to provide opportunities for students to engage in critical literacy practices through the development of four proficiencies. Critical literacy proficiencies are those literacy skills that aid students in accomplishing the critical literacy practices. They include the following: developing a **critical awareness**, engaging in critical conversations, critical reading, and constructing critical questions. Following is a brief description of each of these proficiencies.

First, developing a critical awareness involves demonstrating specific cognitive and metacognitive skills, which include recognizing ideological meanings of text, detecting ambiguities and anomalies, and identifying multiple meanings. Second,

FIGURE 6. Critical Literacy Practices

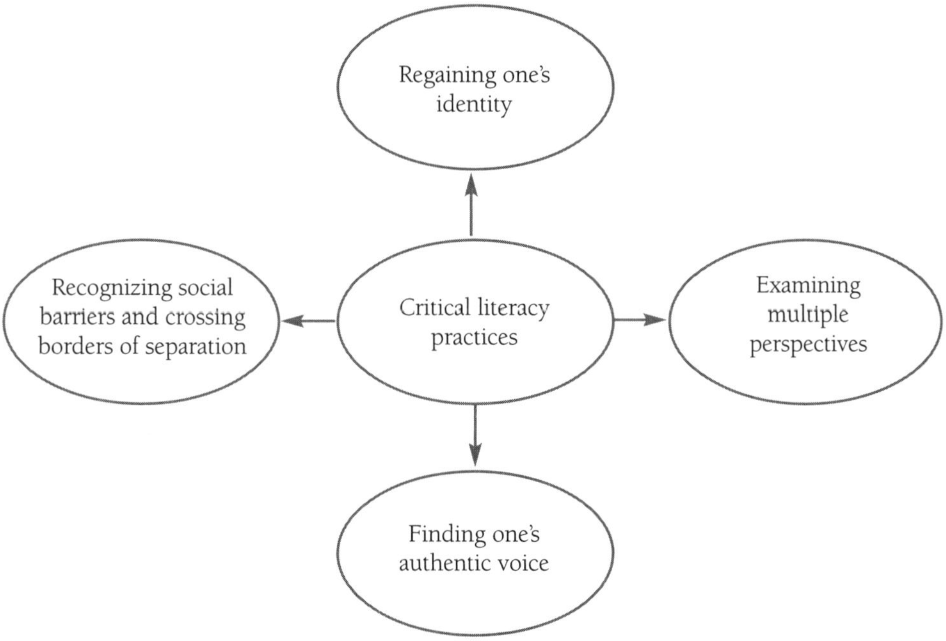

Adapted from Ciardiello, A.V. (2004). Democracy's young heroes: An instructional model of critical literacy practices. *The Reading Teacher*, 58(2), 139.

engaging in critical conversations involves the use of oral discourse to interrogate any text that attempts to position students. This can be done through critical discussions of personal issues, items of popular culture, and stories from young adult literature. Third, critical reading extends on the previous proficiency through the interrogation of content area texts and artifacts. This involves the development of **resistant reading**, or reading against the grain of the text. Fourth, the development of scaffolds and prompts can help students to construct critical questions. The model units in this chapter show how the four literacy proficiencies help students to accomplish the four critical literacy practices. In addition, I provide a rubric to guide teachers in evaluating students' proficiencies for each of the critical literacy practices (see Table 10).

An important objective of this chapter is to give models of student-generated critical questions through four critical literacy practices. A critically literate student does not stay at the surface level but penetrates to the deep meaning of an event.

TABLE 10. Critical Literacy and Question-Finding Rubric

Criteria	Target	Acceptable	Unacceptable
Multiple perspectives • critical awareness • critical conversations • critical reading • constructing critical questions	Demonstrates proficiencies in critical literacy practice	Partially demonstrates proficiencies in critical literacy practice	Unable to demonstrate proficiencies in critical literacy practice
Authentic voices • critical awareness • critical conversations • critical reading • constructing critical questions	Demonstrates proficiencies in critical literacy practice	Partially demonstrates proficiencies in critical literacy practice	Unable to demonstrate proficiencies in critical literacy practice
Overcoming social barriers • critical awareness • critical conversations • critical reading • constructing critical questions	Demonstrates proficiencies in critical literacy practice	Partially demonstrates proficiencies in critical literacy practice	Unable to demonstrate proficiencies in critical literacy practice
Regaining identity • critical awareness • critical conversations • critical reading • constructing critical questions	Demonstrates proficiencies in critical literacy practice	Partially demonstrates proficiencies in critical literacy practice	Unable to demonstrate proficiencies in critical literacy practice

This deep processing of text helps students to find and ask distinctive types of questions called critical questions (Simpson, 1996). Critical questions are those that are concerned with matters of power, authority, and authenticity rather than with literal comprehension of surface meanings. This deep processing also helps students recognize that the social world is composed of unequal discourses and that some voices are silenced and marginalized (Luke, 2000). It is important for the critical reader to listen for the multiple voices in the text and to find critical questions to ask such as the following: Whose voice is not being heard? Who benefits from this reading? How is the text trying to position me? What were the author's intentions and motives in creating this text? Thus, the critical reader interrogates the hidden agendas and assumptions of the text writer (Luke & Freebody, 1997).

It is important to note that the critical questions must be the students own to find. Simpson (1996) explains that it is through students' self-selected questions or "critical perspective toward texts" that the process of the critical exploration of texts can occur (p. 122). This is a process of getting students to recognize that many of the questions that they ask initially will not appear on the surface to lead to critical understanding. This process takes time. As Harste recommends, students need time "to wander and wonder in terms of finding inquiry questions that interest and sustain their curiosity" (as cited in Monson & Monson, 1994, p. 519).

PAUSE AND PONDER

Creating class time for "wandering and wondering" seems counterproductive in today's high-stakes testing environment. Yet, this question-finding disposition and practice can enrich the acquisition of multiple literacies in content area learning. Using the process of question-finding to aid in the development of critical literacy is a novel procedure that will require staff development training.

- What role do you see for teacher training in this light? Would this require a change in classroom pedagogy? To what extent does critical literacy call for a change in educational philosophy as well as classroom pedagogy?

In the remainder of this chapter, I show how a selected critical literacy practice can be accomplished through a focus unit of study in different content areas including American history, physics, and language arts. Each critical literacy practice features the four critical proficiencies needed for its successful execution. Finally, these units of study illustrate how the question-finding process can help to develop a critical orientation to literacy in a specific content area.

Critical Literacy and Examining Multiple Perspectives

One critical literacy practice is examining multiple perspectives (Lewison, Flint, & van Sluys, 2002). To help students understand and execute this practice, teachers can follow a procedure that involves aiding students in the development of the four critical literacy proficiencies discussed in the previous section.

The following procedure can aid teachers in examining multiple perspectives related to a social justice issue. First, introduce the idea of multiple perspectives through personal stories, children's picture books, and young adult literature. Have a critical conversation related to different viewpoints about particular issues in one's family. Ask students if they have experienced times when their parents disagreed about something that involved them. Second, read the narrative and show the pictures from *Voices in the Park* (Browne, 2001), which portrays an incident in a city park from four different accounts involving parents and their children. Relate to students that different participants and observers can view the same event in different ways. Stress that no single version tells the whole story; there are often gaps as well as contradictions in the telling. Third, help students to see the ideological conflict between the opposing sides.

Focus Unit of Study: American History, High School

In a unit of study on Cesar Chavez and the California grape strike (1965–1970), my 11th-grade students discussed the conflicting labor and management positions. They read the opposing views as expressed in Tables 11 and 12. They became critically aware that language often reflects power relationships, and that this kind of language is often used to support ideological positions. One student understood this point when she made a comparison between the ranchers in Delano, California (where the strike originated), who say the farm workers are happy, and the Southern plantation owners who said something similar about the slaves.

TABLE 11. Union Organizer Testifies

What the farm workers in our country are asking for is an opportunity to earn a living wage. Farm workers want union recognition so badly that on September 16 [1965], we began a strike against those employers who paid us $1.10 per hour, no overtime, and no fringe benefits. We went on strike, knowing full well that the Federal laws which protect other striking workers would not help us. And today, six months later, we are still on strike....

Testimony of Cesar Chavez, "Amending Migratory Labor Laws," *Hearings Before the Subcommittee on Migratory Labor of the Committee on Labor and Public Welfare*, United States Senate, 89th Congress, First and Second Sessions, 1966, 361–363.

TABLE 12. Grape Vineyard Owner Responds

The simple truth is...there is no strike in Delano. More than 5,000 of the people who regularly...picked our crops stayed in the job. Instead of striking workers, the picket lines consisted almost entirely of campus agitators, ministers, paid professionals—all people who were trying to maintain the fiction that a strike existed. We have been asked: Why don't you negotiate with the unions [i.e., National Farm Workers Association]? Our answer is simply this: Our workers are not interested in becoming part of these unions. They have rejected all their efforts. We cannot, in good conscience...enter into any type of negotiations with these unions and thereby force our workers into something that is not of their own free choice.

Testimony of Martin Zaninovich, "Amending Migratory Labor Laws," *Hearings Before the Subcommittee on Migratory Labor of the Committee on Labor and Public Welfare*, United States Senate, 89th Congress, First and Second Sessions, 1966, 591–593.

The students were perplexed by the competing messages delivered by each side in the California grape strike and wanted to know if this was a real strike as Cesar Chavez and the grape pickers contended (Table 11) or if it was a "legal fiction" as the owners advanced (Table 12). Upon continued study and discussion of the conflict, students began to recognize that the traditionally marginalized and silenced voices of the grape workers now demanded to be heard. Students raised their own follow-up puzzlement questions (explanation type) and wonderment questions that were critical of the event. One student wanted to know if there was a cover-up on the part of the Delano Grape Company that had to deal with the strikers. Another student's questions related to the activities of Chavez and the grape workers, wondering what hope Chavez had for the migrant workers and how he might have expected the California grape strike to change their lives. Yet another student's reconstruction of the grape strike was very fundamental, wondering whether the strikers (migrant workers) were really striking only because of the problems at Delano, or because of the way they had been treated wherever they went. This student saw the strike in terms of human rights and not just economic issues. She reached a conclusion that the workers were striking in reaction against inhuman labor conditions. Thus, the workers were in need of human rights, too.

These critical, student-generated questions and wonderings paved the way for further investigation and inquiry. Some of the students' responses to their own open-ended research questions included the following:

- Continue to find more documents that Chavez has written in order for me to be fully aware of his role in this situation so I can have a better picture of his accomplishments and what he is doing to help the workers. To find other views of the workers and try to understand what they feel and what they are planning to do in the future so that I can be able to put myself in their places and include their feelings and attitudes in my paper.

- I would go to the library and pull out any article I could find on the California grape strike. I would write to the California Grape and Free Fruit League for information about the strike. I would write to the Delano, California, newspapers asking it [*sic*] for any information they have about the outcome of the strike.

- I'd look up information on Cesar Chavez using articles, newspaper clippings, the encyclopedia, and books written by others regarding the strike that were written during that time. (Adapted from Ciardiello, 2003, pp. 237–238)

The students raised open-ended questions not for the purpose of finding immediate solutions to a problem or to support a position, but as steppingstones to further investigation of a complex issue. As question-finders, the students manifested **tentative exploratory behavior**. They demonstrated that they needed to probe deeper into the problematic situation involving the conflicting testimony about the California grape strike. They realized that their first or preliminary questions did not serve the purpose of finding ultimate satisfying answers. Indeed, the students recognized that their original questions were far less significant than the two or three others that flowed from them (Postman & Weingartner, 1969). Poet John Ciardi expressed this view lyrically when he composed, "a good question is never answered. It is not a bolt to be tightened into place but a seed to be planted and to bear more seed toward the hope of greening the landscape of ideas" (as cited in Christensen, 1987, p. 45).

PAUSE AND PONDER

While teaching in an inner-city high school, I learned that lower achieving students could think and discuss topics at higher levels of cognition. My 11th-grade students revealed this as we studied a complex issue on labor and management (i.e., the California grape strike in the 1960s). One student demonstrated a major principle of critical literacy when she questioned and critiqued the nature of unequal power relationships, manifested in the attitude of ranchers in Delano who professed that the striking workers were really happy with their working conditions just as the Southern plantation owners had once said about their slaves. Another student showed that she could generate questions related to critical issues pertaining to the strike. She perceived the strike as one of a fundamental struggle for human rights beside the more ostensible quest for economic justice. These high-level responses from my apparently low-level academic students helped me gain new insights into the potential of all students to ask critical questions.

> • Do you feel that lower achieving adolescents can deal with advanced literacy and inquiry practices such as question-finding and critical literacy? If yes, how does this attitude conflict with traditional thinking that students need basic literacy skills before being introduced to advanced cognitive processes? If no, what could be done to build up students' basic literacy skills to be able to deal with higher level cognitive instruction?

Finding One's Authentic Voice

Examining texts for multiple viewpoints leads students to recognize the importance of finding their authentic voice as another critical literacy practice. The concept of "voice" refers to the opportunity to express oneself in freedom without regard to power or position. This is often a challenge because the social world is composed of different and unequal discourses (Luke & Freebody, 1997). Faced with inequitable social relationships, marginal groups often need to search and find their own authentic voices. This is a difficult task because those in positions of dominance often silence other voices. The ability to detect the persuasive influence of dominant discourse can help students to distinguish between the different political and social ideologies that attempt to sway their stances and voice on public matters.

One way for teachers to make this complex idea meaningful for students is to help students understand the concept of authentic voice as it relates to their own lives. For example, I modeled this practice with a group of seventh graders in their language arts class by personalizing this critical concept through discussions of family relationships. With the students, I asked the following questions: Who is the boss in your family? Were you ever the boss? Do you have any power yourself in making decisions for your family? Should children have a dominant voice in the family? The answers varied about the nature of the word *boss*. Several students said they became the boss when they were left in charge of younger siblings. Other students claimed that they often made key decisions about purchasing or operating new computer technology gadgets, an area in which they had more expertise than their parents (Ciardiello, 2004).

Focus Unit of Study: Physics, High School

It is important for students to become aware that the critical literacy practice of finding one's authentic voice is socially constructed (D.R. Dillon & Moje, 1998). For example, certain language practices contribute to the domination and oppression of females in the classroom. Gender bias is a cultural norm that prevents the expression of authentic voice. This is particularly evident for females in middle and high school classrooms. Sadker and Sadker (1994) report that this is especially the case with regard to the sciences. Indeed, the researchers claim that "of all the subjects on the curricular landscape, physical science is the most male of all" (p. 123). Thus, the focus unit of study in this section is gender disparities and inequities in the physical sciences (physics). The purpose of this unit is to show how this phenomenon prevents females from engaging equitably in class discussions and generating questions with the overall purpose of finding one's authentic voice.

Instructional practices in the physical sciences contribute to gender inequities in several respects. First, research shows that science teachers often are not aware of how their teaching methods and styles may contribute to gender bias; however, both male and female students consistently report male domination in class discussions and lab presentations (Guzzetti & Williams, 1996). Second, science curricula tend to neglect the topic of gender inequities. Third, teacher-training institutions do not focus on the issue in their undergraduate and graduate courses. Indeed, a national survey revealed that two thirds of education professors spent less than two hours teaching about gender equity (Campbell & Sanders, 1997).

Gender equity is particularly important for question-finding, because male domination in physical science classes prevents females from developing higher level thinking skills, and this disenfranchises them in learning science. Evidence of this occurred in Mr. Williams's high school physics class during a discussion of gravity and projective notions (Guzzetti, 2001). The science teacher presented counterintuitive ideas on the subject in an effort to stimulate inquiry learning (also a key factor in stimulating question-finding). The inquiry training followed the refutational discussion procedure (p. 134). This procedure involves challenges and counterchallenges among participants to maintain or change initial conceptions on a topic. It illustrated the male way of learning that tends to favor the argumentative type activity, and no females participated. Indeed, females remarked that "the boys are loud and obnoxious and they try to show off, so it intimidates girls from asking questions because they might get made fun of" (Guzzetti, p. 142). Clearly, the refutational discussion procedure manifested asymmetrical power relations in favor of males and marginalized females from asking questions in class discussions. Also, because question-finding depends on a learning environment that offers opportunities to detect and interrogate discrepant concepts, this form of asymmetrical discussion definitely puts females at a distinct disadvantage.

Alvermann, Commeyras, and Young (1997) claim that when female students' opinions are challenged, young girls often practice a form of self-deprecating discourse that the researchers called "sorry talk" [I'm sorry, but I disagree] (p. 86).

The researchers created a data-driven poem that expressed this self-deprecating female talk that is particularly relevant to questioning behavior. It reads, "Joy admits she didn't ask that question very well. She's sorry" (p. 86). This kind of attitude is antithetical to question-finding. Male intimidation of females in science classes prevents open-ended and equitable critical conversations.

There is some evidence that science materials and textbooks also reinforce gender inequities (Sadker & Sadker, 1994; Zittleman & Sadker, 2002–2003). A female high school student complained specifically that her physics book neglected to portray women in illustrations and pictures related to physical science activities. The women were portrayed in passive roles (Guzzetti & Willams, 1996). Recently, there seems to be some progress as textbook publishers make attempts to equalize the number of comparable illustrations in textbooks. However, there is still precious little narrative of the scientific contributions of women (Zittleman & Sadker). Students need to be taught to read against the grain of text material that portrays gender stereotypes and reinforces gender inequities.

Even when teachers and texts attempt to practice gender equity, the language and cultural norms of the physical science classroom often shortchange females in the area of higher level thinking. The traditional presentation of physical science topics works against "female ways of learning" (i.e., females' collaborative discussion style and human interest orientation; Guzzetti & Williams, 1996). For example, Heather, a 10th grader, could not get enthusiastic about the nuclear chemistry unit because she did not see the relevance of it to her life (D.R. Dillon & Moje, 1998). She had no impetus to discuss or question the content. She could not develop a critical stance toward the subject matter—a necessary ingredient of deep understanding of content learning (McLaughlin & DeVoogd, 2004). In her words, "the questions did not burn on (my) mind" [did not seem to generate interest or passion] (D.R. Dillon & Moje, p. 221). Students' questions are not generated in a learning atmosphere that stultifies intellectual stimulation and personal relevance.

What could be done to help students such as Heather become engaged in science and generate higher level thinking questions? Teachers can provide opportunities in the classroom to encourage females to use their ways to "talk science" (i.e., collaborative discussion style; Guzzetti & Williams, 1996, p. 6). Teachers can model the kind of questioning behavior that publicly values intuition, intimacy, and insight. But it is not just a matter of increasing the female voice in science. It is more a matter of stimulating the voice of critique against the dominant discourses that marginalize based on gender (D.R. Dillon & Moje, 1998). Students need to be taught how to raise critical questions related to gendered discursive classroom practices that silence female voices in science. Some of the critical questions that could be asked include the following:

- Whose voice is dominant?
- Whose voice is marginalized?
- Who benefits from this practice?
- What can be done to resist this oppressive situation?

It is through raising critical questions such as those above that female students can try to overcome the gendered discursive practices that prevent them from expressing their authentic voices in class.

PAUSE AND PONDER

Fecho (2000) describes an inquiry-based literacy classroom as one that allows for multiple perspectives and listening for students' voices. He tells about the difficulties of establishing critical inquiry pedagogy in schools in which he mentored both new and experienced teachers. He explains that there were no models of critical inquiry teaching in the schools for the teachers to emulate.

- Do you have a similar situation in your school?
- What challenges do you see in incorporating question-finding and critical literacy practices in your school?
- Would the school administration support these practices? Would the parents?

Recognizing Social Barriers and Crossing Borders of Separation

Another critical literacy practice is that of recognizing social barriers and crossing borders of separation. This is a compound critical literacy practice. It consists of both identification and action. Students need to be able to identify the walls of separation before taking action to overcome the barriers of cultural exclusion. Walls and borders establish position (location) and foster exclusion—characteristics that are antithetical to literacy and to democracy. Democracy thrives on openness of ideas and freedom of movement. Dominant political and social systems position people as members or outsiders. Critical literacy is a practice that can break down barriers to communication and borders of separation. It is through crossing over these borders of separation that cultural pluralism, the hallmark of critical literacy, can flourish.

Question-finding is a strategy that can help students to inquire into the "liberating" process of literacy. This was demonstrated by one of my preservice teachers during her field experience of tutoring a middle school student in American history. Specifically, she instructed the student how to use the question-finding process as a critical practice of inquiry into the social injustices inflicted on young slave Frederick Douglass, who was learning, ironically, how to read. The teacher asked her tutee if there was something that he found puzzling or out of the ordinary in learning about Frederick Douglass. This question led to a discussion about how it was strange that people got mad at Frederick for learning how to read when today people might get mad at children who do not want to learn how to read. Eventually, tutor and tutee concluded that the slave-owning society did not want slaves to read. Further questions elicited ideas about why this was so, such as perhaps the slaves would not then concentrate on their work and might also teach other slaves to read. If a number of slaves could read, there might be a revolt and they would stop working because they had new skills and they would be more equal to white people. Although successful, the teacher's attempts to scaffold the question-finding process required a great deal of effort and concentration. Students may be reluctant at first to engage in this process because it is not the way of learning to which they are accustomed. Question-finding encourages students to think more critically about the information. In this case, the history tutoring session was the first time that this student was encouraged to make inferences instead of just accepting facts.

PAUSE AND PONDER

This chapter discusses the liberating process of literacy. Literacy is often used to resist tyranny. In the best-selling memoir *Reading Lolita in Tehran*, Azar Nafisi (2003), an Iranian college professor, secretly gathers seven women at her home once a week to read forbidden works of literature. This literacy practice challenges the laws of the revolutionary Islamic government. In the following excerpt, Nafisi expresses this resistance:

Like a group of conspirators, we would gather around the dining room table and read poetry and prose from Rumi, Hafez, Sa'adi, Khayyam, Nezami, Ferdowski, Attar, Boyhaghi. We would take turns reading passages aloud, and words literally rose up in the air and descended on us like a fine mist, touching all five senses. There was such a teasing, playful quality to these words, such joy in the power of language to delight and astonish. I kept wondering when did we lose that quality, that ability to tease and make light of life through our poetry. In what precise moment was this lost? (p. 308)

• How can the above message be used as an example of resistant reading?
• How can it be used to develop question-finding skills?

Focus Unit of Study: Language Arts, Middle School

A teacher education researcher and language arts middle school teacher created a five-lesson unit of study on the Holocaust and World War II that is a good model for demonstrating the critical literacy practice of overcoming social barriers and question-finding (Busching & Slesinger, 1995). (Earlier, this same unit was used to demonstrate how motivational issues can stimulate question-finding; see chapter 2.) The major purpose of the unit was to teach students to generate authentic questions, which the authors described as "significant human questions," about a social justice issue (p. 341). Indeed, the teaching team stressed the point that the literature readings on the topic should focus on issues rather than personal reactions. Busching and Slesinger (2002) describe their project as a reflection of "socially conscious inquiry" in language arts (p. 12). A social issues topic such as the Holocaust is an appropriate one for developing critical literacy practices.

Another consideration in selecting an appropriate topic for this critical literacy practice is finding one that has content depth and resource availability (fiction, nonfiction, media) for the students to be able to immerse themselves in the topic. The authors stress the point that their students would not have been able to generate higher level thinking without a strong knowledge foundation in the topic. Initially, they discovered that many of the students were not able to discuss the topic intelligently because they were not critically aware that barriers of separation existed between people during the Nazi era. When the students developed a strong factual foundation on the topic, then their critical insights grew naturally out of their new knowledge.

It is often possible and sometimes desirable for teachers to combine critical conversations and critical reading components (i.e., selection of "authentic text") in a single activity when the class does not have enough background knowledge or personal experiences with the topic to sustain an effective critical conversation. Then the introduction of a literature reading can launch a discussion. For example, Busching and Slesinger (1995) used an enigmatic and ambiguous children's book, *Rose Blanche* (Innocenti & Gallez, 1990), to propel a conversation on the injustices of the Nazi regime. The students raised a high number of questions reflecting a broad range of their puzzlement. One student raised the compelling question: "Why wasn't Rose (main young character) caught and arrested for feeding the children in prison?" (p. 345).

In this unit, the students read from a wide selection of fiction and nonfiction literature. They read excerpts from *Anne Frank: Diary of a Young Girl* (Frank, 1952) and novels such as *The Devil's Arithmetic* (Yolen, 1990) and *The Upstairs Room* (Reiss, 1972). They also contacted older relatives through letters and interviews to get information about the human experience of the war. From these readings and experiences, they raised a number of critical questions that became the basis for their follow-up research (a follow-up procedure similar in intent to the one I did with my high school students in the Chavez unit). Some of the responses were so authentic that "some students needed to cry out in question form [to] protest against dehumanizing circumstances" (Busching & Slesinger, 1995, p. 347). Their "protest" questions included, "Why did Hitler hate the Jews so much?" and "Are people so sick they can treat people like toys or something they could turn on or off. Are we really that inhuman?" (Busching & Slesinger, 2002, p. 66).

By humanizing the unit theme, the language arts teacher was able to guide students in relating historical events to their own personal lives. Students then were able to discuss how power structures in their own lives positioned them in their attitudes and beliefs. When students had achieved this level of critical understanding of the topic, they were able to ask authentic questions that challenged barriers of separation between people. These model critical questions included the following:

- How does this text box me in?
- What does this text want to do to me?
- What positions does the text contain?
- What message is it trying to enforce?
- How are dominant boundaries questioned?
- What happens when boundaries between worlds are violated?

Regaining One's Identity

Crossing borders of separation can be uplifting to one's sense of agency and autonomy. Regaining one's identity is an appropriate follow-up critical literacy practice to perform. In trying to help students develop an idea of the importance of self-identity as a critical literacy practice, a highly relevant topic to explore is adolescent girls' images of their bodies and adolescent boys' views of their masculinity. (Recall that this motivational topic was addressed in chapter 2 also.) Researchers and classroom teachers have used these topics in physical education and language arts to foster critical literacy practices (Oliver & Lalik, 2004a; Young, 2001). The critical literacy practice of regaining self-identity can be accomplished through the four critical proficiencies. First, the teacher can instill a critical awareness that one's identity is often molded by ideological systems, and that racial, ethnic, gender, and social identities can be viewed as **cultural constructions**. Also the teacher can help students to realize how victims of prejudice and discrimination often internalize the negative images that the dominant discourse ascribes to them (Gee, 2000–2001). Critical theorists use the term **internalized oppression** to describe a process in which a member of an oppressed group, after a period of abuse, begins to believe the dominant group's portrayal of them as inferior (Leistyna, Woodrum, & Sherblom,

1996). Recognizing the connection between oppression and identity formation is an important element of critical literacy.

A preservice teacher whom I taught, Danielle, practiced her question-finding skills in the context of regaining one's identity as she tutored Robert (pseudonym), an 11th-grade student. Danielle selected a story from a classic television series *The Twilight Zone*. (The story, "Eye of the Beholder," originally aired on November 11, 1960, and is now featured on DVD.) The theme of the show, as the following exchange reveals, highlights the critical literacy feature of internalized oppression.

Danielle: Let me know if you want me to pause [the DVD] or back it up so we can talk about it as we watch, OK?

[After about 10 minutes into the story]

Robert: Something isn't right but I can't put my finger on it. Can you back it up to the beginning?

Danielle: Sure. [Backs up the DVD]

Robert: OK. She [the lady in the hospital] is in the bandages; the doctor is in the shadows. What is it with the camera people and these angles and people's faces? Wait, what's wrong with the patient again? [puzzlement question—awareness type]

Danielle: She's hideously ugly and is in the hospital for treatments to help correct her deformities.

Robert: So we're just supposed to take it on the other characters' words that she's ugly? Why can't we see anyone else's face? Oh my god, that's it, isn't it? The puzzling situation is we haven't seen anyone's face this entire episode! [Robert fills in the puzzling situation on a blank question-finding template; see Appendix B for the template.] I have a question already.

Danielle: Read your question to me.

Robert: In *The Twilight Zone* episode "Eye of the Beholder," why are the faces of the characters hidden? [puzzlement question—explanation type]

Danielle: Do you want to see the rest of the episode, or do you want to work with the question [refine the puzzlement question—explanation type]?

Robert: Let's watch the rest. Maybe I'll come up with something better.

Danielle: OK. [Restarts the DVD]

[The patient's bandages are being removed.]

Robert: I don't want to see it; if she's as horrible as everyone's been saying for the last 20 minutes.... Wait! But she's not ugly. She's gorgeous. But what about.... They all look like pigs! [doctors, nurses, and hospital staff] Look at them with their turned-up noses! Why are they telling her she's ugly and she should kill herself or live in isolation? They're the ugly ones!

Danielle: Listen to the speech. Their leader is making a speech on the television. What's he talking about?

Robert: Conformity. That the group is more important than the individual. That exact sameness is the only way to ever achieve order and happiness. Who are they to tell her she's ugly. How can they be considered beautiful with their pig faces?

Danielle: Do you still want to keep your original question? [puzzlement question—explanation type]

Robert: No. I want to talk about the conformity issue.

Danielle: OK. What's the puzzling situation, then?

Robert: That woman was in the hospital for her, what did they say, 11th reconstructive treatment because she didn't look like everyone else.

Danielle: OK. So what's the question?

Robert: OK. How about this: In this story, why is conformity so highly prized in their society? [puzzlement question—explanation type]

Danielle: Did you come up with any other questions—wonderment or open-ended type?

Robert: What if you were constantly told you were horribly ugly and deformed? Would you subject yourself to correction treatments like that lady did? [wonderment questions]

Danielle: Very good. Do you have any others?

Robert: Yes. Do beauty standards in society cause psychological damage to the members of society?

Danielle: Those are wonderful questions. [They are also good wonderment questions!]

Notice how Danielle guided Robert along the question-finding path as displayed in Figure 2 (see page 9). Also note how Robert practiced critical literacy. He recognized the effects of society's beauty norms on self-identity and realized how this often leads to internalized oppression.

Focus Units of Study: Physical Education and Language Arts, Middle School

In this section, I present procedures for developing units of study on body image and cultural norms in language arts and physical education. Teachers need to guide students to an understanding that dominant cultural narratives often equate female identity with outward appearances. First, help students recognize the conflicting messages that they receive about their bodies and physical health. For example, show how adolescent boys' views of masculinity are also social and cultural constructions and are not based on a single identify formation. Particularly, help students to recognize the ways that texts can position adolescents to internalize the dominant cultural narratives that oppress the development of subjective and multiple identities. It is important for teachers in all content areas to raise awareness levels regarding the socially constructed views of gender (Napper-Owen, Kovar, Ermler, & Mehrhof, 1999).

Second, have a critical conversation about these topics and relate them to students' lives. Discuss with the class why body appearance is such an important feature of adolescent identity in U.S. culture. Also discuss ways that students can challenge, resist, and question cultural narratives that contribute to a distorted sense of self. On the topic of boys' masculinity, discuss how society presents one view of maleness when there are really multiple male identities. For both topics, discuss ways to counter and critique gender practices that stereotype the ways adolescent boys and girls should look and act.

Third, guide students to develop resistant critical literacy practices as they relate to gender issues. Guide students to resist these dominant cultural norms by interrogating that which the larger society characterizes as normal adolescent development. It is especially important to provide resistant reading techniques that challenge patriarchal gender positioning. Oliver and Lalik (2004b) have worked with middle grade girls in physical education by training them to critique the gender discursive elements in teen fashion magazines and the culturally stereotypical pictures of young girls' bodies. Young (2001) also worked with middle school language arts students to help them critique culturally dominant views of masculinity in teen magazines as well as hegemonic practices of television and radio commercials. The teacher researcher also used young adult literature including such books as *Wringer* (Spinelli, 1997), *California Blue* (Klass, 1994), and *The Giver* (Lowry, 1993), which present alternative views of masculinity. Junior high school physical education teacher Paul Martlett applied the Socratic questioning approach using alternative texts to help his students analyze media and peer influence on body image (Martlett & Gordon, 2004).

Fourth, provide scaffolds for helping students frame critical questions that critique stereotypical portraits of identity formation. Oliver and Lalik (2004a) provided scaffolds as they guided middle grade students to create a questionnaire containing critical questions related to gender issues such as girls' body images and girls' roles in sports. The teachers provided the following prompt: "So how can you word a question to get...what people think about inequities and stereotypes of girls and boys?" The teacher then provided the following model question: "Why do girls play softball and not baseball?" This stimulated the following student-generated questions: "Explain what a girl's figure has to do with cheerleading," "How do you think basketball helps a girl's self-image?" and "Explain how softball makes girls feel about their bodies" (p. 183). Some other critical questions related to the critical practice of regaining one's identity include the following:

- Does the text treat both genders fairly?
- Do the genders look like the ones being portrayed in the text?
- What are the messages sent to the genders by the texts?
- Who benefits by the images portrayed in the text?
- What could be an alternate version of gender presentation?
- How do selected versions fuel stereotypes of groups?
- How do stereotypes lead to inequities and injustices?
- How have popular texts perpetuated gender identities?

Through these critical questions, students learn to resist and challenge gender stereotypes and inequities.

PAUSE AND PONDER

One of the main themes of this chapter is that social barriers affect identity formation. This is especially significant in terms of racial barriers. African American author Mildred Taylor (1987) describes her own experiences in a childhood story, *The Gold Cadillac*. She tells of a family car trip from Toledo, Ohio, to her grandparents' home in Mississippi.

> We rolled on, down highway 25 and through the bluegrass hills of Kentucky. Soon we began to see the sign that read: WHITE ONLY, COLORED NOT ALLOWED (we saw them everywhere on our trip). I don't like the signs. I felt as if I were in a foreign land. (p. 29)

- How do racial barriers treat U.S. citizens as foreigners in their own country?
- In what ways are literacy and exclusion antithetical ideas?
- What other critical questions could be generated from the above excerpt?

Critical Questioning

Question-finding provides students with the skills to express a critical awareness that texts represent particular viewpoints while neglecting or silencing others. For this reason and others mentioned below, question-finding is very different from other types of questioning strategies such as "questioning the author" (Beck, McKeown, Hamilton, & Kucan, 1997), which focuses mostly on the cognitive level of literacy learning. The objective of question-finding is not to interrogate the author's surface meaning in terms of clarity and coherence of writing. Rather, question-finding is concerned more with helping students identify the below-surface meanings of an author's text. It looks at the ideological nature of the author's text. It examines intended meanings. In other words, it is concerned not just with the cognitive dimension of literacy but also with a broader or multidimensional nature of literacy including the affective, motivational, and critical domains. Question-finding is a critical inquiry process that engages students in search behavior to uncover the hidden questions within the different layers of text.

Summary

This chapter focused on the critical literacy dimension of question-finding. It showed how question-finding can help the adolescent learner to examine text more critically by interrogating its assumptions and ideological orientation. In contrast to the previous chapters, this chapter looked more at the subjective and discursive practices of literacy rather than the more process-oriented natures of cognitive and motivational literacies. It provided classroom examples of question-finding and critical literacy proficiencies and practices in different content areas. In the next chapter, I will examine an allied dimension of critical literacy—the social literacies.

PONDER AND PRACTICE

1. Question-finding can be stimulated by situations that contain incongruous elements such as the one documented below.

   Situation: African American adolescent interviews a former Ku Klux Klan (KKK) member.

   Adolescent: How old were you when you started with the Klan?

   Former KKK member: 17.

   Adolescent: Only 17?

Former KKK member: Yeah. And I began to read the stuff they gave me, go to their meetings. A lot of it was just pure hogwash, but when you're a teenager and you haven't had a chance to learn and develop critical-thinking skills—at least I didn't when I was in school—then you're kind of ripe for these racist ideas.

(Adapted from King & Osborne, 1997, p. 116)

- Use this brief dialogue to practice your critical questioning skills.
- Does the former KKK member make a case for teaching critical inquiry skills in terms of social justice concerns? Explain.

2. A major theme of critical literacy is that physical characteristics such as age, gender, and race are not necessary conditions of heroism. This theme conflicts with the message presented by the media and society in the United States, which often portray heroes as young, strong, white, and masculine. In an article for a social studies journal, I wrote about how a very young African American girl displayed heroic characteristics in the New Orleans desegregation dispute in 1960 (Ciardiello, 2001). Six-year-old Ruby Bridges represented the "unlikely hero" according to society's standards. The concept of the "unlikely hero" is one that could be used with regard to literary characters as well as real persons. William Faulkner's (1948) novel *Intruder in the Dust* depicts the courage of a white elderly lady and a young boy as these characters risk danger in attempting to help a falsely accused African American male in Mississippi during the Jim Crow era (1876–1964). One of the other characters in the book sums up the theme of the unlikely hero when he states,

> If you got something outside the common run that's got to be done and can't wait, don't waste your time on the men folks; they works on…the rules and cases. Get the womens and the children at it; they works on the circumstances. (pp. 110–111)

A more recent novel, *The Secret Life of Bees* (Kidd, 2002), also provides an alternative portrait of the unlikely hero, a 14-year-old white female and her African American nanny. Both challenge racial segregation in South Carolina in 1964, the era of voting rights and civil rights.

- How can you use this theme of the unlikely hero to teach question-finding skills? One critical question might be, What can the media do to redefine the dominant cultural perception of heroism? Construct other critical questions on this theme.

3. A physical education researcher (Kim) attempted to teach a group of adolescent girls how to generate critical questions for an interview questionnaire on the topic of inequities of girls' roles in sports. The researcher used a strategy in which she walked them through the topic by using a sequence of questions. Below is a short sample of the procedure.

Kim: You want to know whether or not people don't think girls can play sports?

Meg: We wanna know if people compare boys to girls like being equal.

Ashley: Are boys and girls equal in sports?

Kim: That's a yes or no question. [urging students not to ask yes or no questions]

[No response]

Kim: OK, let's think about this.... Why do girls play softball and not baseball? Explain why girls and boys don't play softball or don't both play [together]. [Remember] I'm just thinking aloud.

(Adapted from Oliver & Lalik, 2004a, pp. 183–184)

• Critique Kim's procedure for generating students' questions. Would you use a similar procedure? Review the process for question-finding in this book (see chapter 1). Does Kim follow it? If not, what could she have done to improve her instruction in student questioning?

4. The Federal Writers' Project of the New Deal (1933–1945) collected the oral testimonies of former slaves of the pre–Civil War era. One of the slave narratives contained the following oral report regarding slave literacy:

Ninety-year old Belle Myers Carothers learned her letters while looking after the plantation owner's baby, who was playing with alphabet blocks. One day she found a hymn book and spelled out, "When I Can Read My Title Clear." I was happy, she says, when I saw that I could really read. I ran around telling all the other slaves. (Manguel, 1996, p. 280)

Some scholars question the authenticity of the slave narratives collected by the Federal Writer's Project during the 1930s. They claim that the former slaves were too old to remember the details of their slave existence (before 1865).

• How would you go about checking the accuracy of the above slave narrative? What critical questions would you ask to check the authenticity of this source? Refer to examples from the text to guide your investigation.

CHAPTER 4

Question-Finding and Social Practices of Literacy

IMPORTANT CONCEPTS AND SPECIALIZED TERMS

code-switching	give talk	project-based classroom
covariation questions	guided reciprocal peer	question starters
cultural congruence	questioning	reciprocal questioning
cultural dissonance	indeterminate learning	sense-making
culturally relevant pedagogy	situations	signifying
culturally responsive	intercultural social inquiry	sociocognitive literacy
classroom	iterative nature of generating	sociocultural literacy
dialogic inquiry	questions	sociohistorical literacy
dialogically organized	monologic talk	sociolinguistic literacy
classroom	more knowledgeable other	story-like participation
driving question	open-inquiry lab	structures
funds of knowledge	environments	third space

Staying in Jerusalem were pious Jews from every country under heaven. A crowd of them gathered at the noise being made, and were stunned because each heard the speakers in his own language. They felt awe and wonder as they said: "Wait. These men speaking, don't they all come from Galilee? Then how can we be hearing them in the language of our native land? Parthians and Medes and Elamites, residents of Mesopotamia, Judea and Cappadocia, Pontus and Asia, Phrygia and Pamphilia, Egypt and the district of Libya near Crete, visitors from Rome, Cretans and Arabs—we all hear in our separate languages what they tell us about God's great work." They were awed and puzzled as they asked each other, "What can this mean?"

(Acts of the Apostles, 2.1–2.17, New English Bible as cited in Wills, 2005, p. 168)

The puzzlement and wonderment experienced by the pious Jews assembled in Jerusalem in the biblical account of Pentecost reflects many of the elements of question-finding in a social context. The discrepant event of hearing multiple foreign voices in one's own language created conceptual conflict and induced epistemic curiosity as expressed by the questions, "Then how can we be hearing them in the language of our native land?" and "What can this mean?"

Recall the middle school language arts teacher, Mrs. Mangrum, from the Preface. She used a cognitive–constructivist approach to instruct her students in generating questions. She modeled and scaffolded how to process information independently using student questioning. But Mrs. Mangrum also recognized the importance of the social aspects of constructing meaning. She employed student-questioning strategies that recognized that knowledge is also constructed by social interaction. She guided her students by scaffolding the questioning process in a collaborative manner. After awhile, she disengaged herself and allowed her students to generate questions on their own. In the words of educational theorist Vygotsky (1934/1978), she was able to bridge the "distance between the actual developmental level as determined by independent problem solving and the level of potential development through problem solving under adult guidance" (p. 86). Vygotsky called this area of difference the student's zone of proximal development. After the initial instruction in generating questions, the students began to collectively ask and answer other productive questions related to the young adult novel that they were reading (Moore et al., 1999). This coordinated and collective approach to literacy learning is known as **sociocognitive literacy**. A sociocognitive orientation is helpful in stimulating student questioning (Alvermann, 2004).

This chapter focuses on student questioning induced by social interaction and conceptual conflict. In this chapter, I also examine another literacy dimension, the social nature of literacy. This dimension incorporates many elements of critical literacy, but provides unique insights into questioning behavior that is affected by social constructs such as class, gender, race, and social status. (See Table 13 for resources on social literacies.)

Some of the content area teachers discussed in this book have adopted a sociocognitive approach to student questioning. Mrs. Graham, the middle school science teacher introduced in chapter 2, worked together with her seventh-grade students to investigate the unusual appearance of three trees growing side by side on school property. The investigation was prompted by one student's questions: "Why are those trees different? They used to look the same, didn't they?" (NRC, 2000, p. 6). In a true social-constructivist spirit, Mrs. Graham indicated that she did not know the answer, but that together they would investigate the matter.

In my 11th-grade social studies class, I also used a social-constructivist orientation in the unit of study on Cesar Chavez and the grape strike (see chapter 3). I presented the class with alternative viewpoints on the nature of the strike from labor and management viewpoints. My students and I examined documents supporting both sides to investigate which version was more credible.

The impact of home culture and community is a major dimension of social literacy. This orientation recognizes that text meaning is not culture free, but that it is embedded or contextualized within one's heritage, language, gender, and social condition.

TABLE 13. Resources on Social Literacies

Au, K.H. (1997). Ownership, literacy achievement, and students of diverse cultural backgrounds. In J.T. Guthrie & W.A. Wigfield (Eds.), *Reading engagement: Motivating readers through integrated instruction* (pp. 168–182). Newark, DE: International Reading Association.

Ballenger, C. (1997). Social identities, moral narratives, scientific argumentation: Science talk in a bilingual classroom.*Languages and Education, 11,* 1–14.

Carlsen, W.S. (1991). Questioning in classrooms: A sociolinguistic perspective. *Review of Educational Research, 61*(2), 157–178.

Cole, M., & Griffin, P. (1986). A sociohistorical approach to remediation. In S. de Castell, A. Luke, & K. Egan (Eds.), *Literacy, society, and schooling: A reader* (pp. 110–131). New York: Cambridge University Press.

Delpit, L. (1995). *Other people's children: Cultural conflict in the classroom.* New York: The New Press.

Edwards, B., & Davis, B. (1997). Learning from classroom questions and answers: Teachers' uncertainties about children's language. *Journal of Literacy Research, 29*(4), 471–505.

Gee, J.P. (1990). *Social linguistics and literacies: Ideology in discourses.* Bristol, PA: Falmer.

Gutierrez, K., & Stone, L.D. (2000). Synchronic and diachronic dimensions of social practice: An emerging methodology for cultural-historical perspectives on literacy learning. In C.D. Lee & P. Smagorinsky (Eds.), *Vygotskian perspectives on literacy research: Constructive meaning through collaborative inquiry* (pp. 150–164). New York: Cambridge University Press.

Gutierrez, K., Rymes, B., & Larsen, J. (1995). Script, counterscript, and underlife in the classroom: "James Brown versus Brown v. Board of Education." *Harvard Educational Review, 65*(3), 445–471.

Hudicourt-Barnes, J. (2003). The use of argumentation in Haitian Creole science classrooms. *Harvard Educational Review, 73*(1), 73–93.

John-Steiner, V., & Mahn, H. (1996). Sociocultural approaches to learning and development: A Vygotskian framework. *Educational Psychologist, 31*(3/4), 191–206.

Ladson-Billings, G. (1995). Making mathematics meaningful in multicultural contexts. In W. Secada, E. Fennema, & L.B. Adajian (Eds.), *New directions for equity in mathematics education* (pp. 126–145). New York: Cambridge University Press and National Council of Teachers of Mathematics.

Lee, C.D. (2001). Is October Brown Chinese? A cultural modeling activity system for underachieving students. *American Educational Research Journal, 38*(1), 97–141.

Luke, A., & Freebody, P. (1997). Shaping the social practices of reading. In S. Muspratt, A. Luke, & P. Freebody (Eds.), *Constructing critical literacies: Teaching and learning textual practice* (pp.185–225). Cresskill, NJ: Hampton.

McCarthy, T.L., & Watahomigie, L.J. (1998). Language and literacy in American Indian and Alaska Native communities. In B. Perez (Ed.), *Sociocultural contexts of language and literacy* (pp. 69–98). Mahwah, NJ: Erlbaum.

McMahon, S.I. (1996). Book club: The influence of a Vygotskian perspective on a literature-based reading program. In L. Dixon-Krauss (Ed.), *Vygotsky in the classroom: Mediated literacy instruction & assessment* (pp. 59–76). White Plains, NY: Longman.

Moll, L. (1992). Literacy research in community and classrooms: A socio-cultural approach. In R. Beach, J.L. Green, M.L. Kamil, & T. Shanahan (Eds.), *Multidisciplinary perspectives in literacy research* (pp. 211–244). Urbana, IL: National Council of Teachers of English.

O'Flahavan, J.F., & Seidl, B.L. (1997). Fostering literate communities in school: A case for sociocultural approaches to reading instruction. In S.A. Stahl & D.A. Hayes (Eds.), *Instructional models in reading* (pp. 203–220). Mahwah, NJ: Erlbaum.

(continued)

TABLE   13. Resources on Social Literacies (continued)

Oldfather, P., & Dahl, K. (1994). Toward a social constructivist reconceptualization of intrinsic motivation for literacy learning. *Journal of Reading Behavior, 26*(2), 139–157.

Perez, B., & Torres-Guzman, M. (1992). *Learning in two worlds: An integrated Spanish/English biliteracy approach.* New York: Longman.

Vygotsky, L.S. (1978). *Mind in society: The development of higher psychological processes* (M. Cole, V. John-Steiner, S. Scribner, & E. Souberman, Eds. & Trans.) Cambridge, MA: Harvard University Press. (Original work published 1934)

Warren, B., Ballenger, C., Ogonowski, M., Rosebery, A.S., & Hudicourt-Barnes, J. (2001). Rethinking diversity in learning science: The logic of everyday sense-making. *Journal of Research in Science Teaching, 38*(5), 529–552.

Wertsch, J.V., & Toma, C. (1995). Discourse and learning in the classroom: A sociocultural approach. In L.P. Steffe & J. Gale (Eds.), *Constructivism in education* (pp. 159–183). Hillsdale, NJ: Erlbaum.

This is often described as **sociocultural literacy** (John-Steiner & Mahn, 1996). Mrs. Mangrum recognized the importance of sociocultural literacy. She believed that everyone in her class had something to offer. She organized instruction so students of diverse backgrounds could share their insights in class discussions. Specifically, she "regularly featured discussions of multicultural literature, and she expressed a sincere interest in her students' wide ranging cultural and other differences, learning styles, and needs for respect and security" (Moore et al., 1999, p. 103). Mrs. Mangrum valued her students' cultural experiences and used them as sources for generating students' questions in her language arts class.

This chapter explores how the question-finding strategy can be used in social contexts to enhance literacy learning. In several ways, this chapter and the previous one are interconnected. Both critical and social orientations to literacy view text as rich in value and context. They stress the affective as well as the interactive character of literacy instruction. Both challenge the notion that literacy resides in the text alone and recognize the effects of culture and ideology on text meaning. In addition, both address the concept of authentic voice. Indeed, the critical literacy practice of finding one's authentic voice can be viewed as socially constructed (D.R. Dillon & Moje, 1998).

Aside from this, there are several differences between these dimensions that justify a singular focus on social literacy in this chapter. Social literacy specifically recognizes the social classroom constraints on literacy learning for nonmainstream groups that are reflected in differentiated uses of language and status positions. It also recognizes that the **funds of knowledge** that students bring from their home cultures can enhance literacy learning in content area learning (Moll, 1992). In terms of student questioning, social literacy practices focus on authentic questions that are owned by students and meaningful in their lives. In this sense authentic questions are inherently motivational (which may not necessarily be true for critical questions) as students incorporate their own cultural heritages as building blocks for literacy development.

This chapter focuses on how the strategy of question-finding can be employed in sociolinguistic, sociocognitive, and sociocultural contexts. For the purposes of this chapter, I distinguish between these three aspects of social literacy. In reality, these aspects are interrelated and are often difficult to distinguish from one another. This chapter highlights question-finding as a social practice rather than an individual cognitive act (Cobb, 2005). In this chapter, I briefly review the research on student questioning and the social dimensions of literacy instruction. I also show how the contrasting elements of both **cultural dissonance** and **cultural congruence** can stimulate students to generate questions. In addition, I present examples and procedures of how students can generate authentic questions in classroom learning. Last, I provide sample units of study in different content areas to serve as models of how question-finding procedures can be employed within a social context.

Social Literacies and Generating Questions: A Research Overview

As indicated in chapter 1, cognitive-based literacy has a long association with classroom questioning. Researchers have indicated that cognitive prompts and scaffolds stimulate students to generate questions (King & Rosenshine, 1993; Rosenshine, Meister, & Chapman, 1996). The major thrust of these studies focused on individual cognition and psycholinguistic theories of literacy. However, there are increasingly significant developments in the study of language in the 21st century that point to the need for broader descriptions of literacy.

The case for teaching the multiple dimensions of student questioning is based on the changing nature of literacy in the 21st century (Alvermann, 2004). The emergence of electronic and technological literacies has led to multifaceted views of knowledge and alternate ways of viewing the world. These changing conceptions of knowledge have profound implications for literacy learning and for education. Soltis (1981) has argued in a convincing manner that we need to invent educational strategies that effectively pass on human knowledge in all its forms. Teachers need to keep up with the changing realities and educational demands of the **culturally responsive classroom**, where all varieties of languages and dialects are accepted (Edwards & Davis, 1997). The multidimensional strategy of question-finding addresses the changing conceptions of knowledge and literacy.

Language consists of literacy events, or acts of communication. Beach (1992) argues that in order to understand the nature of literacy events, the researcher must address the full range of the different functions of language. He recommends that literacy researchers adopt multiple stances or perspectives that focus on particular aspects of a literacy event. Social interaction, cultural practices, and cognitive processes shape the communication arts.

Learning the skills of inquiry involves instruction in the language of questioning (Martinello, 1998). Questions have multiple language functions. J.T. Dillon (1982) explains that questions are more than just interrogative tools for requesting information. He states that they "entail cognitive and expressive processes, social relationships, and interactional discourse" (p. 162). Indeed, questions can be viewed as language events shaped by different curricular disciplines. In a review of the literature on student questioning in a dozen different fields, including cognitive psychology, philosophy, survey research, education, and sociolinguistics, Dillon discovered that although the disciplines addressed similar issues, they remained essentially isolated from one another. He called for a multidisciplinary study of questioning behavior. In the context of that research, this book views student questioning as a broad-based literacy practice with implications for the cognitive, motivational, critical, and social domains of literacy. Instruction in self-questioning can provide acquisition of these multiple literacies and higher level thinking skills (King & Rosenshine, 1993). Through understanding the various dimensions of student questioning research, teachers will be better able to advance the cause of multidimensional literacy awareness and development.

Sociolinguistic Research and Generating Questions

Sociolinguistic research indicates that questioning behavior is a part of the social development of language (Carlsen, 1991). Different cultures and societies use questions for distinctive purposes. Questions and other verbal interactions are interpreted differently, depending on social context (Labov, 1972). For example, Boggs (1972) discovered that young Hawaiian schoolchildren refused to ask questions in class. The researcher learned that children's questioning was a form of communication that violated cultural norms. Asking questions was viewed as strictly adult behavior.

Traditional classroom discourse patterns in which the teacher controls the flow of conversation (turn-taking) and asks questions through an initiation–response–evaluation guide (IRE) lead to student passivity in general (Mehan, 1979). Turn-taking and IRE classroom discourse structures violate student ownership of literacy.

In terms of the discourse patterns of Hawaiian children, Au (1997b) claims that the teacher's directive mode of participation structure was too dissimilar to the students' **story-like participation structures** that reflected home and cultural backgrounds. At home, the children routinely cooperated with others on tasks and, in the process, typically collaborated and extended one another's conversations. This scenario includes a great deal of overlapping speech patterns (contrary to the rigid turn-taking and hierarchical nature of the teacher-dominated IRE participation structure). Studies of classroom behavior in Hawaii (Au, 1997a; Boggs, 1972) reveal that the teachers failed to organize culturally responsive classrooms for the students. Teachers did not structure classroom discourse around the communication patterns compatible with the norms and values of the students' home culture. In this sense, these highly structured teaching techniques were inauthentic in that they involved children in tasks that separated school-based literacy activities from the home-based system of social relationships.

Goody (1978) found similar results from a study involving rural African children. These children conceived of questions in terms of adult commands rather than as sources of information seeking. Questions became the property of superior status-holders and belonged to adults alone. In the southeastern United States, Heath (1982) engaged in ethnographic research and also discovered that questioning had various social functions that were used in different ways at home and in school. Specifically, she found that low-income urban African American adult family members rarely asked knowledge-based or informational type questions of their young children—a type of question typically asked in classrooms. Their "home-style" questions generally exhibited a more contextual form and concerned real-world issues. In order to succeed in school, these children had to learn to acquire new functions of language, particularly how to use questions according to the rules of mainstream classroom usage.

A study involving a similar population and setting to the Heath ethnographic investigation (i.e., southeastern United States) also indicated that traditional classroom question-and-answer routines did not reflect the different discourse styles of African American children (Edwards & Davis, 1997). Indeed, the children's discourse patterns contained practical knowledge that helped keep households functioning in the real world. These household funds of knowledge are flexible stratagems and can be adapted to classroom practice (Moll, 1992). Typically, teacher-dominated questioning procedures do not encourage these communication patterns and consequently hinder literacy development for all children.

For most students, asking questions is inappropriate classroom behavior because it is based on authority relationships (Carlsen, 1991). As the power brokers in the classroom, teachers dominate questioning behavior and students are fearful of challenging that authority. In a series of studies, Mishler (1975, 1978) indicates that the nature of classroom discourse was determined primarily by the authoritarian status of the teacher. Indeed, question-and-answer routines between teacher and students were generally one-sided with the former exercising ultimate power for the initiation and order of dialogue. In contrast, when students asked questions of their peers, the nature of the discourse was much more frequent, open, egalitarian, and spontaneous. Children's responses to one another's questions were longer and of greater complexity and thoughtfulness than they were to adults' (Boggs, 1972; Mishler, 1978). Significantly, instruction in peer questioning may hold more promise than teacher modeling for literacy development. Thus, sociolinguistic research reveals that the purpose of classroom questioning has been to maintain teacher control of the social situation and not to promote literacy or inquiry (J.T. Dillon, 1982). There appears to be a strong need for instruction in student questioning that takes factors of **sociolinguistic literacy** into account.

PAUSE AND PONDER

Collaborative or peer learning enhances the social construction of knowledge. My high school students revealed these benefits as they engaged in collaborative question-finding activities related to interpreting discrepant documents from the U.S. Great Depression. While working in groups, one of the members revealed these benefits in an informative manner. She claimed that initially she was very impressed that the others had constructed so many thoughtful questions different from her own. But then again she was satisfied that her own questions were unique and meaningful for the inquiry. The student conveyed feelings similar to a middle school student in a science class who expressed the benefits of a collaborative inquiry project with the words, "Oh...[other students' questions] would really give me a new way to think about this!" (Scardamalia & Bereiter, 1992, p. 191). Developing new insights on a topic is a major benefit of collaborative question-finding.

- Do you give your students opportunities to collaborate while generating questions?
- What role should the teacher play in collaborative inquiry and student questioning?

Sociocognitive Dimensions of Literacy and Generating Questions

Student questioning stimulates literacy development in the sociocognitive realm. Specifically, **reciprocal questioning**, which provides for the interaction and collaboration between teachers and students, is a strategy that offers promise for the social construction of knowledge (Manzo, 1969). Reciprocal questioning provides students with a social context for expressing opposing views and resolving differences of opinions (King, 1992). This cognitive strategy enhances students' comprehension and productive thinking. The collaborative learning context of the procedure also provides a learning environment for the modeling of good questioning behavior either on the part of the teacher or student peers.

To advance literacy instruction for all students, teachers need to change the status environment to one in which students become cointerrogators in the teaching and learning process. Allington and Weber (1993) suggest that teachers need to foster "authentic" student questions in which the questioner does not know the answer and tentative responses are valued. For example, an eighth-grade science teacher set up this type of authentic questioning environment during an open-ended lab assignment in which three students worked together on an experiment separating a salt and sand mixture, a topic from a chemistry unit on the changing physical and chemical states of matter (Chin, Brown, & Bruce, 2002). As coinvestigators, the students had to devise their own method for separating the salt and sand from the mixture. In contrast to other science experiments in which a discrepant event was deliberately introduced by the teacher to stimulate puzzlement (e.g., dancing raisins experiment discussed in chapter 2), in this experiment the students had to detect the puzzlement created by the discrepant events that emanated from the procedure itself. Notice in the following exchange how the students serve as cointerrogators as they ask and answer puzzlement and wonderment questions during the experiment.

> Quin: How about we pour some water in here? [a beaker containing the mixture]
>
> Quin: What do you all think the water is going to do? [wonderment question]
>
> Quin: [Then, answering his own question] I think the water absorbed the salt.
>
> Carl: The dirt [sand] didn't dissolve, so the dirt separated.
>
> Quin: But the water would dissolve the salt. I wish we had something to drain this thing...
>
> Carl: The salt dissolved. It's in there.
>
> Rick: How do you know it's in there? [puzzlement question—awareness type] Take a test, Carl...

[After the students replace the salt solution from the wet sand and place it into an aluminum foil pan.]

> Quin: A lot of sand, but where did the salt go?
>
> Carl: It's in the water. Gone.
>
> Quin: How are we going to bring it back? [puzzlement question—explanation type, seeking resolution of dilemma]
>
> (Chin, Brown, & Bruce, 2002, p. 538)

In this exercise, the students successfully collaborated in asking three different types of question-finding questions. Quin began the cointerrogation with a wonderment question when he asked the group to predict what the water would do to the mixture. Later, Rick asked a puzzlement question (awareness type) when he asked skeptically if the salt was still in the water and mixture solution. Finally, Quin asked a puzzlement question (explanation type) concerning a procedure that could be used to bring back the salt from its dissolved state and resolve the dilemma. Thus, this learning provides an example of students collaborating in a process of generating questions that helps to refine thinking skills, fill in missing gaps in information, and create new ideas.

Vygotsky (1934/1978) explains that learning occurs through collaboration and interaction between people. School literacy grows from social interaction with knowledgeable others within the classroom community of learners (Au, 1997b). The literacy environment needs to be reorganized to include social structures that feature such teaching strategies as collaborative learning, peer mentoring, and reciprocal teaching (Antonacci & Colasacco, 1995). Soltis (1981) labels this new orientation a "sociocentric perspective," which expresses the notion that knowledge and the knower are connected, that all knowledge is embedded in the fabric of social life (p. 97). Resnick and colleagues (1989) argue that it is not possible to assume that thought is a symbolic process divorced from the social and emotional contexts in which it is expressed. Knowledge is situational, not context independent. Egan (1997) modified this sociocentric view by arguing that knowledge and the mind are not only influenced by contemporary society but also evolve from history and culture.

PAUSE AND PONDER

The collaborative social conflict model has implications for question-finding. Some social developmental psychologists have supported the counterintuitive notion that the most effective type of peer collaboration is between two partners, both of whom not only disagree, but disagree using incorrect information (Ames & Murray, 1982; Glachan & Light, 1982). It is through "working out" their incorrect responses that the students become truly engaged in the collaboration and reap the cognitive benefits. Indeed, empirical evidence reveals that at least one of the pair of collaborators makes significant gains. In this case, "two wrongs might make a right" (Glachan & Light, p. 258). (See chapter 5, page 126, for an example of this counterintuitive notion as it relates to conceptual change.)

- Do you agree with these unusual findings?
- Does this research have any implications for question-finding?

Sociocultural Dimensions of Literacy and Generating Questions

A number of educators and researchers stress the cultural nature of literacy instruction. For example, Perez and Torres-Guzman (1992) define literacy as practices that are shared by a group in a particular way in a specific context. In a classic study of literacy in a developing country, Scribner and Cole (1981) concluded that literate thinking among the Vai people of Liberia depended on specific literacy functions and grounded discourse, and that intelligent behavior could not be understood apart from its social context.

Heath (1991) has pursued a sociocultural approach that she calls the "sense of being literate" in a cross-cultural and historical perspective (p. 3). She makes distinctions between literacy skills, which are discrete and disconnected, and literate behavior, which is interpersonal and contextual. She also claims that there is a sociocultural and historical basis for the promotion of literate behavior and reveals in an enlightening ethnographic study conducted in the southeastern United States how different racial groups used reading for different purposes (Heath, 1982). For the African American families, reading served an instrumental function and was executed mainly in a social setting; whereas for the white families, reading served a more analytical function and was facilitated individually. The former used literacy as an aid to everyday life situations and included out-of-school skills, uses, and contexts. The latter's literacy pattern reflected more of the school-based type with its focus on academic achievement.

Gee (1990) advances the notion that all school activities and, indeed, all literacy activities are bound to what he calls particular "Discourses," or socioculturally determined ways of thinking, feeling, valuing, and using native language for communication. Indeed, the author identifies these ideas as the basis of new literacy studies dedicated to the examination of language and cognition from a variety of disciplines such as linguistics, psycholinguistics, anthropology, sociology, political theory, and education.

Scholars have also developed procedures for instruction in student questioning using **sociohistorical literacy**. This rationale views school literacy as a social process affected not only by present realities but also by past circumstances and realities (Au, 1997a). Cole (1996) and Cole and Griffin (1986) indicate that language is a uniquely human development that evolves from historically accumulated experiences. Using scripted role-playing, groups of students were taught to model adult reading behavior by learning to ask questions that focused on the construction of meaning rather than on memorization of a topic. Specifically, they learned to ask text analysis questions that involved recognition of main idea, hypothesizing, and prediction. Instruction revolved around a broader view of literacy that was not limited to school matters but expanded into the home, workplace, and society. Cole and Griffin claim that critical thinking and questioning skills are more serviceable to the future lives of learners.

The Impact of Cultural Dissonance and Cultural Congruence Factors

In this section, I discuss two seemingly contradictory items. First, I examine the cultural dissonance that many ethnic minority and linguistically different groups face in school. I show how a cultural dissonance condition (sometimes referred to as a cultural conflict state) that exists between home and school practices can serve as a catalyst for question-finding and literacy. Then, I show how cultural congruence factors regarding language practices of ethnic minority students carry literacy benefits for question-finding behavior as well. I use classroom discourse to reflect these themes.

Cultural Dissonance and Question-Finding

As the research on sociocultural and sociolinguistic factors of student questioning discussed in the last section reveals, a cultural dissonance exists between school and home and cultural norms. But this kind of cultural conflict also can play an important role in question-finding behavior. Teachers can encourage students to generate questions by serving as mediators between the opposing cultural orientations. Delpit (1995) demonstrates how this has been done in a tutoring situation involving an African American teenager from the U.S. South, who spoke African American Vernacular English, and his African American language arts teacher. In the following exchange, notice how both the teacher and the student were interacting in a co-constructive inquiry format, one in which the teacher raised a noninterrogative-type question for which she herself did not know the answer. The "challenging" question related to events in a children's book written in African American Vernacular English that the student had been reading.

Teacher: What do you think about that book?...

Joey: It use more of a southern-like accent in this book.

Teacher: Uhmn-hmm. Do you think that's good or bad?

Joey: Well, uh, I don't think it's good for people down this a-way, 'cause that's the way they grow up talking anyway. They ought to get the right way to talk.

Teacher: Oh. So you think it's wrong to talk like that?

Joey: Uhmn-hmm, that's a hard question. But I think they shouldn't make books like that...

Teacher: Uhmn-hmm. Well, that's a hard question for me to answer, too. It's, ah, that's a question that's come up in a lot of schools now as to whether they [teachers] should correct children who speak the way we speak all the time. 'Cause when we're talking to each other we talk like that even though we might not talk like that when we get into other situations, and who's to say whether it's—

Joey: [Interrupting] Right or wrong.

(pp. 42–43)

As evidenced in this exchange, both the teacher and the student expressed puzzlement about the topic in a genuine inquiry session. It is genuine because the teacher and the student raised questions for which they did not have ready-made answers. This is unlike the conventional teacher–student interaction in which the knowledgeable other or mentor poses typical school-based and test-like questions for which the teacher already knows the answer. Delpit states that it is important for teachers to value all students' language dialects but that these linguistic structures must be integrated within the codes of power that traditional mainstream language imparts. She asserts that exclusive or dominant use of one's own language dialects in school will only lead to further marginalization for language-minority children.

PAUSE AND PONDER

During 1870–1933, many Native American children were sent to off-reservation boarding schools to begin a process of assimilation into white mainstream culture. Almost immediately, the boarding school officials instituted a system of renaming the new students. Often, the new names were selected from the Bible or from famous historical figures. Sometimes, the new names were inaccurate and offensive English translations of Native American children's names.

A boy from the Sioux tribe described the process of renaming after attending a few days of school:

We had the names of white men sewed on our backs.... When the teacher called the roll, no one answered his name. Then she would walk around and look at the back of the boys' shirts. When she had the right name located, she made the boy stand up and say "Present." She kept this up for a week before we knew what the sound of our new names was. (Adams, 1995, p. 111)

• Is this system of renaming an appropriate example of cultural dissonance as described in this chapter?

- The renaming process has been labeled as an example of "education by extinction" (Adams, pp. 15–16). Is this label warranted?
- Can you find any additional probing questions to ask about the renaming process?

The teacher in a whole-class setting (as well as in individualized instruction) could strive to resolve tensions between students' home cultural practices and school cultural norms. Fecho (1998) demonstrated this mediation activity in an action he called **code-switching** (p. 94). This practice is one in which the teacher assists students in shifting between home language and school language patterns based on audience and social expectations. In a unit of study on the importance of everyday language, Fecho utilized "code-switching" between African American Vernacular English and standard English in class discussions. He began the unit with his own framing question, "How does learning about language connect you to your world?" His students took the teacher's framing question and added their own questions in a true spirit of collaborative inquiry. One of their questions was, "What happens when the language of rap music is studied for what it says about Blacks [African Americans] in America?" (pp. 90–91). In reflecting on a similar experience he had with former students, Fecho admitted that those students' questions still "reverberate within these walls today" (p. 97). In the true spirit of question-finding, the language arts educator related that some of the questions generated by his students had no definite answers but were still worth asking.

Cultural conflict also provides opportunities for teachers in other content areas to create classroom environments that are conducive to collaborative inquiry and question-finding. Gutierrez, Rymes, and Larsen (1995) examined a ninth-grade social studies class consisting of mostly African American and Latino students. The topic of the lesson was the historic legal case *Brown v. Board of Education* (1954), involving school desegregation. In the classroom, a discourse pattern evolved that contained three distinct social language features that the researchers labeled, "scripts." The first script was teacher dominated and involved mainly **monologic talk**. The second script was student constructed and often consisted of answers or comments that showed a misreading or inappropriate reaction to the teacher script. For example, one of the students associated the name Brown (in the court case) with the rock singer James Brown. The third script was unscripted, which in classroom discourse was also described as the "**third space**" (Gutierrez et al., p. 466). This is the place where the two scripts intersect and create potential for authentic interaction to occur. It is often a student's genuine question that opens up the unscripted third space. In the following exchange, a ninth-grade student of mixed African American and white ancestry posed a personally relevant question related to the separation of African American students and white students in public schools.

S: What if they're half Black and half White...

T: What if who's...what

S: What if the kid's half White and half Black where do they go—what school do they go to?...

T: In the South you weren't half anything.

S: See?

T: In the South if you were even a teeny weeny...eentsy bit Black...you were Black.

(p. 465)

It is in this third space that collaborative inquiry and question-finding occurred. According to the researchers in this study, "the personal and social relevance of this line of questioning may in fact be what draws the students and teacher in the same key, or into the unscripted third space" (p. 466). Indeed, it was the cultural dissonance and "conflict" learning situation that set the stage for **dialogic inquiry** (third space) and student questioning to take place.

PAUSE AND PONDER

Holden Caulfield, the adolescent character in Salinger's (1951) *The Catcher in the Rye*, remarked about his high school social studies teacher,

> He hardly ever listened to you when you said something. He read my paper anyway. You can't stop a teacher when they want to do something. They just do it. (p. 15)

This sentiment has often been expressed by students in real life as well as fiction. For example, Rop (2003) recorded high school science students' remarks about their teachers that were essentially similar. The students said that their questions were too often greeted by what they called, "the teacher slam," which they defined as being so busy slamming content that the teacher brushes off the question. The teachers would say to the students, "We'll get to that later" (p. 25).

A major theme in this chapter is the dissonance between teacher talk and student talk in the classroom. Teachers talk and students listen. Many educators believe that this dissonance is based on the asymmetrical power relationships in the classroom. Kohl (2003) recommends what he calls "topsy-turvy" teaching to increase student talk and questioning in the classroom. It means literally to upend the classroom format so teachers encourage and "try to understand what students are saying in a context where they [teachers] are not accustomed to listening and students are not accustomed to speaking openly and honestly in class" (p. 106).

- Is the "teacher slam" an accurate description of the state of student passivity in the classroom?
- Are you in favor of Kohl's recommendation for increasing student voice and questioning in the classroom?
- What implications does Kohl's recommendation hold for question-finding?

Cultural Congruence in a Language Arts Classroom

In some classroom situations, ethnic minority and linguistically diverse students may not experience cultural dissonance or cultural conflict. Indeed, they may be able to express home language practices that are congruent with school norms of behavior. Ethnographers and literacy researchers of diverse American ethnic minority cultures have discovered patterns of cultural behavior that actually benefit students in different content areas (Hudicourt-Barnes, 2003; Lee, 1993; McCarthy & Watahomigie, 1998). Thus, in this section, I examine culturally congruent school and home practices that support the development of student questioning behavior and literacy learning in the classroom.

In a ninth-grade language arts classroom, Lee (1993) demonstrates how the use of an African American genre of talk serves as a scaffold for a literary interpretation of novels and short stories. Lee believes that African American adolescents bring a powerful intellectual tool into classrooms, which is too often undervalued. The teacher researcher calls this genre of talk "**signifying**," an African American dialect rich in historical and literary tradition. Specifically, signifying is a form of social discourse that stresses figurative language, body language, and rhythms of speech (e.g., rapping). It means "to speak with innuendo and double meanings, to play rhetorically upon the meaning and sounds of words, and to be quick and often witty in one's response" (p. 11). When the teacher opened up the lesson to discussion, students raised their own questions related to a literary discussion of Alice Walker's *The Color Purple* (1982). The teacher began with a focus question, "What is the image of God in the book called *The Color Purple*?" In the following exchange, the students working in a group demonstrate the practice of signifying.

Yvonne: What's that writing on your paper?

Willard: We talking about it now.

Laverne:	You were supposed to have read the whole book. What is [the] image of God?
Willard:	I did read the whole book.
Laverne:	Then what was the image of God?
Willard:	He looked like me.
Laverne:	Stupid. How ghetto can you be?...
Janet:	I think that this is [referring to a reading passage in the book]. It says, "God is different to us now. After all these years in Africa, more spirit than ever...and more internal. Most people think that he has to look like something or someone...but we don't and (not) being tied to what God looks like frees us."
Willard:	That's Nettie discussing what God is to her. What does Celie think He looks like?
Laverne:	...we found some pages about the way that Celie thinks about God...
Willard:	She believes in Him and she really cares about what He thinks but on one page... [she] was talking about Him, blasting Him....

(Lee, 1993, pp. 116–117)

In other lessons on the same theme, the teacher modeled the kind of questions that her students needed to ask. She scaffolded with the following prompt: "it ought to be a question that you don't know the answer to, and preferably they should not be questions like how old was Celie or those kinds of questions? They should be things that you really worry about" (Lee, 2000, p. 218). The teacher passed out index cards for the students to write their individual questions. Some of their questions included, "Why did she [the author] start each letter off with dear God and then later on change it to dear Nettie?" "Why did Celie stop writing to God?" and "Why did Celie start bad mouthing God?" (p. 218). The teacher was satisfied that these were all provocative questions and stated that they would discuss a few questions like these every day during the remainder of the unit.

Cultural Congruence in an After-School Literacy Program

The influence of cultural congruence on question-finding also can be observed in after-school literacy programs for adolescents. For example, a team of university researchers, graduate students, and schoolchildren worked together on a literacy program that tapped into sociocultural concerns (Alvermann, 2002). The students were allowed to select and study a problem of interest to them over a 14-week period. Ned, an African American student, designated his unit, the "freedom activity," a project built around socially conscious rap music. He worked closely with Kevin, a graduate student member of the research team, who had similar interests and also had personal contacts in rap music. The graduate student served as the **more knowledgeable other** and scaffolded how to engage in a problem-solving activity. Kevin prompted Ned to find his own initial unit question. Kevin evaluated the efficiency of Ned's initial question and then prompted the adolescent to find other research questions, but only after the mentor had explained and modeled the **iterative nature of generating questions**. In a social-constructivist vein, Kevin related that he himself expected to learn something from Ned's research, which revealed the co-constructed nature of the literacy exercise.

Cultural Congruence and Question-Finding in Science Classrooms

In secondary science classrooms, teachers and researchers have used the language practices of linguistically diverse students to scaffold instruction successfully (Ballenger, 1997; Hudicourt-Barnes, 2003; Warren, Ballenger, Ogonowski, Rosebery, & Hudicourt-Barnes, 2001). These studies revealed that scientific ways of talking do not always have to be rational and analytical. Lemke (1990) explains that there are ways of talking science that are subjective and affective, and that science does not have to be a cold and emotionally detached subject.

Such challenges to traditional scientific literacy orientations have been the focus of a number of studies involving Haitian Creole, middle-grade students (Ballenger, 1997; Hudicourt-Barnes, 2003; Warren et al., 2001). Teachers and university researchers have demonstrated how selected cultural characteristics including forms of argumentation and **sense-making** can be used as scaffolds for learning science. These scaffolds are important support structures for generating questions. In the following exchange, seventh- and eighth-grade Haitian students revealed a cultural facility for argumentation called "Bay odyans" or "**give talk**" while engaged in a heated discussion about organisms in pond life. Notice how one student served as the theoretician (Steve) and the other as a challenger (Danielle), which are defining characteristics of "Bay odyans," as they discussed the specific topic of snails in pond life. The issue in question is Steve's claim that he had taken 10 snails home from the pond and discovered after three weeks the number had spontaneously generated to over 30. Danielle is surprised by Steve's claim and raises questions (challenges) about the validity of Steve's assertion.

> Danielle: You say you have thirty snails. How long does each snail take to have babies? Like, does a snail, that is, if it is born today, could it make babies tomorrow?...
>
> Teacher: Good question.
>
> Steve: I myself said that! I said when they grow. I said when they grow they have babies.

Teacher: Ok, kids let me say something. That's something I would like to know because we are also researching it. Steve, respond!...

Steve: Ok, myself, here is what I said...

Danielle: Let me ask you a question again before you finish answering.

Steve: You could not wait till I finish?

Danielle: Before you respond in that way, let me ask you something... Since you said that they had babies, and what you said, how long does it take for a snail to grow?

Steve: How do I know?

Danielle: Well, Steve...

Steve: Snails are always small.

(Hudicourt-Barnes, pp. 85–86)

An analysis of this exchange reveals some interesting implications for cultural congruence and question-finding. Notice how Danielle used her Haitian Creole form of argumentation in a scientific way. She called on Steve to support or give evidence for his claim, which can be considered a linguistic structure for forging norms of scientific accountability (Warren & Rosebery, 1996). After Danielle's challenge, Steve admitted that he could not support his earlier implicit claim (that he could distinguish snails by their growth and size) when he exclaimed, "How do I know?... Snails are always small" (Hudicourt-Barnes, p. 86). As a result of Steve's counterintuitive assertion and observation that snails form multiple generations almost spontaneously, both the students and the teacher began to ask inquiry questions. In showing a sincere interest in Steve's surprising claim, the teacher established a collaborative learning situation. He, too, wanted to know what method of verification Steve used to identify the multiple generations of snail babies.

In the next example, the cultural practices of Haitian Creole, middle-grade students also supported scientific literacy. The sixth-grade students engaged in a discussion of the metamorphosis of mealworms and used their everyday reasoning to try to understand the topic of growth and development. This discussion took place in what the teacher called a "science circle"—a time set aside to hear students' questions, share observations, read aloud from journals, tell stories, joke around, and argue among themselves using everyday language. The following exchange illustrates how Haitian Creole students used their cultural practice of "sense-making" to generate questions comparing the metamorphosis of mealworms and physical changes in humans.

Manuelle: Why, if people eat and eat, don't they change their skin, don't they transform, the way insects do?...

Fabiola:	God did not create us like insects.
Stefan:	People and animals aren't the same thing.
Jean-Claude:	Manuelle, skin changes. It's like, the larva, when it was inside the egg, you, like you were inside your mother's stomach. It's like,...when you were born, when you were a little baby, you had hardly any hair. Didn't that change? Don't you have hair?

[Manuelle listens to this and then stands up to exclaim.]

Manuelle:	Do I change my skin like this, vloop, vloop? [pretending to unzip her skin and climb out of it]

(Warren et al., 2001, p. 536)

Clearly, Manuelle took the initiative in using her culture-based reasoning and sense-making as a means of stimulating student questioning in a science lesson.

Finding Authentic Questions

Establishing cultural congruence between home and school environments sets up authentic learning situations in the classroom. When there is cultural continuity between home and school, adolescents see the relevance of learning. Heather, in chapter 3 in the discussion of student questioning and critical literacy, didn't care enough about the science topic (nuclear chemistry) under discussion to show concern about critiquing its message. She did not see the relevance of it to her life. She expressed a "why bother with it" attitude that does not stimulate authentic student questions.

Which types of social learning situations stimulate authentic questioning? In the next section, I suggest three types of classroom environments that stimulate authentic questioning. They are the **dialogically organized classroom**, the culturally responsive classroom, and the **project-based classroom**. Each kind of learning environment relates to the social dimensions of literacy learning. It is important to note that although each social learning situation is presented independently, there often will be overlap among and between these authentic social learning environments.

The Dialogically Organized Classroom

The dialogically organized classroom is based on the language discourse theories of philosopher and literary theorist Mikhail Bakhtin. According to Bakhtin (1981), dialogical discourse is characterized by a plurality of voices within the boundaries of a single utterance. One voice or utterance refracts off the others as a composite act of communication. In Bakhtin's words, "the actual meaning of an utterance is understood against the background of other concrete utterances on the same theme, a background made up of contradictory opinions, points of view and value judgments..." (p. 281). Discourse is dialogical because utterances are continually structured by tension between the conversants, as one voice refracts another. It is this tension among competing voices that gives shape to discourse and lies at the heart of comprehension and understanding (Nystrand, Gamoran, Kachur, & Prendergast, 1997).

The typical recitation type of learning environment is monologic, in that the teacher asks questions, the students give answers, and the teacher evaluates students' answers. As indicated earlier, this type of classroom discourse is often referred to as IRE (teacher initiation, student response, and teacher evaluation). This environment is inauthentic because the questioner (the teacher) asks questions for which he or she already knows the answer. Questions are not used to find unknown information, but to evaluate student responses in a test-like fashion. This condition leaves little space for student voice. Students' cognitive-based questions, on the other hand, are almost always authentic because they are based on students' desire to know an unknown answer.

Clearly, the recitation method or monologic type of teaching is inauthentic in terms of classroom questioning behavior. This method of teaching questioning is not only inauthentic but also asymmetrical. It is almost entirely dominated by the teacher, whose voice, too often, is the only one heard in the classroom. On the other hand, authentic classroom questioning behavior is dialogical.

Authentic questions thrive on uncertainties, and a dialogic inquiry learning environment provides these **indeterminate learning situations** (Dewey, 1938; Dudley-Marling, 1997). However, it should be kept in mind that it is possible for real inquiry (and question-finding) to take place in classrooms in which a teacher-posed question initiates the inquiry process. Students' questions do not have to necessarily initiate inquiry learning. Teacher questions can be authentic or real if they awaken a wondering on the part of the students. The essence of authenticity is that the teacher's focus questions must be taken over and eventually "owned" by the students (G. Wells, 2000).

Teachers can set up a dialogical classroom by "priming the possibility for discussion" and inviting students to speculate about sociocultural issues (Nystrand, Wu, Gamoran, Zeiser, & Long, 2003, p. 189). For example, in a ninth-grade language arts classroom, a teacher took this role by engaging the class in a discussion about racism in Mark Twain's *The Adventures of Huckleberry Finn* (1931). In the following exchange, the teacher scaffolded the dialogical lesson by posing the lead question.

Ms. Turner: Can you recall things from *Huck Finn* that, um, seemed racist to you?

Tasha: Miss Watson's, that guy she's always calling "Miss Watson's nigger."

Ms. Turner: Ok...Jim?

Jim: Well, they sell the slaves. Also, they said in one part, "fetch in the nigger"...and it's like, you know, it's like you're saying to a dog, "Here, boy."

Ms. Turner: Right—"We fetched in the niggers to have prayers." Yeah, that's in probably the first couple of pages. Good. Sam?

Sam: Isn't he [Mark Twain] being historically accurate when he says "those niggers"?

Ms. Turner: Oh, yes, absolutely.

Sam: So why is it racist?

Ms. Turner: Well...Twain is really just trying to mirror the society and especially the society of Missouri at the time. But Twain is using the word rather sarcastically. I mean, you're right, he's being historically accurate, but he's also trying to make a point, um, about the different people who are saying things like that...

Cassie: Everyone claims it's so historical, you can find that anywhere "nigger," you know, you just hear that and people always think it's so historical.

Ms. Turner: Like, oh, we wouldn't do that anymore.

Cassie: Yeah, like, oh we're not so primitive [now]...but [today] people do that—people can't get in[to] apartment buildings because they're black...

Jim: You know, it's just, I mean, everybody is always saying how historical it is, and it's right here, and it's right now.

(Nystrand et al., pp. 189–190)

Notice how the dialogical nature of this exchange prompted the students and the teacher to collaboratively find authentic questions to ask about the nature of racism in this classic work of American literature and its current implications.

Teachers also can scaffold the question-finding process with preadolescent students in sociocognitive contexts. For example, in a fifth-grade language arts classroom, the teacher initiated the inquiry process by modeling how students should use their learning logs to write questions collaboratively. She scaffolded their inquiry by posing a focus question related to a Book Club activity (McMahon, 1996). The focus question related to Winnie, the main character in *Tuck Everlasting* (Babbitt, 1975). The teacher asked, "Would you have liked to live in the same time period (i.e., 1880s) as Winnie?" This question served as the focus of a collaborative dialogic inquiry in which one student (Crystal) acted as the more knowledgeable other. As the teacher-type surrogate, Crystal used scaffolding to encourage another student, Trenton, to respond to the main question.

Crystal: Okay, what do you think? What did you write in your log?

Trenton: I wrote, "No."

Crystal: Why?

Trenton: Because they don't have no cars.

Crystal: Oh yeah, and what else?

Trenton: What would we do without cars? They ain't got no Nintendo. They have wooden spoons. Um, they have wooden floors. We have classic floors. Um, um, they have a whole bunch of trees and I don't want a bunch of trees in front of my house. They got snakes out there and stuff.

Crystal: And that's why you think you wouldn't want to live in her time.

(McMahon, p. 63)

Notice how both Crystal and Trenton treated their utterances as thinking devices and generators of meaning. They do not regard their utterances as information to be received, encoded, and stored. Rather, the students took an active stance by questioning and extending their own utterances (Wertsch & Toma, 1995). The social application of the question-finding process with its dialogical basis created a collaborative space for the generation of meaning and not the production of self-enclosed messages. In contrast, a monological instructional sequence provides few opportunities for students to take a teacher's utterance as an object to be questioned. Generally, teachers' utterances are accepted without question (Wertsch & Toma).

An authentic learning environment can occur even without a teacher-directed query to guide the discussion. The teacher can simply scaffold a number of **question starters** and leave the rest of the question for the students to complete. Recall how I used cue cards containing question prompts with my 11th-grade American history students (see chapter 1). Mr. Garcia used a similar approach with his ninth-grade world culture class (King, 2002). After teaching his students to recognize 15 question starters (e.g., How does...influence...? What would happen if...?), Mr. Garcia directed his students to use them in a peer discussion on the concept of culture. Following is an excerpt from that discussion in which students practiced what King called a **guided reciprocal peer questioning** procedure (p. 34). Notice how students' questions and answers bounce off one another spontaneously and authentically, guided by the structure of the "given" question starters.

Jim: How does a culture influence the language of a society?

Barry: Well...the language is made up of words that are important to the people of that culture. Some cultures may not even have a word for telephone, because they don't have any [telephones]. But, phones are important in our culture, so we have lots of different words for them...

Barry: I've got a great question! You'll never be able to answer it. What would happen if there was a group somewhere without any spoken language? Maybe they were all born not being able to speak... How would that affect their culture, or could there even be a culture?

Sally: Well, it would mean they couldn't communicate with each other...

Barry: But wait! Why couldn't they communicate? Maybe they would develop a nonverbal language system, you know, the way [deaf] people use hand signs...

Sally: I didn't think of that! But it would be difficult for them to communicate with anyone who was out of their line of sight...

Barry: Well, not if they could hear...they could communicate with drums or clackers of some sort.

Sally: Then maybe drums would become very important to them...the drums might even become a status symbol...

Jim: What made you think of that?

Sally: We learned about status and status symbols last year in social studies.

(King, p. 35)

Reciprocal peer questioning correlates well with the idea of question-finding. Both are generative thinking processes. One student's question prompts other students to find additional questions and answers to carry on the dialogical interaction. Each member contributes and at the same time learns from the others. Notice how Sally exclaims, "I didn't think of that!" to Barry's alternate way of looking at culture and communication. This is a good example of the sociocognitive dimension of student questioning.

The following examples show how students in various content areas can serve as substitute mentors or more knowledgeable others in sustaining a dialogically organized classroom. Students who serve in this capacity can model authentic questioning behavior in peer learning situations.

In my 11th-grade American history class, I set up an inquiry strategy in which the class had to predict the unrevealed period (i.e., the 1920s) in which an immigrant story took place. (The story was adapted from Levin's [1937] *The Old Bunch*.) One student was selected as the leader, or more knowledgeable other. The story involved a confrontation over hair fashion between an immigrant mother and her American-born teenage daughter. The hair fashion was a bob style that resembled a man's short hairstyle. The mother angrily railed against her daughter's adoption of "modern" ways. In groups, the students analyzed the story and searched for clues to identify the time period. The student leader facilitated the inquiry interchange by modeling questions. For example, he asked, "Can we really assume that the story took place a long time ago?" In the discussion, some students thought it was an early period such as the 1940s because the mother was angry with her daughter for cutting her hair, whereas in modern times, one's mother would not be so angry. Others disagreed and thought that a drastic haircut would shock some parents even today. However, the strictness of the mother's reaction to the bob haircut led some students to conclude that this was very different from today's parents, who might be more understanding. The leader guided the questioning process so his questions modeled dialogic inquiry. Throughout the dialogue, he posed the following fundamental question: "Do you still think it is different today?" There was no way to predict the direction in which the dialogue would move. The cultural conflict incident (immigrant versus first generation) generated its own conceptual conflict among the students. The group began to take ownership of the inquiry process through the leader's authentic questions—ones that were very relevant to these adolescents' lives (haircut style, reaction of parents, and so forth).

In an 11th-grade mathematics classroom, Adam served as a more knowledgeable other as he and Luke worked on a cantor set problem. A cantor set is formed by taking a line segment and removing a fractional part in the middle on a continuous basis. In this learning experience, the students worked on a middle fifth-cantor set. This set is a fractal or a line that is broken off into fifths. The students were given a line with a length of one (the whole number), and they had to start by first removing the middle fifth, then removing the middle fifth of the remaining segments, and repeating this procedure continuously. The theoretical purpose of the exercise was to explain the infinite repetitions underlying fractals. After repeating this process continually, it might appear that the total amount of space removed would leave nothing of the original line. Instead, however, the exercise revealed that the sum of all the lengths removed is equal to the length of the original line. For most students, this is a surprising and counterintuitive result (Goos, 2004).

In the following excerpt, Adam takes on the role of a teacher in a teacher–student-type dialogical pattern. He helps scaffold the steps of the cantor set problem through question-finding procedures. Specifically, Adam assists by asking questions that lead Luke to locate any errors or reconsider his solution plan of action.

Luke: [Thinking out loud] It's going to be a fifth [the fractal to be removed].

Adam: Work through it!...

Luke: [Looks up puzzled.] What am I doing? [Checks example] The size remaining [is right] isn't it?

Adam: OK, just do it.

Luke: OK, fine...

Adam: [Opens his book and checks Luke's work] Wrong!

Luke: [Expression of disbelief] How and where? I cannot see where it could possibly be wrong!

Adam: OK, explain this to me [points to Luke's work].

Luke: [Pointing to his work] What we've lost is the original fifth, and...[turns to Adam] two fifths [sounds hesitant]

Adam: No, you're doing each section, you haven't added them up yet. So you haven't lost the original fifth yet, we're ignoring that.

Luke: OK. Out of each portion we...

Adam: OK, how big is the section?...

Luke: A fifth of...two fifths! ["Aha" expression on his face...both laugh...] Now it gets tricky! [Luke circles the incorrect working and crosses it out] Phew? [to Adam] You've given me food for thought.

(Goos, 2004, p. 280)

Adam serves as an effective model in scaffolding the question-finding process because he does not just point out mistakes to Luke. He encourages Luke to question the assumptions about his (Luke's) answers to the problem. Adam wants Luke to work out the puzzlement created by the counterintuitive nature of the problem. He models by asking, "How big is the section?" Adam asks the kind of puzzlement questions that Luke should have asked himself. That question leads Luke to recognize the iterative nature of the problem—that by continuously doing the same removal process, one surprisingly arrives at the original amount.

In an 11th-grade language arts class, another learning situation occurred in which a student served as a more knowledgeable other (Rex, 2001). In a discussion of Chaucer's *The Canterbury Tales* (1978), a student, Kora, expressed confusion about certain Christian practices. Specifically, Kora asked, "What is a rosary?" (Rex, p. 309). The teacher took the opportunity to redirect Kora's question to the whole class. The teacher called on Patricia, a student well versed in Christian rituals and practices, to address Kora's question. Patricia sought to clarify Kora's question by asking, "Is it the rosary beads, or the rosary itself that you need [an] explanation [for]?" Then, Patricia explained the significance of the rosary practice to Kora. Thus, the teacher set up a situation in which one student (Patricia) joined her knowledge of a cultural text with another student's (Kora) need to know. The teacher adapted Patricia's contributions, elaborated on them, and retold them to Kora and to the class.

PAUSE AND PONDER

This chapter has focused on the importance of collaborative social interaction as prompts to question-finding behavior. For example, we examined the Vygotskian perspective concerning the benefits of the "more knowledgeable other" as a model of questioning behavior. Yet, we also discussed the idea that sociocognitive conflict is beneficial. Indeed, some developmental social psychologists believe that only peer conflict is beneficial, and that a situation in which partners argue and search for solutions stimulates cognitive development (Bell, Grossen, & Perret-Clermont, 1985; Doise & Mugny, 1984). In fact, they say that the more knowledgeable other often imposes his or her thinking and leaves little room for cognitive growth for both parties. That is, modeling is less effective for cognitive development than conflict. Apparently, both of these alternative ideas of peer modeling and peer conflict can stimulate question-finding behavior.

• Which of the two ideas do you feel has a stronger impact on question-finding behavior?

The Culturally Responsive Classroom

Previously, I referred to the theoretical benefits of culturally congruent practices on question-finding behavior. In this section, I describe how some teachers and researchers have set up specific classroom learning environments that incorporate the main elements of cultural congruence. This type of classroom environment is sometimes described as the culturally responsive classroom, or one in which students' home and cultural experiences are adapted to serve literacy instruction (Au, 1993). A culturally responsive classroom is different from the traditional learning environment in that the teacher seeks to incorporate students' cultural ways of thinking and reasoning into mandated curriculum goals and activities. The idea behind this inclusiveness is to find ways to integrate school and home cultural practices to help all students achieve.

As previously mentioned, Au (1997b) showed how this could be done with Hawaiian children in mainstream school settings. Specifically, she demonstrated how the teacher could use the distinctive participation structures (face-to-face interaction patterns) of the Hawaiian children to enhance literacy learning. Hawaiian children are raised using a talk-story-like participation structure that is distinctive from the mainstream directive interactions. With this talk-story structure, children do not respond well to teacher-dominated questioning and rigid turn-taking answering. Their cultural preferences are for collaboration in producing answers to teacher's questions, rather than competition with peers. In the following exchange, a language arts teacher used the Native American children's story *Annie and the Old One* (Miles, 1971) that contains the theme of learning from grandparents, one that is very prominent in the Hawaiian culture, too. The following classroom discussion centers on the grandmother's dying as symbolized by the fading of the cactus flower.

Teacher: But she [grandmother] also compared it [to old age and dying]...

Joey: The cactus.

Teacher: Okay, tell me about the cactus, Joey.

Joey: Oh. I know about the cactus.

Teacher: [What did you] find out about the cactus?

Joey: [Reads from text] "The cactus did not bloom forever. Petals dried and fell to earth."

Teacher: Okay, what is she trying to tell Annie by using that analogy of the cactus?

Ross: That people die of old age. That people just don't die when they say so.

Teacher: Well, yeah, okay, that's—that's true. But what did they mean when they said, "The cactus did not bloom forever"?

Ross: That people, they got to die.

Kent: That means that when it starts blooming a life will start, but when it falls the life will end.

(Au, 1993, pp. 115–116)

Notice how the teacher allows the students to respond to one another's comments without designating each speaker's turn. The students worked collaboratively on the problem, responding to one another and building their answers to the teacher's initial focus question. This learning situation contains the elements of a culturally responsive classroom. The teacher affirms students' cultural identity by using a story containing grandparents' wisdom and encourages cultural genres of communication by allowing for the talk-story participation structure to evolve.

In this example, the teacher provided a competent model of questioning behavior, but she could have elaborated on her role. She could have used this opportunity to scaffold additional questions by referring back to specific events in the story. For example, Annie's reaction to the death of her grandmother provided one such opportunity. Annie eventually comes to the realization that her grandmother's dying fits into the Native American belief system of the earth's giving and taking of life. At this juncture, the teacher could have scaffolded the following questions: Does this story have any personal meaning for you? Can you think of any ways Annie could have reacted differently to her grandmother's passing? Then, the teacher could have elicited additional puzzlement and wonderment questions from her students.

The idea of the culturally responsive classroom has implications for other content areas such as mathematics. Research pertaining to mathematics and cultural diversity indicates that children from different cultural backgrounds often approach the same mathematics problems from different vantage points or "relational perspectives" (Cobb & Hodge, 2002, pp. 251–252). Evidence for this was revealed by Ladson-Billings (1995), who described specifically how inner-city students and their suburban counterparts interpreted the same real-world mathematics problem in different ways. The problem was stated in the following way:

> It costs $1.50 to travel each way on the city bus. A transit system fast pass costs $65 a month. Which is the more economical way to get to work, the daily fare or the fast pass? (p. 131)

The suburban students assumed that the task was about a person who commuted to work in the city and calculated a cost of $3.00 per day for five days each week. Therefore, they selected the daily fare as the most economical. In contrast, the inner-city students asked a number of questions including, "How many jobs are we talking about?" and "Is it a part-time job?" After obtaining responses to their questions and realizing that the fast pass offered them better benefits as everyday commuters, they selected the fast pass as the most economical means of transportation. These authentic responses reflected differences in the economic practices of the students' local communities. Ladson-Billings asserts that the creators of the above math problem identified with the practices of the suburban students' home community. They did not expect different answers depending on the economic practices of the students' home communities. However, it is important for teachers to consider the cultural backgrounds of their students when constructing curriculum topics and problems. This procedure has been described as **culturally relevant pedagogy**.

This cultural dissonance between the inner-city and suburban students provides an opportunity for question-finding. Teachers could model the following puzzlement question (explanation type): Why do the two "cultural groups" react so differently to the same math problem? Teachers also can model the following wonderment questions: What are some ways to construct math word problems that are value free? Can you create a math word problem that does not reflect societal values?

Culturally relevant pedagogy advocates incorporating students' home culture as an effective means for academic learning. It also stresses the need to critique the cultural norms, values, mores, and institutions that produce and maintain social inequities (Ladson-Billings, 1995). The Algebra Project is an educational intervention program that incorporates the idea of culturally relevant pedagogy (Moses & Cobb, 2001). The Algebra Project is a community initiative started by Robert Moses, an African American civil rights activist in Mississippi during the 1960s. The goal of the project is to provide economic access and full citizenship opportunities for African Americans through mathematics literacy. It conceives of algebra for all students as the "new" civil rights. It claims that African Americans have been denied the opportunity to succeed in mathematics, that mathematics instruction should be available to every middle school student so that upon entering high school, all students will be prepared to take algebra.

The motto of the project is "each one teaching one" (Moses & Cobb, 2001, p. 178). In essence, the program is a tutorial program involving older students tutoring middle school students in algebra preparation by making the subject "cool" and by using home culture as the scaffold for math literacy. One tutee explained why the program appealed to him:

> I like [the way the program is trying] to teach other folks, kid to kid, teenager to teenager. And teenagers can explain something to teenagers. They're not going to look at grown-ups like they'll look at somebody just like them. I ain't saying all grown-ups are slow, but if a grown-up says something to you, they might say it, like, in a grown-up way—a longer way. (p. 192)

Some school districts have incorporated the Algebra Project into the eighth-grade curriculum (Martin, 2000). In particular, the program stresses the development of student questioning skills. A math teacher involved in the program articulated one of its main goals in the following manner:

> Now why is it that children at a young age have all this WHY? Then when they get older, they don't have any WHYs? What happened? What are the schools doing to get rid of the WHY? If you take away the WHY, then there is no potential. (Moses & Cobb, 2001, p. 152)

Martin, a sixth-grade student enrolled in the Algebra Project, displayed the proper question-finding attitude while working on a math problem with his classmates. He stated,

> I remember once we were trying to figure out how to show the six routes of a train with unifix cubes that only went in four directions. Finally after thinking about it I said, "Why don't we put two more routes on top of two of the [bottom] routes." Some of the group I was in objected. "They didn't say we could do that." But I convinced them. "They didn't say we couldn't either." (Moses & Cobb, 2001, p. 190)

The Algebra Project is based on the counterintuitive idea that mathematics is not just numerical computation, but includes writing, drawing, and discussion. When the program was introduced as a transition curriculum in Oakland, California, it was resisted by many students because of its discrepant nature. Students raised the following questions: "How is writing part of math? How is art a part of a math?" (Martin, 2000, p. 118). These seventh graders openly questioned whether the math in the Algebra Project was the "real" math as they had traditionally learned it.

Programs that involve modifying the traditional format of a curriculum are often resistant to change. This is often the case with children, who sometimes find it more difficult to adapt than adults. (See chapter 5 for a more detailed discussion of conceptual change.)

Project–Based and Research–Oriented Instruction

In this chapter, I have noted that authentic-type questions can be generated across the curriculum. I also examined authentic questions as legitimate information-seeking queries. Further, I presented authentic questions that have personal and cultural relevance for the asker. In this section, I discuss questions that are authentic in the sense that they are of the type that subject specialists ask. This type of authentic question can be asked in any content area that uses project-based instruction. As an illustrative example, I demonstrate how this type of authentic question can be generated in the field of science.

Science educators often label this type of authentic question as a **driving question** or as a question that simulates a scientist's mode of inquiry and contains personally relevant goals (Krajcik, Blumenfeld, Marx, & Soloway, 2000). Four main features characterize driving questions: First, they are scientifically worthwhile—that is, they are related to what scientists really do. Second, they are feasible—that is, they are framed in terms that make the subsequent investigations and experiments doable and achievable. Third, they are collaboratively constructed with input from teacher and students in a "social framework in which scientific work can be understood" (K. Roth, 2001, n.p.). Fourth, they are based on one's desire to really want to know something personally. In a word, they are anchored in real-world experiences.

In science, anchored learning experiences often take place in laboratory settings. Driving questions are most often generated in **open-inquiry lab environments**, in which procedures are not prescribed in a cookbook fashion, but are often flexible and ill defined. Clearly, driving questions are often inquiry oriented and experimentally based. W.M. Roth (1995) further describes these types of authentic lab questions as **covariation questions**, which attempt to establish a causal relationship between variables. Covariation questions are those most often asked by scientists in their quest for sets of experimental variables (Roth). Question-finding, as described in this book, is an inquiry tool that can be used by scientists in their quest for sets of variables that can be tested experimentally. Indeed, scientists take steps to revise and reframe their initial covariation questions in order to make room for serendipitous findings (Roth).

In a unit of study on biome life in their school neighborhood, eighth-grade students posed the following covariation questions that mimicked scientists' mode of open inquiry:

Does the amount of light affect the growth of plants?

How does the soil temperature affect plant growth?

How does acidity affect plant growth? (W.M. Roth, 1995, p. 111)

In the process of finding covariation questions to investigate, the students took a very important step in rigorous scientific experimentation. They set out to test the relationship between the above variables (i.e., amount of light and growth of plants). Based on the following statement from Einstein (Einstein & Infeld, 1938), he would have approved of the students' question-finding strategy:

The formulation of a problem is often more essential than its solution, which may be merely a matter of mathematical or experimental skill. To raise new questions, new possibilities, to regard old questions from a new angle requires creative imagination. (p. 92)

Einstein, himself, needed to change his concepts of time and space when he formulated his theory of relativity. He believed that the creative imagination often requires a conceptual change in one's knowledge and attitude toward disciplinary learning. In the next chapter, I examine how the different dimensions of question-finding (i.e., cognitive and metacognitive, motivational, critical, and social) can be used to stimulate conceptual change in different content areas.

Summary

This chapter examined three subtypes of the social literacy dimension and their relationships to question-finding. These included the sociocognitive, sociolinguistic, and sociocultural dimensions of literacy. Conceptual conflict teaching and epistemic curiosity factors were incorporated into the social literacy perspective, just as they were used in the other dimensions (i.e., cognitive, motivational, and critical). These factors of question-finding were induced through dialogic inquiry and peer argumentation. This chapter also highlighted the notions that cultural and linguistic diversity practices were not considered deficits but assets to student questioning behavior.

PONDER AND PRACTICE

1. Examine the following photograph of a toy lending library in Jackson, Mississippi. The program was operated by the Works Progress Administration in several cities such as Jackson and Milwaukee, Wisconsin, during the Great Depression in the United States. In Milwaukee, where the first toy lending project opened in 1937, public officials decided to open toy lending libraries in poor neighborhoods where juvenile crime was the highest. The officials reasoned that the absence of toys in poor families was the "chief cause" of crime, and that if toys were provided to delinquent and potentially delinquent children that crime could be prevented (Webb, 2004).

Toy lending project in Jackson, Mississippi. Mississippi Department of Archives and History, Mississippi Historical Society, Jackson, Mississippi.

- What are your feelings about this program? Is the program discrepant?
- Do you detect any sociocultural bias in the Milwaukee program? Explain.
- Use the question-finding process (see chapter 1, pages 7–12) to generate puzzlement and wonderment questions.

2. The concept of biculturalism, an accommodation of two distinctive cultural heritages, is an important one in U.S. society. Very often this accommodation is strained and sometimes conflicted. As an example, I have used the children's book *Grandfather's Journey* (Say, 1993) to focus on this theme in which the author describes his own personal conflict in the following way: "the funny thing is, the moment I am in one country, I am homesick for the other" (p. 31).

- Practice your question-finding skills using the above theme. Refer to other examples of children's literature that contain a similar theme (e.g., S. Roth, 2001, *Happy Birthday Mr. Kang*).

3. In chapter 3, I introduced the term crossing borders as a critical literacy practice. This term, with its attempts to overcome barriers of separation between social and cultural groups, is also significant in attaining social literacy. Here too, question-finding can be an important educational intervention, particularly in fostering **intercultural social inquiry**, a process of promoting inter-group understanding through collaborative discovery learning (Flower, Long, & Higgins, 2000). Tyrone, an African American Muslim male teenager, demonstrated this inquiry practice in a collaborative writing assignment with an Asian American female partner. At first, Tyrone had to overcome a few cultural stereotypes. He wondered if he would be able to communicate with her. He stated,

> I come from a male-dominated home. Can I work as well with a woman as I would with a male? My partner was the first Asian American [I ever worked with]. Through TV, I...associated being Asian American with karate and Bruce Lee. I asked her did she know any karate or anything. She says, "no, no, no." I told her...how I was all tied up by that, and how my parents didn't teach me that [stereotype]. I just kind of picked it up off the street.... It showed me...that I could work with someone who was not male.... (Long, Peck, & Baskins, 2002, pp. 154–155)

- How does this example show the benefits of working with people who are different from us as an opportunity for mutual learning? Use this example to practice your question-finding skills.
- What questions can be generated from the inquiry experience?
- Can question-finding in dialogical learning environments also help to dispel cultural stereotypes?

4. The following two excerpts are from different literary genres that have implications for social literacy and question-finding. The first excerpt is a poem taken from Pulitzer Prize–winning poet Adrienne Rich's (2004) collection *The School Among the Ruins*:

> Today this is your lesson:
> write as clearly as you can
> your name home street and number
> down on this page
> No you can't go home yet
> but you aren't lost
> this is our school. (p. 24)

The second excerpt is from a classic novel by Betty Smith (1943), *A Tree Grows in Brooklyn*. In the novel, the author describes how Francie, a lower class Irish American adolescent, feels about her first day of school.

She had been in school but half a day when she knew that she would never be the teacher's pet. That privilege was reserved for a small group of girls...girls with freshly curled hair, crisp clean pinafores and new silk hair bows. They were the children of the prosperous storekeepers of the neighborhood. (p. 23)

- How does the poem address the theme of cultural dissonance that many children from nonmainstream cultures feel about school?

- In what ways does Francie express a dissonance with school culture similar to that suggested in the poem?

- Practice generating puzzlement and wonderment questions related to cultural dissonance between school and home cultures.

5. Middle school students in a Montclair, New Jersey, language arts and social studies interdisciplinary classroom were assigned a project to learn about their town's desegregation movement in the 1970s. They did research on the topic through readings (newspapers and other print sources) and conducted interviews with residents who had been involved in the movement. Particularly, they examined *The Montclair Times* "to identify emotional and racially charged words (and) to understand how these words are connected with stereotypes, prejudice, and privilege" (Anand, Fine, Surrey, & Perkins, 2002, p. 68). *The Montclair Times* of October 3, 1968, presented the following report that the students examined for fairness and objectivity:

   An intolerable situation at Montclair High School [occurred, in which] the Black Student Union, some 500 strong, decided on a sit-in demonstration.... The high school has been plagued with demonstrations, physical attacks by Negro students upon White students and conditions in the high school not conducive to the democratic process.... Everyone in the community, Negroes and Whites, have much at stake in this critical situation and already many White families, fearful of attack upon their children, are considering withdrawing them from the high school and moving or sending them to private schools. Montclair can ill afford such a movement, for it wouldn't take long for our schools to become predominantly Negro and the community a ghost town. (as cited in Anand et al., p. 39)

- How would you use the question-finding strategy to teach this assignment? Refer to the question-finding process in chapter 1.

- Can you formulate critical questions about the "objectivity" of the newspaper account? Refer to chapter 3 for examples of critical questions.

CHAPTER 5

Question–Finding and Conceptual Change

IMPORTANT CONCEPTS AND SPECIALIZED TERMS

affective entrenchment	guided inquiry approach	radical conceptual change
cognitive closure	intentional conceptual change	reconceptualizing prior
cold conceptual change	meaningful conflict	knowledge
conceptual change	multiple entry point teaching	self–monitoring questions
conceptual conflict strategy	naïve presuppositions	tolerance for ambiguity
conceptual ecology	peripheral conceptual change	whole–number bias
epistemic freezing	question-driven conceptual	
exposing preconceptions	change	

---

*I didn't know there were different types of questions. I just thought a question was
just a question. When my teacher told us that there were different types of
questions...I thought wow—I didn't know there were several different kinds of
questions. I learned that there are types of questions that I didn't know before. That
it's not always "Who?" "What?" and "When?" There is a better chance of asking
those [new] types of questions today than before we started.*

11TH-GRADE STUDENT (ADAPTED FROM CIARDIELLO, 1990)

This statement is representative of the student remarks I compiled from several
classroom lessons in 11th-grade American history during one semester. I had
taught my students how to recognize, categorize, and construct questions from
discrepant social studies documents. Prior to this instruction, they had had very
little experience with generating questions in school. As it was incorporated into the
course content, they were experiencing a kind of "mental shift" in their thinking
about the role of student questions in classroom learning. They were experiencing,
perhaps for the first time, a learning environment that encouraged and respected the
expression of their own self-selected questions. The question-finding exercise itself

provided them with a counterintuitive learning experience. Typically, students answer the teacher's preformulated questions; now the students were being asked to focus not on answers, but on questions—and not the teacher's questions—but their own. In these classes, the social dynamics of classroom questioning were being upended. Question-finding provided these students with a mental shift in their thinking that, in this chapter, is referred to as **conceptual change**.

What Is Conceptual Change?

Conceptual change is a theoretical model that explains an alteration in one's knowledge and belief systems. Educational researchers and philosophers in science from Cornell University, New York, first articulated this theory in the 1980s (Posner, Strike, Hewson, & Gertzog, 1982). Specifically, the creators explained the dimensions of the process as a profound change "from one set of concepts to another set, incompatible with the first" (p. 211). Even though this model of conceptual change was derived largely from the sciences, the theory "can illuminate [all] learning in general" (p. 212). Thus, in this chapter I show how question-finding can help to induce conceptual change in several content areas.

Conceptual change theory is founded on constructivist principles of learning. It presupposes that the construction and transformation of prior knowledge, interests, and beliefs is an active process of meaning making. It attempts to explain how preconceptions change with the impact of new ideas, information, and experiences. The creators of the theory envisioned the connection among conceptual change, constructivism, and student questioning. They believed that prior knowledge is the foundation upon which new knowledge is based and reconstructed. Without current concepts, it would be impossible to ask about the phenomenon or to even know what would count as appropriate answers to one's questions (Posner et al., 1982; Strike & Posner, 1985). Therefore, the student takes an active role in reconceptualizing and restructuring his or her knowledge base.

According to conceptual change theory, there are four conditions necessary for any mental shift to occur: First, the student must express dissatisfaction with his or her current concepts. This condition is very similar to the first stage of the question-finding process, which begins with the introduction of a discrepant or counterintuitive event. This "new" idea poses a challenge to the current conception. That is, the conceptual conflict created by the discrepant event sets up the condition of dissatisfaction. This condition is a necessary but not sufficient condition for conceptual change to occur. In order to convert the dissatisfaction into a modification or replacement of the "old" idea, the new idea needs to provide the three remaining conditions, the second of which is that it needs to make sense or appear logical to the student (it must not be confusing or foreign to the mental representations of the student). The theory creators called this condition intelligibility. Third, the new idea needs to be plausible; it should possess some consistency with the student's other well-established beliefs. Fourth, the new idea should be applicable to different situations; it should be able to provide new insights and greater explanatory power than the current idea about the focus topic.

The Revised Conceptual Change Model

In the 1990s, the classic conceptual change model was revised (Strike & Posner, 1992). This was done largely in response to challenges from science educators and cognitive scientists who claimed that the model was too rationally and cognitively oriented (Pintrich, Marx, & Boyle, 1993). Indeed, one team of researchers labeled the classic model **cold conceptual change**. What the critics were saying was that the model did not take into account motivational and affective factors, and that the classic theory was too rational and individualistic. In their revision of the original theory, the Cornell researchers advanced the idea that students brought more than just rational misconceptions to a new learning experience; that indeed, they carried with them a **conceptual ecology** of attitudes, ideas, and beliefs that were entrenched and tied to a network of personal factors and set in epistemological and psychological structures (Strike & Posner, 1992). Other researchers claimed that the classic model also did not take into consideration sociocognitive and sociocultural factors (Dole & Sinatra, 1998; John-Steiner & Mahn, 1996; Oldfather & Dahl, 1994; Swafford & Bryan, 2000). They claimed that conceptual change took place in social situations. The social literacy researchers recognized the impact of the "more knowledgeable others" in learning situations and believed that the only real change occurred within a student's zone of proximal development (McMahon, 1996; Vygotsky, 1934/1978). These social factors helped to explain the multidimensional nature of conceptual change and how it reflected the broad scope of reality.

Students at every grade level are resistant to conceptual change. Perhaps the multidimensional nature of conceptual change can help explain some of the reasons why students are so resistant to change. Children come to school not as empty slates, but with developed schemas about the world. They bring with them not just knowledge, but also attitudes and belief structures that are deeply held or entrenched. When students' preconceived ideas and belief structures are in harmony with school-based learning, then there is an enrichment and extension of their new knowledge. Piaget (1985) called this an assimilation process. However, when the students' preconceptions conflict with the new knowledge, then a different learning situation is presented. Piaget labeled this an accommodation process. With this process, students need to alter their preexisting frameworks because this process requires a reconceptualization and reorganization of initial ideas. For example, Heather, a ninth-grade biology student (who appears again later in this chapter), had naïve views about the change of seasons, which needed to be assimilated and accommodated.

After learning from the teacher's lecture, class discussions, and student experimentation, Heather did make some changes and accommodated her thinking in favor of a scientific account for seasonal change, but she still refused to give up other **naïve presuppositions** and unscientific beliefs. Students such as Heather overlook or even modify experiments in order to maintain their deeply believed conceptions. For example, Heather continued to believe the erroneous ideas that direct sunlight rays travel in a straight line from the sun and that indirect sunlight bounces off points in space before reaching the earth. She maintained her naïve presuppositions even after viewing diagrams and working on an experiment that showed the astronomical explanation of direct and indirect sunlight rays. She refused to abandon her beliefs and continued to trust her sense that direct and indirect sunlight rays perform just as light reflecting off a mirror.

Particularly resistant to change are ideas that are based on cultural and religious beliefs. Resistance is often encountered when content challenges one's family and cultural beliefs and traditions. Chin and Chia (2004) recognized this when they observed a ninth-grade biology lesson dealing with food and nutrition. Particularly, the researchers learned that family folklore played an important role in supporting students' misconceptions about the topic. Students' initial questions for the unit on food and nutrition revealed the nature of these misconceptions included in the following questions:

> Does drinking "Ginseng" tea have a "cooling effect" and help one to do better on studying for tests?
>
> Does MSG [monosodium glutamate] cause hair loss?
>
> Is it true that if you perspire a lot you are fat?
>
> Can we improve color blindness with nutrition? (pp. 715–716)

Researchers also have documented resistance to new topics that carry highly charged and emotional contexts such as life issues, health concerns, and biological factors (e.g., abortion, evolution, cloning; Dole & Sinatra, 1998). Students tend to ignore, rationalize, or just defend such ideas even when presented with what scientist Thomas Kuhn called events that are "awash in a sea of anomalies" (as cited in Strike & Posner, 1992, p. 149). Some researchers believe that resistance is so strong that the teacher needs to present multiple discrepant events related to a topic to induce conceptual change (Clement & Steinberg, 2002).

Traditional instructional strategies such as direct instruction and recitation generally are not successful in affecting conceptual change. Strategies that directly involve students in constructivist activities using discussion, discovery, and inquiry learning have the greatest potential for affecting conceptual change. In the next sections, I review some of these strategies, including the question-finding strategy, which all contain a common element—they all induce conceptual conflict in students.

Conceptual Conflict and Conceptual Change

As previously mentioned, conceptual conflict is a state of puzzlement created by ambiguous, surprising, and often contradictory information (see chapter 1). In addition, the state of puzzlement or conceptual conflict stimulates question-finding behavior. In the same vein, conceptual conflict is a condition that can induce conceptual change. Indeed, one of the conditions for conceptual change is the creation of dissatisfaction with existing ideas and beliefs. The authors of the classic conceptual change model emphasize that the presentation of an anomaly, which stimulates dissatisfaction with current conceptions, is one way to induce conceptual change (Posner et al., 1982).

As important as conceptual conflict is, by itself, it is not sufficient to overcome resistance to conceptual change. There are additional conditions necessary for the kind of radical restructuring that conceptual change requires: First, students need to become aware of the discrepancies between their prior conceptions and the new conception. Without this awareness factor, there can be no conscious will or desire to change. Second, there needs to be what Dreyfus, Jungwirth, and Eliovitch (1990) call a state of "**meaningful conflict**" created by anomalous data that are very compelling (p. 557). Students must really feel the strong need to alter their ideas and be actively engaged in that alteration. Third, students need to be shown how to make the changes through modeling and scaffolding. This requires strategic direction and strategy instruction. To be effective, these strategies need to utilize students' conceptual ecologies including motivational, affective, and social dimensions of literacy learning (Strike & Posner, 1992). Teachers need to consider the following fundamental question in strategic planning: Do my educational strategies solve problems and resolve anomalies by making the new concept intelligible, plausible, and fruitful?

Cognitive Conflict Strategies and Conceptual Change

There are several different types of cognitive conflict strategies that have been used to induce conceptual change. (Note that the terms *cognitive conflict strategy* and *conceptual conflict strategy* can be used interchangeably. Conceptual conflict strategy is discussed in more detail later in this chapter.) These strategies use the following designs: text-based comprehension connections, graphic organizers, intertextual connections, and social structures such as cooperative learning and reciprocal teaching. Some of these strategies integrate the different designs.

TEXT-BASED COMPREHENSION CONNECTIONS
A strategy with strong empirical support is refutational text (Guzzetti et al., 1993). Refutational text uses a text alteration technique in which the common misconception is generally presented at the beginning of a reading. Then the misconception is explicitly and directly challenged by the "scientific" explanation in the same or next paragraph. The confrontation between the clashing ideas is the focus of the refutational text. A similar idea is behind the strategy augmented activation that was discussed earlier in this book (Anders & Guzzetti, 1996). Instead of intertextual conflict, this type of strategy uses counterintuitive demonstrations and experiments to challenge common misconceptions and induce conceptual conflict.

GRAPHIC ORGANIZERS
The next grouping of cognitive conflict strategies utilizes graphic organizers as scaffolds to help students become aware, understand, and alter misconceptions. The discussion web is a strategy in which students work in small groups to discuss and frame their arguments on a given topic (Alvermann, 1991). Their conflicting positions are recorded on a graphic web and need to be supported by evidence from the text. Another graphic-type strategy is the think sheet (Dole, 2000). This strategy taps students' prior knowledge on a topic and calls for students to record these conceptions on an organizer, and then contrast and challenge these ideas with those from the text. Another graphic tool is called the conflict map (Tsai, 2000). This visual display helps students to map out the conflict between their preconceptions and the scientific conceptions. This strategy contains a metacognitive structure to help learners visually monitor their ideas and processes involved in conceptual change.

INTERTEXTUAL CONNECTIONS
An intertextual approach to conceptual change is advanced by psychologist Howard Gardner (1991). He frames his approach around events that produce cognitive conflict. He labels these events "Christopherian confrontations" (p. 229), named after Italian explorer Christopher Columbus, who was one of the first individuals to challenge the intuitive impression that the earth was flat. "Christopherian confrontations" stimulate cognitive conflict in that they are "situations where students' misconceptions are brought into sharp focus because of an experience that directly challenges the viability of the model they have been favoring" (pp. 157–158). As noted earlier in this chapter, just presenting discrepant events, or in this case "Christopherian confrontations," is not sufficient for conceptual change. Gardner (2004) recognizes this factor and recommends a strategy that uses **multiple entry**

point teaching. In other words, he recommends a method of teaching that presents multiple versions of the same topic using varied resources. These multiple entry routes using varied resources correspond to the different intelligences that make up Gardner's theory of multiple intelligences, which include linguistic ability, spatial representation, logical-mathematical analysis, and understanding of ourselves (intrapersonal) and others (interpersonal).

SOCIAL STRUCTURES

The last grouping of strategies, sociocognitive conflict strategies, involves interactions that also enhance cognitive conflict. Indeed, some researchers believe that it is the dialogical learning environment itself that plants the seeds for conceptual change (Hatano & Inagaki, 2003). The motivation for conceptual change is amplified through social means. Conflict is engendered naturally through an honest difference of opinions about the topic. It is the nature of the social interaction and disagreement that matters most. Peer teams in which members hold similar viewpoints lack the "conflict" ingredient necessary for cognitive development (Perret-Clermont, 1980).

One strategy that successfully incorporates these features is academic constructive controversy (D.W. Johnson & R.T. Johnson, 1992). This is a cooperative learning strategy in which students are paired off in teams and take different advocacy positions on a controversial topic. First, the teams confront each other and argue their respective positions. Second, they attempt to recognize the merit and credibility of the opposing position. Last, they attempt to arrive at a compromise or synthesis of the conflicting positions. This strategy enhances epistemic curiosity or the motivation to understand and acquire new knowledge. The important point of this strategy is that the cognitive conflict is not competitive or competence driven, but actually seeks conflict resolution (Buchs, Butera, Mugny, & Darnan, 2004).

PAUSE AND PONDER

The conventional wisdom about the relationship between people and plants is that people are active and plants are passive. Their relationship is one of give and take. People are the takers, and plants are the givers. Science journalist Michael Pollan (2001) has challenged this concept in his counterintuitive study *The Botany of Desire: A Plant's Eye View of the World*. Pollan sees plants in a more active light and tells how this enlightenment induced questioning.

> That May afternoon, [my] garden suddenly appeared before me in a whole new light, the manifold delights it offered to the eye and nose and tongue no longer quite [seemed] so innocent or passive. All these plants, which I'd always regarded as the objects of my desire, were also, I realized, subjects, acting on me, getting me to do things

for them they couldn't do for themselves.... And that's when I had the idea: What would happen if we looked at the world beyond the garden this way, and regarded our place in nature from the same upside-down perspective? (pp. xv–xvi)

- How is this "upside-down" perspective counterintuitive?
- Would it require conceptual change to subscribe to it?
- What additional questions could be generated from this alternative perspective of plant life?

Motivation and Conceptual Change

Conceptual conflict is a motivating force. As we learned in chapter 1, it stimulates what Berlyne (1960) calls epistemic curiosity and is the main impetus behind question-finding. In like manner, conceptual conflict is a motivating force behind conceptual change. Learning environments that create conceptual conflict stimulate dissatisfaction in the learner. Students are driven to know the way(s) to resolve the tension created by the anomalous situation. Recall that dissatisfaction is one of the four main conditions of the classic model of conceptual change (Posner et al., 1982). Reading and science educators believe that dissatisfaction may be the critical motivational element when scientific ideas conflict with intuitive ideas (Dole & Sinatra, 1998). Indeed, the moments of surprise that create dissatisfaction are often themselves motivators of conceptual change (Clement & Steinberg, 2002).

As indicated earlier, the classic conceptual change theory did not account for affective and motivational factors. A number of challenges to the theory led to a reformulation of the theory to include what many scholars call **intentional conceptual change** (Sinatra, Southerland, McConaughy, & Demastes, 2003). This revised version takes into account the inner and purposeful dimensions of personality besides the rational and external. Some of these personal dimensions include the following: need to know, need to believe, levels of commitment, and the need for **cognitive closure**.

These personal dimensions address the fact that there is a strong inner resistance to changing one's initial conceptions. Particularly, resistance is often encountered when content is challenging to one's cultural systems and religious beliefs. For example, in a lesson on creationism versus evolution, some students could not accept the idea that humans were animals because they were strongly committed to the notion that human beings are a special creation. They had what Dole and Sinatra (1998) call a "need to believe" (p. 118). Students who express strong personal commitments to their existing ideas are much less likely to change. In addition, there are some students who display what is called a need for cognitive closure (Kruglanski & Webster, 1996), which is a tendency to seize on early information and neglect the quest for further scholarly investigation. Evidently, there is this urgent desire to attain definite and certain knowledge because of a low **tolerance for ambiguity**.

The introduction of anomalous information can be threatening to a person committed to cognitive closure. Some researchers have labeled this state **epistemic freezing**, or a locking up of thinking on a topic (Kruglanski & Webster, 1996). This condition is opposite to epistemic curiosity, a main feature of question-finding. Epistemic freezing is a condition that is not conducive to conceptual change.

Question–Finding and Conceptual Change

Question-finding is a cognitive conflict strategy that can also be used to induce conceptual change. It satisfies the classic conceptual change model in that discrepant events are introduced to stimulate puzzlement and cognitive dissatisfaction. It satisfies the revision of the classic model as well in that it incorporates motivational, affective, and sociocognitive elements. Question-finding, however, contains distinctive features that distinguish it from other cognitive conflict strategies (i.e., refutational text). It provides cognitive and metacognitive (chapter 1), motivational (chapter 2), critical literacy (chapter 3), and social (chapter 4) dimensions. It uses direct instruction and inquiry instructional strategies.

Question-finding opens both convergent and divergent thinking pathways. It provides models to guide the development of puzzlement questions (explanation type) to help solve problems and resolve anomalies in the quest for conceptual change. It provides scaffolds for the generation of divergent questions to explore the realms of wonder and imagination. Wonderment questions are the kind that scientists refer to when they speak of the serendipitous elements of inventions and discoveries. Indeed, Einstein is quoted as saying that he "succeeded in good part [in discovering the theory of relativity] because he kept asking himself questions concerning space and time which only children wonder about" (cited in Holton, 1978, p. 279).

Procedure for the Question–Driven Conceptual Change Model

Conceptual change is a complex process that involves the reformulation of ideas. This reconceptualization involves three major phases that can be used before, during, and after the conceptual change instructional strategies are applied (adapted from Nussbaum & Novick, 1982; West & Pines, 1984). First, reconceptualization begins with an awareness phase, in which students' initial concepts are exposed or brought to surface. Second, this awareness phase leads to a state of disequilibrium when a conflicting idea is presented that challenges the initial conception. Third, a culminating phase ensues in which the new or school-based conception replaces the old intuitive ones and additional knowledge is presented to reinforce the new framework. Each of the phases is brought into existence by distinct teaching events involving student-generated questions. (See Table 14.)

The first phase, **exposing preconceptions**, requires a procedure that brings to light students' initial conceptions. Nussbaum and Novick (1982) define this type of strategy as a "phenomenon carefully selected for its ability to evoke students' preconceptions in order to understand it" (p. 187). The second phase, conceptual conflict, requires a procedure that challenges, contradicts, and refutes the initial conceptions with the presentation of an anomalous or discrepant source. The third phase, **reconceptualizing prior knowledge**, requires a procedure that restructures, reconceptualizes, and reinforces the new conceptions. Students need rich and appropriate learning events to restructure misconceptions and prior conceptions in the context of content learning (Maskill & deJesus, 1997).

Each of these phases is driven by student-generated questions. These questions guide students in the deeply personal and challenging conceptual change process. Student-generated questions help teachers diagnose and evaluate the extent to which their students are successfully revising and internalizing the alternate conceptions that are being taught. Refer to Table 14 for model questions that drive each phase. Students' authentically generated questions help to bridge the divide between everyday knowledge and school-based learning. Students' questions help fill in what Watts, Gould, and Alsop (1997) call "points of plasticity" (p. 59), or instructional spaces between students' initial conceptions and scientifically formulated conceptions.

PAUSE AND PONDER

> I write quite differently in emails...especially in the punctuation. I feel it's OK to use dashes all the time, and exclamation marks. And [I also use] those dot, dot, dot things. (Truss, 2003, p. 198)

This comment from an adolescent student appears in *Eats, Shoots & Leaves: The Zero Tolerance Approach to Punctuation* (Truss, 2003). The author challenges this viewpoint and proclaims that punctuation is necessary for reliable communication and clarification of syntax. She claims that e-mails and text messages should be blamed for the decline in punctuation standards. Many students disagree and feel that their messages can be conveyed clearly in unpunctuated discourse.

- Which side poses the stronger argument?
- Do you believe that instruction in conceptual change with regard to punctuation and writing standards is needed today? If you agree, then can the question-driven conceptual change model be helpful? Explain.

TABLE 14. Phases of the Question-Driven Conceptual Change Model

Phase	Student-Generated Questions
Phase 1: Exposing preconceptions	What are my ideas about this topic? How did I arrive at these ideas? Are these ideas based on my daily life experiences? How are these ideas/beliefs supported by my world view? What social and cultural factors shape these beliefs? How are my beliefs influenced by advertisements and media? Can I express these beliefs in different ways? (art, music, and so forth) Am I disposed to questioning or altering these beliefs? Am I open to considering alternative viewpoints?
Phase 2: Conceptual conflict intervention	Should I take this new idea seriously? Does this new concept truly puzzle me? Do I sense a problem or conflict here? Does this conflict create a feeling of personal dissatisfaction? How does this new idea conflict with my original concepts/beliefs? How does this new concept differ from my own knowledge and beliefs?
Phase 3: Reconceptualizing prior knowledge	Is this alternative concept credible? Is this alternative concept logical? Does this alternative concept clarify any doubts I may have about the topic? How will this new concept help me reinterpret past experiences and prior knowledge? How can I reconcile these contradictory beliefs/ideas? Do these alternate concepts solve problems and resolve anomalies that my initial concepts could not? Can I think of any metaphors, similes, or analogies that may help me to better comprehend the new concept? What can I do to sustain this altered view of my world? Does this alternative concept help me explain new meanings and explore other possible worlds of learning?

Question–Driven Conceptual Change Across the Curriculum

Teachers can use student-generated questions to stimulate conceptual change in selected content areas. In the following sections, I focus on specific content area units of study as prototypes of **question-driven conceptual change**. In science, I focus on the causes of seasons. In the social studies, I focus on the institution of slavery in the United States. In mathematics, I focus on comparing decimals and common fractions. In some of these units, I present my own classroom experiences. In others, I display what other content area teachers and teacher educators have accomplished. In all of the selected sample units, I demonstrate the instructional sequence of the question-driven conceptual change model. (See Figure 7.)

Each of the conceptual change phases involves the different literacy dimensions of question-finding that form the basis of this book. In some cases, one particular literacy dimension predominates. For example, in phase 1 on Table 14, the metacognitive literacy dimension of question-finding occupies a prominent place. Here the objective is to encourage students to ask questions related to developing an awareness of the basis and scope of their initial conceptions on a topic. In phase 2, the motivational literacy dimension plays an important role. This is because the introduction of discrepant events generally creates a feeling of dissatisfaction and a state of puzzlement. The quest to stabilize this process generates the motivational condition of "epistemic curiosity," or the quest to know. In phase 3, the sociocognitive literacy dimension plays a leading part. This is because social interaction helps students restructure and replace their initial conceptions, particularly, if the content is within the students' zone of proximal development (Vygotsky, 1934/1978).

Focus Unit of Study: Physical Sciences, Middle School

A major misconception held by adolescents relates to the seasonal changes of the earth. Indeed, even advanced-level students and some of their professors hold misconceptions about this astronomical event. Recent Harvard University graduates (including some physics majors) and professors revealed uninformed conceptions about the change in seasons that was documented in the educational video *A Private Universe: An Insightful Lesson on How We Learn* (Schneps & Sadler, 1988). Indeed, the viewer is informed that 21 of 23 of the participants in the video held incorrect notions about the seasons.

The most scientifically accepted explanation for the change in seasons is that the earth's axis is tilted with respect to the plane of the orbit around the sun. As a result, different amounts of solar energy reach the two hemispheres at different times. But this idea is not readily accepted as the reason for seasonal change. When I asked preservice teachers in a content literacy course I taught to tell me what they knew about the causes of the change of seasons, most of them replied that the position of the sun was the main reason for the change in seasons. One student responded, "The position of the sun is what causes the changes of the seasons. As the sun is at a higher angle to us, the warmer it is—making it summer. The lower the angle, the cooler it is and therefore winter."

This common misconception is based on what science educators call the distance theory (Newman, Crowder, & Morrison, 1993). This theory stipulates that the distance between the earth and the sun causes the seasons. Therefore, it is reasoned

FIGURE 7. Instructional Sequence of Question-Driven Conceptual Change Model

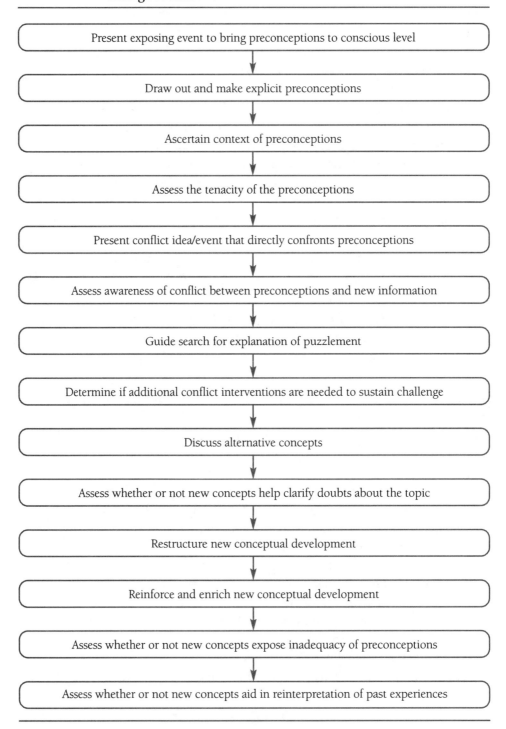

Present exposing event to bring preconceptions to conscious level

Draw out and make explicit preconceptions

Ascertain context of preconceptions

Assess the tenacity of the preconceptions

Present conflict idea/event that directly confronts preconceptions

Assess awareness of conflict between preconceptions and new information

Guide search for explanation of puzzlement

Determine if additional conflict interventions are needed to sustain challenge

Discuss alternative concepts

Assess whether or not new concepts help clarify doubts about the topic

Restructure new conceptual development

Reinforce and enrich new conceptual development

Assess whether or not new concepts expose inadequacy of preconceptions

Assess whether or not new concepts aid in reinterpretation of past experiences that the earth is closer to the sun in the summer. Several of the preservice teachers also believed that the higher angle of the sun's elevation in the summer (the movement of the sun itself) causes the seasons. Clearly, there is a widespread misconception that the position of the sun, the source of sunshine, is responsible for the change of seasons.

Another popular misconceived explanation of seasonal change is called the facing theory. This theory states that the reason for seasonal change is that the side of the earth facing the sun has summer while the other side has winter. As described by a middle-grade student, "winter is placed on the side of the globe away from the sun, summer on the side facing the sun, and spring and fall on the twilight areas between the back and the front" (Newman et al., 1993, p. 19). This idea does not scientifically account for the seasons.

To address these misconceptions and others related to seasonal change, some science teachers have presented classroom strategies that have implications for question-driven conceptual change. For example, a sixth-grade science teacher began her unit on the causes of the seasons with the following instructional exposing event. She called on her students to pantomime the relationship between the earth and the sun associated with their idea of seasonal change. For example, "one boy, seated in the middle, represented the sun while other students used their bodies to model the earth's orientation to and movement around the sun" (Newman et al., 1993, p. 32). Other students described and pantomimed their versions of the facing theory of seasonal change as indicated below.

Caitlin: When it [the earth] is not facing the sun it causes winter, so you don't have much light, or much warmth, and, in the summer, it's facing the sun, so it's warm, and we have a lot of light.

Paul: [N]ight time is when it's [the earth] not facing the sun...and when we're facing the sun, we get a lot of heat and...[when we are not] we get a lot of cold.

(Newman et al., p. 32)

These two children did not seem bothered by the apparent contradiction in their explanation that the earth's spin accounted for both day and night and the seasons (p. 34). But another student, Chrystal, did notice the contradictions and offered the following challenge:

Chrystal: I don't think that when it's dark that it all of a sudden turns winter, 'cause that's when it gets night out and when, it spins around...see, it takes a day for it to spin around, but it takes a year for it to go around the sun....

[Chrystal continues her challenge of the facing theory but this time she stands up and illustrates using her body to represent the earth.] Everybody else is saying that, when it's [earth's] facing this way [faces her body toward the "sun"], that it's daytime and this way [faces away from the "sun"] that it's night-time, and that's what it really is. But then they're also saying that this [toward sun] is summer and that this [away from sun] is winter, but it's not, because it...takes, to go around the sun, the whole year....

(Newman et al., pp. 35–36)

In summary, Chrystal's challenge that the turning of the earth explains day and night, but that it could not also explain the seasons, proved to be effective. The facing theory was never brought up again. Her refutation of the prevailing facing theory opened the way for alternative theories. But no alternate theories were offered. Chrystal's challenge altered the misconception but did not provide a replacement theory of seasonal change. Her challenge provided what Chinn and Brewer (1993) call **peripheral conceptual change**. That is, change that was not deep enough to truly alter entrenched beliefs. Without the replacement of a viable alternate theory, conceptual change is not likely to be strong enough to be sustained (Chinn & Brewer).

The question-driven conceptual change model could provide a deeper processing of contradictory information to construct lasting conceptual change because the model uses a **guided inquiry approach** in which students' own authentic questions drive the investigation of the target issue. By becoming more personally involved with the issue through their own questions, students are more likely to process the contradictory information. Indeed, it is the personalized and contextualized nature of question-driven conceptual change that aids deep processing.

In addition, deep processing is aided through the reinforcement of the sequence of learning events as detailed in the question-driven conceptual change procedure. Recall that the procedure begins with an instructional exposing event, continues with an instructional challenging event, and culminates with an instructional reconceptualizing event (see Figure 7, page 114). Repetitions of the sequence of learning events are crucial to developing an accurate understanding of the targeted concept. Student questioning is more likely to foster theory change because it is based on the multidimensional nature of literacy and thinking (Chinn & Brewer, 1993).

According to the question-driven conceptual change model, students' questions spearhead the three different phases of the conceptual change process. In the previous teaching episode related to seasonal change, each phase could have benefited from the question-driven model. In accord with the first phase of the model, there was some evidence of reflective student questioning. The students asked themselves (with teacher scaffolding) about how they could express their existing conceptions of seasonal change through words and pantomime. But this could have been developed further. The teacher could have encouraged students to be more metacognitive in their questioning. (See Table 14, page 112). For example, the teacher could have assigned a reflective writing exercise in which students ask themselves such questions as, Am I disposed to questioning or altering my initial ideas? Am I open to considering alternative viewpoints on the causes of seasonal change? In this manner, the teacher could have further diagnosed the nature of students' misconceptions and monitored any possible conceptual changes.

Related to the second phase, a challenging situation did evolve as Chrystal challenged and questioned the accuracy of the facing theory. Chrystal's challenge created a state of conceptual conflict for the class, and especially for Caitlin and Paul who supported the erroneous facing theory. This conflict condition provided both Caitlin and Paul with an opportunity to ask **self-monitoring questions** similar to those presented in the second phase of the question-driven conceptual change model. For example, either Caitlin or Paul could have asked the following: How does Chrystal's challenge conflict with my personal beliefs and ideas about seasonal change?

Full conceptual change never took place. Neither Chrystal nor the other students provided an alternative theory to replace the facing theory. The teacher could have presented a strategy to capitalize on Chrystal's challenge. She could have used a physical model of the solar system and positioned the earth at some specific point relative to the sun. Then she could have asked students to predict what season(s) it would be in the northern and southern hemispheres. Through scaffolding, students could have raised such questions as, Is this alternative idea credible? Does it help me to understand and explain the change in seasons in a more logical and scientific way? (See Table 14.)

Focus Unit of Study: Social Studies, High School

Most of the research on conceptual change has been done in science education. As previously mentioned, science educators were the founders of the conceptual change model. This model has guided most of the science education studies on conceptual change. The field of science is most adaptable to the model because it deals with concrete objects and experimentation (Torney-Purta, 1994). Scientific concepts are observable and verifiable and can be assessed directly in terms of conceptual change. However, in recent years, there has been increasing research in fields other than science. One content area that is receiving increasing attention is history and the social studies (Domizi, 2003; Limon, 2002; Wade, 1994).

Conceptual change research in history and social studies has incorporated the classic conceptual change model and, significantly, has stressed the application of cognitive conflict strategies (Domizi, 2003; Limon, 2002; Limon & Carretero, 1999; Wade, 1994). One of the strategies that has been used successfully is the juxtaposition of opposing viewpoints on controversial issues. In this section, I show how I used an opposing viewpoint strategy (cognitive conflict) in regard to the alternative and contradictory views held by Abraham Lincoln on slavery. I show how I used the question-finding process to attempt to facilitate conceptual change on this topic.

The topic of slavery in the United States is a familiar one to students. It is taught in elementary school, middle school, and high school social studies classes. One might possibly think that with so much exposure to this topic that students would have few misconceptions or stereotypes. However, I have observed that students still harbor many misconceptions about slavery.

PAUSE AND PONDER

Palmer, J.A. (1876). Collection of the New-York Historical Society, New York. Negative number 48099. Public domain.

Many students have misconceptions about slavery and literacy. This rare photograph shows that some slaves learned how to read. This literacy event was considered very subversive to the society and government of the antebellum South.

- How can this photograph be used to expose students' preconceptions about slavery and literacy?
- Can this photograph be used to generate student questioning?
- Can it be used to induce conceptual change on the topic?

In this section, I present some of these misconceptions and how I have addressed them through the application of a question-driven conceptual change model. I worked on conceptual change with preservice teachers in a social studies methods course I taught. I began with an instructional exposing event to bring into conscious awareness their prior knowledge regarding slavery. The instructional exposing event was a self-reflection essay on the students' knowledge about slavery guided by questions from the first phase of the question-driven conceptual change model. I asked my students to reflect on the following questions: What do you know about slavery? How did you learn about this topic? Some of their responses included the following:

- Slaves were brought over from Africa.
- Slaves were treated cruelly.
- Slaves were owned only by wealthy and prominent white people.
- They worked on plantations.
- Harriet Tubman and other abolitionists tried to free them.
- President Abraham Lincoln fought against slavery and freed them.

The last item generated strong support from my students. One student revealed this general confidence by stating, "I was always taught in school that Lincoln was one of the best presidents of the United States. He wrote the Emancipation Proclamation."

As part of the strategy for conceptual change, I introduced a conflict or discrepant event (the second phase) to challenge the students' conceptions on the topic. I presented the following two apparently contradictory statements made by Abraham Lincoln (in speeches that he delivered when campaigning in different sections of Illinois for the United States Senate in 1858).

Statement #1 July 1858

Let us discard all this quibbling about this man and the other man, this race and that race and the other race being inferior, and therefore they must be placed in an inferior position. Let us discard all these things and unite as one people throughout this land, until we shall once more stand up declaring that all men are created equal.

Statement #2 September 1858

I will say, then, that I am not, nor ever have been, in favor of bringing about in any way the social and political equality of the white and black races; that I am not, nor have ever been, in favor of making voters or jurors of Negroes, nor of qualifying them to hold office, nor to intermarry with white people....

And inasmuch as they cannot so live, while they do remain together there must be the position of superior and inferior, and I as much as any other man am in favor of having the superior position assigned to the white race. (Abraham Lincoln, cited in Hofstadter, 1973, p. 115)

Students reacted to the above discrepant statements with puzzlement. They were puzzled by the second statement and didn't believe it was true, thinking that the nickname "Honest Abe" meant he always told the truth. It was confusing to them as to how he could be honest if he completely contradicted himself with the two opposing viewpoints. Students began asking a sequence of questions such as, What was happening in 1858? Where was he when he made these statements? Was it an election year? Who was his audience? Where did these sources come from? Some students offered possible hypotheses such as that Lincoln was just acting like a politician—talking out of two sides of his mouth. The following student-generated questions (adapted from the second phase) were pertinent to this exercise: Is the idea that Lincoln expressed ambiguity about slavery credible? How does it conflict with my original beliefs and concepts?

Students decided to do research to find the reasons for Lincoln's contradictory statements. While acknowledging that Lincoln wanted to free the slaves and wanted everyone to be equal regardless of race or color, they opined that he might have told people what they wanted to hear when making his (campaign) speeches. Perhaps Lincoln's way of making discrepant statements was exactly what he intended. Making statements that are discrepant is a safe way to please many people with many different beliefs. In this process, some students' research experience changed their initial ideas about Lincoln. Students found it interesting that, as seniors in college, they had never been presented with this discrepancy regarding what Lincoln stated in his speeches on slavery. Not all of the students changed their initial concepts of Lincoln and slavery. Some thought that because the initial information was found on a website about Lincoln's views on slavery, it was possible that anyone could write statements and put them on a website. Also, they were suspicious as to why they had not learned about this event in their previous years of education. Some wanted to keep pursuing the question by gathering more evidence to support or oppose the idea that Lincoln had conflicting views on slavery. Still, a few students did not alter their initial conceptions regarding the image of Lincoln as the "Great Emancipator." Limon (2002) called this persistence of initial preconceptions "**affective entrenchment**," or a tenacious belief and value related to one's prior knowledge (p. 279). Thus, this exercise shows how the presentation of the conflicting viewpoints of a historical figure can stimulate students to ask puzzlement questions as a means of inducing conceptual change.

Social studies educators and researchers have used these contradictory statements by Lincoln on slavery as a venue for stressing the importance of contextualized history teaching (Wineburg & Fournier, 1994). These researchers worked with pairs of preservice teachers using think-aloud procedures to elicit students' reactions to Lincoln's contradictory statements. One pair of students was strongly divided. One student believed—just as one of the preservice teachers in my course did—that

Lincoln was acting like a typical politician trying to get as many votes as possible. This student took into account the context of Lincoln's remarks and stated that "Lincoln's remarks disclose more about the social situation than the naked truth about the man" (p. 295). The other student felt that these statements showed Lincoln to be a bigot.

Lincoln's ambiguous and inconsistent views on slavery can be explained in some manner using the question-driven conceptual change model. For example, an appropriate guide question that students could ask is, Can I think of any analogies that may help me better comprehend the new concept? (See Table 14, Phase 3, on page 112.) Hofstadter (1973) used the following analogy in an attempt to reconcile Lincoln's contradictory ideas. He suggested that the discrepancies in Lincoln's view on slavery (based on the two conflicting statements) revealed some interesting insights about the 16th president that perhaps could best be understood by a famous statement that Lincoln himself once uttered. The historian explained

> that it is not easy to decide whether the true Lincoln is the one in the first or the second statement. Possibly the man devoutly believed each...utterance at the time he delivered it; possibly his mind too was "a house divided against itself." (p. 115)

As he stated in his 1858 Senatorial campaign speech, the phrase "a house divided against itself" may be an appropriate analogy to describe Lincoln's ambiguous view of slavery.

Focus Unit: Mathematics, Middle School

The field of mathematics consists of many principles and concepts that are domain specific and highly resistant to change. This section addresses some of these concepts related to whole numbers and fractions that have been investigated in conceptual change research. Similar to conceptual change research in the sciences, conceptual change in mathematics challenges what are called naïve presuppositions that are formulated in childhood and are very powerful. However, in contrast to the sciences, which rely on experimental procedures and the manipulation of variables to challenge naïve conceptions, mathematics often depends on deductive proofs and logical reasoning to change misconceptions.

Naïve conceptions in mathematics have been labeled as intuitions. These misconceptions are often presented as intuitive rules that have been defined as "well-stabilized clusters of expectations—self-evident, premature with respect to certain situations" (Fischbein, 1987, p. 204). One of the major intuitions in mathematics is about numbers and what is more numerous and less numerous (Gardner, 1991). An important intuitive number rule is that multiplication always makes numbers bigger and that division makes numbers smaller (Graeber & Campbell, 1993). Middle and high school students continue to have trouble with fractions (especially related to this number rule). Indeed, "early knowledge of numbers might...serve as a [continued] barrier to learning about fractions" in later school years (Hartnett & Gelman, 1998, p. 343).

Another important number rule has been labeled as the "More A–More B" (Stavy, Tsamir, & Tirosh, 2002, p. 225), which means that the bigness of Object B reflects the bigness of Object A. This rule applies to comparison tasks such as comparing common fractions. It states that when comparing objects, the object in question (e.g., Object B) is related to the salient quality of another object (e.g., Object A). In other words, if A is bigger than the object, then B also will be bigger.

One of the preservice teachers whom I taught witnessed the common expression of this intuitive rule while tutoring a sixth-grade student in the comparison of the fractions $\frac{11}{16}$ (representing the A fraction) and $\frac{3}{4}$ (representing the B fraction). The middle school student answered that $\frac{11}{16}$ was the larger fraction. She reasoned that because the number 11 (numerator) in the A fraction is bigger than 3 (numerator) in the B fraction and the 16 (denominator) in the A fraction is larger that the 4 (denominator) in the B fraction, that therefore $\frac{11}{16}$ is bigger than $\frac{3}{4}$—that is, "More A–More B."

The sixth grader based her answer on prior knowledge and the expectation that fractions follow the same principle rule of counting as whole numbers, that is, the higher the digit, the higher the value. This, of course, is not the case. She did not view the proportional relationship between the fractional numbers and instead treated the numerators and denominators as if they were whole numbers. This misapplication of whole numbers is often called the **whole-number bias** (Ni & Zhou, 2005). The student expressed the idea that bigger numbers always mean larger value and applied this to fractions. She did not understand that fractions do not follow the same counting principles as whole numbers (Stavy, Tsamir, & Tirosh, 2002).

Decimals also pose problems for students who are oriented toward the whole-number bias. In another situation (which I will explore in more detail later in this section), 10th-grade students revealed their strong belief in the intuitive rule that "the number with more decimal places is the larger one" (Resnick et al., 1989, p. 9). For example, they believed 4.63 is greater than 4.8. They treated the decimal portion of the number as a whole number. Because they believed 63 is larger than 8, then 4.63 must be larger than 4.8. Students used their knowledge of whole-number values and erroneously applied it to decimals. They believed that the length of a number is an indicator of the magnitude of the decimal part of the number (an application of the whole-number bias). They did not recognize that the number's decimal portion represented a fraction of the whole.

The Need for Radical Conceptual Change in Mathematics

The intuitive rules mentioned in the preceding section begin to develop early in a child's life. Indeed, Gardner (1991) proclaimed that these intuitive understandings of the world are expressions of the "youthful theorist" (p. 248) and must be addressed in school. Even before being formally taught, children experience the one-to-one correspondence between objects and whole numbers in their daily lives. It is a part of their "everyday cultural context" that for every object there is a next object (Merenluoto & Lehtinen, 2002, p. 236). It is also believed that this intuitive idea is neurobiologically based, and that there is only one way to express a number (Vosniadou & Verschaffel, 2004). Further, these core principles and presuppositions are often viewed as not being under the conscious control of the learner (Vamvakoussi & Vosniadou, 2004). These deep-seated beliefs and concepts appear to persist into adolescence and beyond.

Related to the previously stated reasons is the idea of the permanence of first impressions. Fischbein (1987) described these first impressions as "the primary effects" (p. 198). These first global interpretations tend to disregard the consideration of later sensible alternative arguments. The student reaches a state of premature cognitive closure characterized by epistemic freezing (the opposite condition of the question-finder) in which no further exploration or investigation is considered necessary (Fischbein).

The influence of the "primary effect" of intuitive rules retards advancement in mathematics. This is especially the case in progressing from whole numbers to fractions and decimals. The study of fractions often conflicts with that of whole numbers. Many adolescent students do not see this. They believe that fractions are an add-on to whole-number learning. They begin to develop erroneous "synthetic models," in which new concepts are built on unrelated initial ideas (Vosniadou & Verschaffel, 2004, p. 447). Unwittingly, students often ascribe properties of whole numbers (i.e., the idea of discreteness) to fractions (i.e., the idea of density). Indeed, a conceptual shift in mathematical thinking is needed when this occurs (Moss, 2004). Further, many mathematics educators believe that because intuitive rules are anchored so strongly in a person's mental framework that **radical conceptual change** is required (Fischbein, 1987; Moss; Stafylidou & Vosniadou, 2004; Vamvakoussi & Vosniadou, 2004; Vosniadou & Verschaffel). Indeed, mathematics researchers believe that there must be a substantial shift in students' mathematical thinking as they transition from the study of whole numbers to fractions (Merenluoto & Lehtinen, 2002).

Question–Finding and Conceptual Change in Mathematics

Intuitive rules are so strongly entrenched that traditional strategies (e.g., recitations) are not adequate to effect conceptual change (Mestre, 1994). An effective conceptual change strategy must provide a multidimensional approach to change intuitive mathematical thinking; it needs to consider the cognitive, motivational, and social-cognitive dimensions of learning. Question-finding is a multidimensional strategy that can address these varied requirements.

As previously mentioned, mathematics educators believe that intuitive rules are supported by a need for cognitive closure. This kind of close-mindedness reflects the mental state of epistemic freezing, which, as stated earlier, retards inquiry learning. More than anything else, this state of mind is dominated by the desire for equilibrium and stability. In contrast, question-finding is grounded in epistemic curiosity theory and relies on openness of investigation, or "the drive to know" (Berlyne, 1954, p. 187). This condition is highly motivating and is driven by surprise, novelty, and a tolerance for ambiguity. Question-finding provides a counterpoint to the premature cognitive closure of mathematical reasoning.

Radical conceptual change needs to be question driven. Students' self-selected questions and concerns should guide the way. As with science and social studies, the question-driven conceptual change protocol model (Table 14, page 112) also can be useful in mathematics.

PAUSE AND PONDER

A number of literacy educators have proposed that popular culture has benefits for in-school literacy learning (Alvermann, Moon, & Hagood, 1999). Recently, researchers have stated that popular culture is actually "giving us a cognitive workout," or making us smarter (Johnson, 2005b, p. 55). In particular, they claim that reality television shows and dramatic narrative shows with their multiple story lines (e.g., NYPD Blue, E.R., The West Wing, and so forth) present complex and ambiguous events that stimulate the development of mental neural networks. Researchers advance that these shows stimulate adolescents to analyze complex social networks and track subtle narrative intertwining. Indeed, one social critic (Johnson, 2005a) has proposed the counterintuitive notion that everything bad is good for you when it comes to media and television today, and that what our parents and teachers tell us about the negative intellectual effects of popular culture is a myth.

- Do you agree with this counterintuitive idea about popular culture?
- Does it require radical conceptual change to alter one's views on the effects of television?
- What questions come to your mind with regard to this issue?

Discussion of the Procedure for the Question–Driven Conceptual Change Model

In this section, I provide an example of how question-finding can assist mathematics teachers in conceptual change teaching in regard to whole numbers and fractions. I provide specific examples of how teachers can use exposing, conflict, and reconceptualized teaching strategies to prompt conceptual change related to the topic.

Exposing Preconceptions

In a content literacy course I taught, one of the preservice teachers, Suzanne, practiced conceptual change instruction (i.e., understanding fractions) in the following tutoring session with a sixth-grade student, Nicole. (This example is adapted with permission from Suzanne Masotto and the parents of Nicole.)

Suzanne provided a sequence of fractions (in ascending order low to high) consisting of $\frac{9}{16}$, $\frac{5}{8}$, and $\frac{3}{4}$ and a sequence of whole numbers of 1, 2, and 3 and told Nicole that both sequence groups were in correct ascending (low to high) order. Suzanne recorded her experience as follows: "At first, she [Nicole] didn't believe me, and simply said 'No.' Then that 'No' turned more into a confused stare at the paper, and then she said, 'I don't get it.'" This state of puzzlement led Nicole to ask, "Why are these fractions in correct order when some smaller ones look bigger?" By answering her own puzzlement question, Nicole could have recognized her application of the whole-number bias in comparing fractions.

A teacher–student tutorial is not the only way to expose intuitive rules (e.g., whole-number bias) in mathematics. A more interactive instructional exposing strategy occurred in a 10th-grade mathematics classroom. This time the students were asked to work collaboratively in dyads on the topic of ordering and sequencing decimals. They were provided with six cards containing the digits 0, 0, 5, 8, 4, and a decimal point (Schwartz, Neuman, & Biezuner, 2000). The objective was to write the biggest and smallest numbers using the combination of digits. For example, for the smallest decimal, one student (Si) wrote 0.0854, while her partner (Ve) wrote 00.458 from the six cards. Both answers were wrong, and both students gave incorrect reasons for their answers, resorting to different intuitive rules to justify their answers. Ve justified her answer by saying, "The number after the period go smaller. The number 458 is smaller than 854, and because of that, my number (458) is smaller" (application of the whole-number bias; p. 472). Si incorrectly reasoned, "If you take a pie and divide it into 458 parts, every part will be larger than if you divide by 854. You have 458 parts and I have 854 parts, so I have more parts than you do. So mine are smaller" (incorrect application of the fraction rule; p. 472).

By referring to Table 14 (page 112), we can search for the kind of cognitive and metacognitive questions that would help both students become aware of their incorrect use of intuitive mathematical rules. For example, they could ask themselves, What are my ideas on this topic? and How did I arrive at these ideas? In answering these puzzlement questions, both students could have become more aware of their preconceptions about the incorrect use of the whole-number and fraction rules, respectively.

Conceptual Conflict Strategies

Conceptual conflict strategies can serve to induce conceptual change. The preservice teacher, Suzanne, successfully exposed her student's erroneous understanding of fractions. Because this first step is not enough to bring about conceptual change, Suzanne realized that she needed to support these first efforts by generating conceptual conflict. She accomplished this when she told Nicole that the fractions ($9/16$, $5/8$, $3/4$) were in correct ascending order just like the numbers 1, 2, 3 were in correct ascending order. This baffled Nicole, who exclaimed in exasperation, "I don't get it!" followed by her sincere question, "Why are these fractions in correct order when some smaller ones look bigger?" Nicole's question revealed her state of puzzlement and created a feeling of dissatisfaction. This learning event helped pave the way for conceptual change.

In the peer collaboration activity discussed above between the 10th-grade students (Ve and Si), the conflict generated can be described as sociocognitive in orientation. The two students disagreed and argued their (incorrect) respective positions. The design of the task itself triggered argumentation and conflict. Therefore, the teacher encouraged the students to demonstrate the accuracy of their positions. Using calculators, Ve multiplied 00.458 by 10 and obtained 4.58, and Si multiplied 0.0854 by 10 and obtained 0.854. Ve responded, "Yours is less, but I don't understand! Why?" Si countered by stating, "I have 854 thousandths and you have 4,580 thousandths. So mine is smaller because the two are thousandths" (Schwartz, Neuman, & Biezuner, 2000, p. 473). Eventually, Ve accepted that Si's number was smaller. This conceptual conflict strategy provided the two 10th-grade students with the opportunity to ask and answer a key question: Am I open to considering alternative points of view? (See Table 14, page 112.)

Reconceptualizing Prior Knowledge

The previously mentioned teaching strategies can culminate in the reconceptualization of prior knowledge. It is important for the teacher to scaffold the kinds of questions that transition to the last phase of question-driven conceptual change. (See Table 14, Phase 3.) As indicated earlier, when dealing with intuitive rules in mathematics, conceptual change requires a radical transformation. Both Nicole (a sixth-grade student) and Ve (a 10th-grade student) followed the whole-number bias and incorrectly ordered and sequenced fractions and decimals, respectively. They both needed to replace the whole-number bias when dealing with fractions. Nicole viewed the larger values of the numerator and denominator separately (i.e., $^{11}/_{16}$ versus $^{3}/_{4}$) and assumed that $^{11}/_{16}$ was larger. She needed to unlearn the concept that the larger digit means higher values when it comes to fractions. By asking herself the following guide questions, Nicole could have transformed her initial conceptions regarding numbers: Do I need to reexamine this rule? Is this rule valid for all occasions? How is this rule based on my own personal experiences?

Ve, on the other hand, needed to transform her intuitive rule that the length of a number is an indicator of the magnitude of the decimal part of the number (e.g., 4.63 > 4.8). Here, also, is an application of the whole-number bias, but this time with regard to decimals. By asking herself the following guide questions, Ve could have transformed her initial conceptions regarding decimals: Does the alternative concept (that the length of a decimal rational number does not by itself determine value) make sense? Does this alternative concept solve problems and resolve anomalies that my initial concept could not? Will this new concept help me to explain new meanings and explore other possible applications of decimals? If these questions are successfully answered, then students (i.e., Nicole and Ve) can progress to higher levels of mathematics.

Teacher Conceptual Change

Conceptual change teaching often requires a radical reorientation in classroom pedagogy and teachers' personal attitudes. In terms of teaching procedures, it means a decrease in teacher control and domination and an increase in student freedom and autonomy. Teachers need to become comfortable with the idea of their students asking questions for which they might not know the answers (Chin & Kayalvizhi, 2002). They also need to become comfortable with the idea that skepticism, dissonance, and uncertainty are valuable assets in the classroom. This requires a transformation in pedagogy because school culture in the United States prizes unity, predictability, and certainty (Dudley-Marling, 1997). A number of content area specialists have recommended the value of uncertainty and skeptical thinking in their respective disciplines. (See Table 15 for recommended readings on this topic.)

A 10th-grade biology teacher provides an example of pedagogical conceptual change stimulated by a student question in a lesson on genetically inherited diseases. Her student, David, asked, "Given that fetal hemoglobin has a greater affinity for oxygen, is it more reluctant to release it in the embryo?" (Watts, Alsop, Gould, & Walsh, 1997, p. 1033). The question made the teacher, an experienced biologist, stop and think about the topic anew. She pondered, "I'd never really thought about what happened in the tissues before." She began to test her own constructs and reconsider her understanding of the topic. She described further how this critical incident changed her view of student questions as well. She added: "[M]y responses are changing. Because I am paying more attention to questions.... As my pupils see me giving status to their questions, they in turn are more prepared to listen to their colleagues...in class" (pp. 1033–1034). Thus, this example focuses on teacher conceptual change induced by a student's question. Students' high-level thinking questions can be powerful change agents of traditional teaching practices.

Teachers need to view the multidimensional nature of question-finding as not only an instructional strategy for the construction and enrichment of learning but also a scaffold for the reconstruction and transformation of prior knowledge and experiences. This involves modeling questioning techniques that elicit, challenge, and restructure students' misconceptions of content area topics. Thus, teachers need to become agents of change in their own teaching disciplines.

TABLE 15. Resources on the Value of Uncertainty and Skepticism in Content Area Learning

Language Arts

Dudley-Marling, C. (1995). Uncertainty and the whole language teacher. *Language Arts, 72,* 252–257.

Villaume, S.K. (2000). The necessity of uncertainty: A case study of language arts reform. *Journal of Teacher Education, 51*(1), 18–25.

Mathematics

Brown, S.I. (1993). Towards a pedagogy of confusion. In A.M. White (Ed.), *Essays in humanistic mathematics* (pp. 107–121). Washington, DC: The Mathematical Association of America.

Frykolm, J. (2004). Teachers' tolerance for discomfort: Implications for curricular reform in mathematics. *Journal of Curriculum and Supervision, 19*(2), 125–149.

Science

Mackenzie, A.H. (2001). The role of teacher stance when infusing inquiry questioning into middle school science. *School Science and Mathematics, 101*(3), 143–154.

Whitin, D.J., & Whitin, P. (1998). Learning is born of doubting: Cultivating a skeptical stance. *Language Arts, 76,* 123–129.

Social Studies

Houser, N. (1996). Negotiating dissonance and safety for the common good: Social education in the elementary classroom. *Theory & Research in Social Education, 24*(3), 294–312.

Perfetti, C.A., Britt, M.A., Rouet, J.F., Georgi, M.C., & Mason, R.A. (1994). How students use texts to learn and reason about history uncertainty. In M. Carretero & J.F. Voss (Eds.), *Cognitive and instructional processes in history and social sciences* (pp. 257–284). Hillsdale, NJ: Erlbaum.

Summary

This chapter presented a different orientation from the preceding ones. It examined how the different dimensions of literacy could register a cumulative impact on the conceptual change process. It used a question-driven conceptual change model as a guide to the process. It presented classroom practices that revealed how this model could alter adolescents' misconceptions and naïve presuppositions and reconceptualize learning in content areas.

PONDER AND PRACTICE

1. One of the major principles regarding how children learn asserts that new knowledge is strongly influenced by prior knowledge. Learners conceive new ideas on the basis of preconceptions. This message is conveyed and illustrated in a delightful way in the children's book *Fish Is Fish* (Lionni, 1970). In this story, a tadpole ventures out of its familiar environment (water) and onto dry land. There it sees for the first time "unusual" creatures such as birds, cows, and humans. When it returns to the water, it tells its friend, a young fish, about the strange new things that it saw. In its mind, the young fish begins to envision each of these creatures as modified forms of fish, with scales and gills. This story has strong implications for conceptual change learning and question-finding. Instruction that does not explicitly address students' everyday preconceptions cannot advance new knowledge. Just as the fish constructed an image of a human as a modified fish, children use what they know to shape their new understandings (Donovan & Bransford, 2005).

   • Do you believe it is important to address students' preconceptions directly?

   • What experienced-based preconceptions do students bring to your classroom? Have you found them to be strongly resistant to change?

   • How can the question-driven conceptual change model provide a guideline for changing students' misconceptions?

2. How many times have you heard someone say, "I'm going to feed my plants." Scientists tell us that this is a misconception. Plants develop their own food through a process of photosynthesis—a process in which plants take water and carbon dioxide and combine them in the presence of light energy to create food matter in the form of sugar and starches. Thus, plants grow food (defined as an energy source) in their own leaves, and unlike human beings are not fed from outside sources.

Every child learns about photosynthesis in science at different times throughout their school career; yet, students of all ages exhibit the same misconceptions. For example, Kevin, a seventh-grade student, continued to maintain his initial conception that mineral fertilizers are food for plants, even though he learned that the minerals only help plants grow better, but do not supply plants with energy (food). One of the main reasons for this misconception is that students such as Kevin cannot see any evidence in their daily lives that plants make their own food. They erroneously believe that, just as people, plants get their food from the environment (Roth, 2001).

Students also believe that water is food for plants. The most typical reaction is "If water isn't their [plant] food, then why does my mom water her plants?" Traditional instruction in photosynthesis does not change this highly resistant idea. Even after scientific demonstrations, students still persist in what Bruner (1986) calls the maintenance of "folk theories" about plant nourishment (p. 49). Puzzled by this conceptual conflict situation, students have been found to react in the following way:

> Water must be food...because they [plants] cannot live without it, but water does not provide energy to living things so water cannot be food. I'm confused! (Roth, 2001, n.p.

Science educator Roth tells us that this type of confusion (i.e., puzzlement) helps create a questioning stance toward the topic. She asserts that student questioning holds promise for conceptual change.

- How would you use the question-driven conceptual change model to induce alterations in students' misconceptions about photosynthesis? Review the question-driven conceptual change model as provided in Table 14 (page 112).

3. The following dialogue occurred between three speakers on the topic of video games and learning.

First Speaker:	Playing video games is a waste of time.
Second Speaker:	Well, it does build hand–eye coordination.
First Speaker:	Yes, that may be true, but there isn't any content learning.
Second Speaker:	I see your point—I guess it could be called meaningless play.
Third Speaker:	Playing a video [game] is not a waste of time. Playing these games is learning "content" but not the type of passive content learned in school with its emphasis on learning school-based facts. Playing video games embodies experiences to solve problems in a multimodal space and involves real and imagined social relationships. (adapted from Gee, 2003, p. 21)

This discussion presents a conversation between two opposing viewpoints related to the cognitive benefits of playing video games. The first and second speakers present a more traditional argument against the educational value of video games. The third speaker presents the alternative view that video games are beneficial to literacy and learning. This position is the actual view of social linguist James Paul Gee (2003), who asserts "when people learn to play video games, they are learning a new literacy, one that includes images, symbols, graphs, diagrams, artifacts and many other visual symbols" (p. 13).

- How does the alternative position on the benefits of video games require a conceptual change for the first and second speakers?
- Explain how the question-driven conceptual change model could help foster conceptual change for these speakers.

4. This chapter presented an example that focused on seasonal change in middle school science. Following is another classroom scenario that focuses on seasonal change, but this similar learning situation occurred in a high school. Heather, a bright ninth-grade student, explained that the earth orbits the sun in a bizarre "curlicue" pattern and that the seasons are caused by the proximity of the earth to the sun at different points along the orbit (Schneps & Sadler, 1988). Further, Heather explained that during the summer, direct rays from the sun traveled in a straight line to the earth, whereas during the winter the rays from the sun bounced off somewhere in space before reaching the earth. She called these indirect rays. After two weeks of direct instruction, lab experiments, and diagramming of seasonal patterns, Heather changed some of her initial misconceptions: she agreed particularly that the earth did not revolve around the sun in a "curlicue" fashion, and that the earth's distance from the sun did not vary significantly during the year. However, Heather still maintained her naïve beliefs about the sun's rays. She maintained her entrenched beliefs that were supported by daily experiences. She resorted to the analogy of light bouncing off points in space before hitting the earth as similar to light reflecting off a mirror.

- How would you use the question-driven conceptual change model to help students who share Heather's misconceptions?
- Use the following illustrative questions as a guide: How do real-world experiences (mirror reflections) interfere with an understanding of the difference between direct and indirect rays? How is the idea of bouncing light unscientific?

CONCLUSION

For some time, I have been inclined to believe that our compulsory education laws, as they exist, contribute somewhat to the criminal class. In this State, a youth, until sixteen years of age, is prohibited from working and compelled to attend school. There are a large number of boys not bent toward a school education, and in addition to avoiding study, we find them loitering around street corners, pool rooms, etc., with the result that when they arrive at sixteen years of age, they have not been trained to work, and it is practically impossible to persuade them to work. From that class, come many of our hold-up men, gunmen, etc....

(A.B. Geary, Law Offices of Geary & Rankin, Letter to Law Enforcement Commission, June 6, 1929; U.S. National Archives, Washington, DC)

Puzzle Them First! begins with an excerpt from a provocative and puzzling letter and ends with an excerpt from another one, as shown. The first letter (see Preface) made the surprising connection between cigarette smoking and crime. This type of discrepant source stimulated a process that I called question-finding. The above excerpt from another letter is also discrepant and should be of even greater interest to educators. This is because the writer of the letter (a lawyer writing to the Law Enforcement Commission, an agency of the U.S. federal government) makes the startling assertion that "compulsory education laws" contribute to the rise of the criminal class. The puzzling assertion of this letter also leads us to generate questions that attempt to resolve the discrepancy between our background knowledge and experiences and the claims made in the source.

Question-finding is the process of searching for the "hidden" or the below-surface questions that could resolve the anomaly or explain the puzzlement. This process is closely allied to the epistemic quality of curiosity. But the question-finding process is even more; it also guides the seeker to probe deeper by posing creative or divergent type questions, those that do not generate explanations but create alternative hypotheses. In this situation, the epistemic quality of the question is one of wonderment. The differences between the epistemic qualities of curiosity and wonder are articulated well by education philosopher Paul Martin Opdal (2001), who claims that whereas "curiosity is a motive to do exploration within definite and accepted frames, wonder is a state of mind that signals we have reached the limits of our present understanding and things might be different from how they look" (p. 332). In this context, curiosity and wonder reflect different types of question-finding activity; the former reflects a convergent thinking orientation whereas the latter reflects a divergent thinking orientation. In this book, I have demonstrated how these different orientations relate to different types of questions—convergent thinking is reflected in the generation of puzzlement questions (awareness and explanation types), and divergent thinking is reflected in the generation of wonderment questions (see Figure 2, page 9).

The following brief example reviews specifically how a perplexing learning situation can stimulate convergent and divergent thinking in the generation of puzzlement and wonderment questions, respectively, in the field of science. Middle schools were studying the topic of the reproduction of sponges (one-cell animal structures). The class learned the startling idea that sponges have three ways of reproducing. One student asked the following puzzlement question (explanation type): "Why do they [sponges] need more than one way to reproduce when animals use only one way?" A number of comments were generated and numerous hypotheses were advanced. After the original question was answered, another student raised an additional question of a wonderment nature. This student asked, "If having several ways to reproduce is so advantageous, why don't other animals have them as well?" The second question led the way to what Scardamalia and Bereiter (1992) call "divergent progressive inquiry" (p. 195). This wonderment type of question pushes against the limits of current knowledge and can lead in many different directions.

Review the cartoon of the daring student at the beginning of this book. Notice how the cartoon reveals the direct connection between student questioning and genuine learning. Indeed, all learning is really a search for the right question to ask. In the following excerpt, poet Rainer Maria Rilke (1954) expresses this profound insight beautifully.

> Try to love the questions themselves as if they were locked rooms or books written in a foreign language. Don't search for the answers, which could not be given to you now, because you would not be able to live them. And the point is to live everything. Live the questions now. Perhaps, then, someday far into the future, you will gradually without even noticing it, live your way into the answer. (pp. 34–35)

The quotation summarizes the proper attitude of the question-finder as presented in this book. It is a disposition that many creative people possess. Poet Alice Walker (1983) acknowledged her fellow poet Rilke (quoted above) in a poem entitled "Reassurance." Walker claimed that she, too, needed reassurance "to love the questions themselves." She associated her own questions "with locked rooms full of treasure to which my blind and groping key does not yet fit" (p. 40). It is the intent of this book to provide a tool that can open the locks that shut out authentic student questioning behavior in the classroom.

Question-finding is based on the belief that self-questioning is an important life-time literacy disposition and skill in its own right. My 17-year-old student, Eduardo, displayed this orientation when he stated that one asks questions even though one can never know or discover the answers. Twelve-year-old Elie Wiesel, Holocaust survivor and future author, learned this same lesson from his elder, Moshe the Beadle, as depicted in the autobiographical account *Night* (1982). The young Wiesel learned from his mentor that "every question possessed a power that does not lie in the answer" (p. 2). In his quest for spiritual enlightenment, Wiesel learned a truth that can be applied to all phases of learning. The older man related that he prays to the God within him that He will give him the strength to ask the right question. Finding the right question is a timeless pursuit that should be the foundation of effective literacy and living for all age groups. As one of my former students once said, "Questions are everywhere." All we need to do is to find them.

APPENDIX A

Selected Materials and Resources That Foster Question-Finding

The materials and resources annotated in this appendix can be adapted for all content areas in the adolescent curriculum. Many of the themes explored in the various genre selections touch on universal themes such as self-expression, self-identity, self-worth, freedom, equality, justice, culture, heritage, imagination, humanity, and hope.

Autobiographies, Memoirs, Personal Narratives

Bartoletti, S.C. (2000). Exploring the gaps in history. *Book Links*, *10*, 16–20.

This award-winning children's author has written several books about the exploited coal mining families in Pennsylvania. In this personal memoir, Bartoletti demonstrates the question-finding process during a slide show presentation. One of her photographs shows a poor coal miner's wife stooped over a wooden washtub surrounded by six barefoot children. Dark crescents lie beneath her eyes, but she's smiling. The audience watching the presentation feels there is something puzzling about this picture. They want to know why the wife is smiling under these unfortunate conditions. One participant asks, "Is this the way women really were then?" Another asks, "Is this an example of faulty history that results when we do not question our early perceptions?" These are examples of puzzlement questions.

Hoose, P. (2001). *We were there, too.* New York: Farrar, Straus and Giroux.

This critically acclaimed book consists of 67 brief stories of young people from diverse cultures who tell about their role in the making of the United States. It is based on primary sources (i.e., first-person accounts, journals, interviews). Many discrepant themes emerge including the unexpected role of children as strike leaders and civil rights activists.

King, C., & Osborne, L.B. (1997). *Oh, freedom! Kids talk about the civil rights movement with the people who made it happen.* New York: Knopf.

This book consists of 31 interviews conducted by children with family members, friends, and civil rights activists. It is an ideal source for question-finding and critical inquiry because, as Rosa Parks says in the Foreword, "children can relate to this book because it is the children who ask the questions." Note in particular the provocative and surprising interview by the African American adolescent girl with a former Ku Klux Klan leader (see pp. 115–117). Excerpts from this interview appear in chapter 3.

Steinbeck, J. (1962). *Travels with Charley: In search of America*. New York: Viking Penguin.

Travels With Charley is a memoir of the famous writer's journey across the United States with his dog. One of his trips took him to New Orleans in the fall of 1960, where he witnessed and recorded 6-year-old African American Ruby Bridges' experiences at a desegregated school. Steinbeck describes the infamous actions of the "Cheerleaders"—middle-aged women shouting invectives and racial epithets toward a defenseless 6-year-old Ruby. This discrepant incident prompts several puzzlement questions such as, Why were the adults so hateful toward a young child?

Children's Artwork and Poetry

Atkins, S.B. (Ed.). (1993). *Voices from the fields: Children of migrant farm workers tell their stories*. Boston: Joy Street.

In poems, interviews, and first-person narratives, Mexican American children reveal their hardships and hopes. In particular, the provocative poem "La Fresa/The Strawberry," by adolescent Silvino Murillo, stimulates questions about child labor and human dignity.

Coles, R. (1992). *Their eyes meeting the world: The drawings and paintings of children*. Boston: Houghton Mifflin.

This book by a child psychiatrist shows the artwork (crayon, paint, and pencil drawings) of minority children from around the world. In particular, the crayon drawings of African American Ruby Bridges, showing the distorted figure drawings of herself in relation to other children during her desegregation ordeal, are especially poignant and stimulate question-finding.

Kafka, S., & Coles, R. (1982). *I will always stay me: Writings of migrant children*. Austin, TX: Texas Monthly Press.

This collection of poetry, personal essays, and short fiction by the children of migrant farm workers is the result of a creative writing program introduced in classrooms throughout south Texas in the 1970s. One poem written by a sixth-grade student, from which the title of the book derives, expresses the hopeless beliefs of migrant children that their marginal lives will never change.

Children's Literature and Picture Books

Bartoletti, S. (1999). *Kids on strike!* Boston: Houghton Mifflin.

This is a graphic story of working children who fought against powerful company owners in the late 19th and early 20th centuries. The book contains more than 100 photographs that display several discrepant events and stimulate question-finding.

Cohen, B. (1983). *Molly's pilgrim*. New York: Lothrop.

This chapter book tells the story of the meaning of the U.S. Thanksgiving holiday, as seen through the eyes of a Russian-Jewish immigrant girl and her Yiddish-speaking mother. The theme presents the stimulating view that new immigrants can be considered American pilgrims, too. This idea raises questions related to the topic of Americanization.

Coles, R. (1995). *The story of Ruby Bridges*. New York: Scholastic.

This illustrated picture book is written by a Pulitzer Prize–winning child psychiatrist who interviewed the young African American girl who attempted to desegregate a school in 1960. A highlight of the book is the scene in which the besieged first grader, Ruby, offers a prayer of forgiveness as she stands before a hateful mob of adults blocking her entrance into school. This counterintuitive act prompts puzzlement questions such as, Can you explain how such a young child could display such high moral behavior?

Cronin, D. (2000). *Click, clack, moo: Cows that type*. New York: Simon & Schuster Books for Young Readers.

This delightful fable presents a battle between Farmer Brown and his barnyard animals over living and working conditions. The cunning and wit of the "farm employees" to win concessions from the boss present several discrepant incidents that prompt student questioning.

Ringhold, F. (1991). *Tar beach*. New York: Crown.

In this picture book, a young African American girl dreams of flying over her Harlem home and her father's segregated union building as an escape from prejudice. The idea of flying can be viewed as a metaphor for escaping from slavery and other forms of persecution (as discussed later in this appendix in regard to the African American folk tale "People Can Fly"). This is a stimulating theme for question-finding.

Say, A. (1993). *Grandfather's journey*. Boston: Houghton Mifflin.

In this story, a young Japanese American boy reminisces about his grandfather's immigration to the United States and his return to his home country. This is expressed emotionally when the narrator states, "just when you get used to one country you become homesick for your homeland" (p. 31). The discrepant idea of dual citizenship and conflicting loyalties offers opportunities for question-finding.

Folk Tales

Courlander, H. (1947). *The cow-tail switch and other West African stories*. New York: Holt, Rinehart and Winston.

"The Cow-Tail Switch," one in the collection of West African folk tales in this book, stimulates readers to develop hypotheses about who among a chief's sons should receive the valuable cow-tale switch. Readers may be surprised by who is finally selected.

Hamilton, V. (1985). *The people could fly: American black folktales*. New York: Knopf.

"The People Could Fly," one in this collection of American black folk tales, is a fantasy tale about escaping from slave oppression by flying away from one's masters. The theme of flying over one's oppressors is a popular motif in American black folk tales. Wonderment questions can be raised such as, Could the expression "come fly with me" have been used as some sort of code message for runaways? Were there metaphorical ways of escaping from slavery?

Paintings

Farny, H. (1904). *The song of the talking wire*. Taft Museum, Cincinnati, Ohio.

This oil-on-canvas painting shows a Native American hunter stopping to listen to the reverberating telegraph wires, a symbol of culture clash and expansion by the "white man." Reproductions of this painting are available from the Taft Museum. One may ask the provocative question: Were industrial advances a prelude to the decimation of Native Americans?

Lawrence, J. (1992). *The great migration: An American story. Paintings by Jacob Lawrence*. New York: HarperCollins.

Through a series of 60 panels, African American painter Lawrence tells the bittersweet story of black migration in the United States from the rural South to the urban North during and after World War I. Observers see from the sequence that the movement northward did not bring the migrants to the "Promised Land." Among the puzzlement questions beneath the surface of these art panels is, To what extent was this painful experience worthwhile for the migrants?

Rockwell, N. (1964). *The problem we all live with*. Norman Rockwell Museum, Stockbridge, Massachusetts.

This is a famous painting of the young African American girl Ruby Bridges being escorted into school under the protection of United States marshals. It appeared in *Look Magazine* on January 14, 1964, and copies are available from the Norman Rockwell Museum. Among the puzzlement questions one might ask is, Why would Norman Rockwell give his painting this unclear title, instead of just saying what the problem was?

Photography

Buckland, G. (1980). *First photographs: People, places, and phenomena as captured for the first time by the camera.* New York: Macmillan.

This book presents 300 photographs with captions. Photographs include one of the first Native Americans to gaze at a "white man's" picture box. Another is the earliest known photograph (August 1913) of agricultural laborers on strike in America, which appears with the caption, "They are hop-pickers.... They seem to be organized in non-violent protest, with a tot here and there." The involvement of young children as labor strikers is a counterintuitive event that prompts question-finding.

Heiferman, M., & Kismaric, C. (1994). *Talking pictures: People speak about the photographs that speak to them.* San Francisco: Chronicle.

The authors interviewed 69 individuals (celebrities, artists, laypeople) and asked them to choose an image or photograph that has affected their lives. For example, in terms of social justice issues, two very powerful photographs have had a pronounced effect on the lives of two well-known individuals: Civil rights attorney and social activist William Kunstler selected one of Margaret Bourke-White's photographs showing the discrepancy of living conditions between African American people and white people during the U.S. Great Depression, with the ironic title "World's Highest Standard of Living." Civil rights leader Jesse Jackson chose a heart-breaking photograph of young civil rights demonstrators being blasted by jets of water from fire hoses in the segregated city of Birmingham, Alabama, in the 1960s.

Websites and Electronic Books

http://www.archives.gov/digital_classroom/index

This website is the "digital classroom," an educational resource of the National Archives. It contains primary sources in several periods of U.S. history. One collection on the topic of social justice is the "Photographs of Lewis Hine: Documentation of child labor," which contains 16 photographs from the U.S. investigative photographer. One of these photos shows very young boys and girls who were so small they had to climb up on to the spinning frame to mend broken threads and to replace the empty bobbins on the machine.

http://www.historyplace.com

This website displays photographs, captions, and narratives on major topics in U.S. and world history, in particular, migrant farm families. Of particular interest is the feature entitled "Dorothea Lange and Migrant Farm Families," which contains 24 U.S.Great Depression photos of the living conditions of families hired to work in cotton fields in Arizona and California. One very poignant photograph is of a 10-year-old cotton picker fixing his family's car, with the caption, "I do not go to school because my father wishes my aid in pickin' cotton."

Mindtronics: Inquiry alive

Mindtronics: Inquiry alive is an e-book available at www.hometreemedia.com/carpool.htm. This e-book describes 100 discrepant events in the fields of social studies and science. These discrepant events stimulate puzzlement questions (explanation type) and wonderment questions.

Young Adult Literature and Novels

Jones, E. (2003). *The known world*. New York: Amistad.

This Pulitzer Prize–winning novel tells the discrepant story of free African Americans owning slaves. One of the main characters, Moses (an African American slave), expresses that this is a strange world "that made him a slave to a white man, but God had indeed set it twirling and twisting every which way when he put black people to owning their own kind"(p. 9). This discrepant situation of African American ownership of other African Americans is a rarely told story in U.S. history and is a stimulus for question-finding.

Merrill, J. (1964). *The pushcart war*. New York: W.R. Scott.

This is a humorous story of the battle of the haves (i.e., the trucking business) and the have-nots (i.e., the pushcart peddlers) during the 1970s in New York City. This Cinderella tale of the successes of the powerless over the powerful presents multiple discrepant events from which one can find questions at different levels of cognition.

Morrison, T. (1970). *The bluest eye*. New York: Penguin.

This award-winning novel tells the story of a young African American girl who is raped by her father. It deals with powerful issues of racial self-loathing. It uses physical features as metaphors for self-acceptance. This theme prompts the reader to search for questions about the harmful effects of racial discrimination and child abuse on one's personal identity.

Paulsen, G. (1993). *Nightjohn*. New York: Delacorte.

This young adult novel reveals the threatening influence of literacy on the institution of slavery. The protagonist risks his life (and limb) to teach a young slave girl how to read. The theme is an effective stimulus to student questioning. This novel prompts the following puzzlement question: Why was slave literacy such a deep fear among slaveholders?

Smith, B. (2005). *A tree grows in Brooklyn*. New York: HarperPerennial. (Original work published 1943)

This classic novel tells the story of an Irish American family living in tenement slums during the early part of the 20th century. The young daughter, Francie, rises above her impoverished conditions by entering the world of literacy (i.e., reading every book in her local library and writing realistic stories). This brings her into conflict with her high school English teacher, who wants the young girl to write about beauty and not the harsh features of her family life. Among the wonderment questions that this story prompts is, Should writing be used to portray things as they are or as they might be?

Question–Finding Template and Sample Question–Finding Lesson Plan

This appendix includes the question-finding template I created, which is based on the question-finding process and can be used as a conceptual guide, as well as a sample lesson plan that incorporates the template and demonstrates the question-finding strategy. The sample question-finding lesson plan included in this appendix is one of five lessons that I require in the social studies methods course for preservice teachers that I teach. Christie Raimondi, one of the preservice teachers in my course, created the lesson plan in this appendix for middle school students as part of a unit on the U.S. Great Depression. The standard that Christie chose to focus on is based on the standards for social studies identified by the National Council for the Social Studies (1994).

The lesson plan is presented as a graphic organizer in which key elements of the lesson are presented. These elements include multiple objectives (i.e., process and value), related activities, appropriate assessments, and differentiated instruction. In this lesson, Christie chose question-finding as the process strategy to inquire into the despair and hopelessness of Americans during this period of history. Note that the question-finding template and process can be adapted to any content area.

Question–Finding Template

Identify puzzling situation

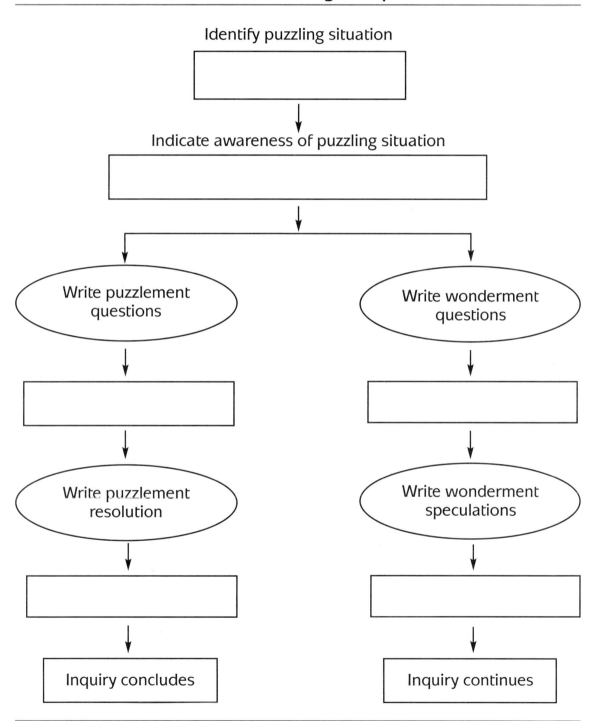

Indicate awareness of puzzling situation

Write puzzlement questions

Write wonderment questions

Write puzzlement resolution

Write wonderment speculations

Inquiry concludes

Inquiry continues

Question-Finding Lesson Plan

TOPIC: Analyzing photos of one migrant mother and her children from the U.S. Great Depression

---

Materials: Each student receives copies of five photos of the migrant mother, Florence, and her children (see page 150).

Standard/Evidence

Standard: Individual Development and Identity

Evidence: Students will learn how culture shapes personal identity. For example, students will be able to understand how the culture or way of life during the Great Depression personally affected the life of one migrant mother and her children, which is made evident through the photos.

Process Objective: Students will work together as a class in order to construct a question-finding template. Students will develop the question-finding template by analyzing five photos taken by Dorothea Lange of a migrant mother, Florence, and her children.

Value Objective: Students will be able to empathize with one of the children in the photos by writing a paragraph response to their wonderment questions.

Activity (Process Objective): Model the question-finding strategy for the students. In addition, explain the differences between a puzzlement and wonderment question. Provide the students with examples of each type of question. Next, allow the students to observe the five photos of the migrant mother and her children for a few minutes. Then, allow the students as a whole group to develop their question-finding template. Draw the question-finding template on the chalkboard and fill it in as students respond. Have students write three puzzlement (explanation) questions and three wonderment questions related to the effects of the Great Depression on family life. Then, allow the students to answer their own questions and draw conclusions with this information. Provide support and guidance when needed during this activity. When the question-finding template is complete, allow the students to copy it into their social studies notebooks. (See sample on pages 148–149.)

Activity (Value Objective): After the students have copied their question-finding template into their social studies notebooks, they will write one paragraph answering their wonderment questions from their question-finding diagram. After the students have completed this assignment, conduct a class discussion for students to share their responses. (See sample written response on page 151.)

(continued)

Assessment (Process Objective): Evaluate students through observations. Observe the students' participation levels during this class activity, listening carefully to each student during the activity and recording in an anecdotal form a few observations.	Assessment (Value Objective): Collect all the students' paragraphs. Using a teacher-created checklist (see page 152), assess whether the students respnded to their own wonderment questions from their question-finding template.

For gifted students: After the students have written their paragraphs, instruct them to go to the website www.english.uiuc.edu/maps/depression/photoessay.htm. Here, the students will be able to view and study more pictures of families and children of the U.S. Great Depression.

For struggling students: If the below average learner is having trouble completing his or her paragraph, allow him or her to work with another student. If the below average learner does not complete the work for this lesson in the given time, allow the student to finish his or her work during free time throughout the rest of the school day or for homework.

Sample Completed Question-Finding Template

Puzzling photographs: A migrant mother and her children destitute in a pea picker's camp in Nipomo, California. Dorothea Lange, a famous photographer, took these pictures in February or March of 1936.

Awareness of puzzlement: In all of these pictures, the migrant mother looks extremely worried, tired, and depressed. In the pictures, the migrant mother's children are clinging to her. In some of the pictures, we do not see the children's faces because they are turned away from the camera. In all of the five pictures, the migrant mother and her children look very poor and their faces and clothes are dirty. In the fifth picture, it appears as if their home is a tent and the migrant mother and her children are living in the wilderness.

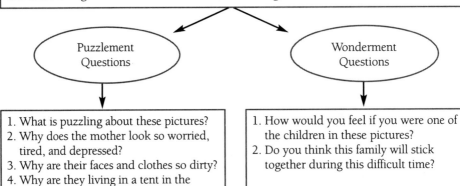

Puzzlement Questions

Wonderment Questions

1. What is puzzling about these pictures?
2. Why does the mother look so worried, tired, and depressed?
3. Why are their faces and clothes so dirty?
4. Why are they living in a tent in the wilderness?

1. How would you feel if you were one of the children in these pictures?
2. Do you think this family will stick together during this difficult time?

The migrant mother looks very worried, tired, and depressed because this picture was taking [sic] right after the family found out that there was no work for them in these fields because during the night a freak frost had frozen the peas in the field. The faces of the mother and her children are dirty because they have no water. Their clothes are dirty because it was probably the only piece of clothing that they each now owned. The family became poor during the Great Depression. The family had to set up a tent as shelter in the wilderness because they had nowhere else to go and their car broke down.

I cannot imagine myself being in one of the children's shoes in the pictures. I would be very worried about my family. I would be very upset and angry that my dad does not have a job. I would be scared to live in a tent in the wilderness with no water. Yes, I believe that this family will stick together. Families are supposed to be there for one another and stick by each other's sides through the good and bad times.

(continued)

Inquiry concludes: Many families, such as the one seen in these pictures, had to travel the country in order to find jobs during the Great Depression. Many families became poor during this time period.

Inquiry continues: What would you do if you were the president of the United States when this picture took place? Would you turn your head away and accept this reality or would you do something different? What would be the best plan to help these families, who are struggling to make ends meet?

A   B   C

D   E

Lange, D. (1936). Migrant Mother collection. Prints and Photographs Division, FSA/OWI Collection, Library of Congress, Washington, DC. (A) LC-USF34-9058-C (B) LC-USF34-9093-C (C) LC-USF34-9095 (D) LC-USF34-9097-C (E) LC-USZ62-58355. Public domain.

I cannot even imagine what life must have been like for the children in these pictures. If I were one of the children in these pictures, I know that I would be very worried about my family. I would be upset and angry that my dad cannot find a job to support my family. I believe that I would cry a lot in fear of not knowing what to do or how a small person like me could help my family. I would be very scared to live in a tent out in the wilderness with no water or food. I would be very nervous about the baby because the baby needs food to survive. I think that the family in these pictures will stick together. Families are supposed to be there for one another and stick by each other's sides through the good and bad times.

Checklist for Students' Paragraphs

Students' Names	The students responded to their own wonderment questions from the question-finding template.
1. Student A	✔
2. Student B	✔
3. Student C	✔
4. Student D	✔
5. Student E	✔

Everyday Motivational Sources for Question-Finding

Following are samples of sources from everyday life that teachers can use with students to generate questions. Included among the samples are childhood photographs, family and human interest stories, signs, and television shows.

Childhood Photographs

Childhood photographs are powerful inducers of curiosity. See the childhood photograph below of the author as a young boy wearing a heavy winter coat during a summer's day. This photo generated a classroom discussion on preventing common colds and wearing warm clothing. This source also led to a discussion on the scientific idea of heat and conduction. My students believed (just as my mother believed) that the heavy coat conducted body heat. See also a childhood photo of my wife as a child and her other young relatives on a tar roof in July. The roof served as their "tar beach." The use of rooftops as recreational areas is counterintuitive to children today. Thus, these images are effective sources of question-finding.

A family photograph of the author (as a child) wearing a winter coat on a summer's day. The two neighbors are dressed more appropriately.

A family photograph of the author's future wife and relatives sun-bathing on a tar roof.

Family Stories

Family stories provide a rich source of discrepant artifacts. I encourage my students to interview relatives and friends about unexpected or counterintuitive anecdotes in their (relatives') lives. Following is an example of a discrepant family story provided by a preservice teacher whom I taught. (This example is adapted with permission from Jeanine Surace, a current inservice teacher.)

> One night my grandfather and his buddies were playing poker at my grandparents' home. While in her bedroom, my grandmother overheard one of Grandpa's friends talk about a large plot of land for sale for $1000. Grandma reached for the sock where she saved her money and counted out $1000. The next day, she bought the property where we still live today. The couple built two businesses on the land, one of which was still in operation 15 years ago. My grandmother worked full-time and raised three girls. Mothers working full-time jobs were unheard of in the 1930s. The children worked after school at the family's grocery store. Grandma stopped going to school after sixth grade. Despite her limited education, she was an intelligent woman. It was typical for her to read the newspaper to find the best rate for bank CDs and transfer funds, always getting more for her money. Grandpa died of cancer in 1964 at the age of 66. Grandma worked full-time until the age of 81, when she retired. She died in 1993 at the age of 92.

"Generation Gap" Literature and Visuals

Fiction and nonfiction that present conflicting views between generations provide highly motivational contexts for question-finding. I have used selections from *The Old Bunch* (Levin, 1937), a novel that portrays the conflict between a mother and her daughter over a hairstyle called the "bob" that was popular with adolescents in the 1920s (see chapter 4 for a discussion of this example). The extent of the mother's anger over what today's adolescents would consider a minor matter stimulates active discussions with my students and generates some interesting questions. I also have used a cartoon from the 1920s as a further motivational prompt on the topic. (See opposite a cartoon from the 1920s on a similar theme, entitled "If grandpap could only return with some of his discipline.") As you might expect, the cartoon proved quite perplexing to my students.

Human Interest Stories

Human interest stories such as those from newspapers can stimulate question-finding behavior. For example, I recently found the article "Black Collectors Hate and Buy Them: Surprising Popularity for Jim Crow Items" in the *New York Times* (Ramirez, 2006). The article explains that Mary Taylor, an African American businesswoman, owns a gift shop in Harlem, New York. What is interesting about this shop is that Mary sells memorabilia from the Jim Crow era (1876–1964). Some of the objects for sale include objectionable and racist items such as white hoods and robes from the Ku Klux Klan and mammy dolls. Surprisingly, the store is located in the heart of the most famous African American community in the United States. Perhaps even more surprising is that most of the patrons are African Americans.

Signs of All Kinds

Signs are often counterintuitive and a source for question-finding. Following is the text for a consumer sign that was displayed in a candy store and ice cream shop in the 1950s that warned

NO DRINKING OF INTOXICATING BEVERAGES ON OR AROUND THESE PREMISES.
THERE WILL BE NO 'PROFANE' LANGUAGE AT ANY TIME.

From Norfleet, B. (2001). *When we liked Ike: Looking for postwar America*. New York:
W.W. Norton, p. 106.

The following discrimination sign could use a lesson in spelling.

Source: New York Public Library Picture Collection, New York.

Following are two photographs of signs enforcing racial discrimination.

Vachon, J. (1939). Sign in a beer parlor window. Farm
Security Administration, Office of War Information. LC-
USF33-1661-M3. U.S. Library of Congress, Washington, DC.

Bubley, E. (1943). A rest stop for Greyhound bus passen-
gers on the way from Louisville, Kentucky, to Nashville,
Tennessee, with separate accommodations for colored
passengers. Farm Security Administration, Office of War
Information. LC-USZ62-62919. U.S. Library of Congress,
Washington, DC.

Viewer-Participation Television and Radio Shows

The old-time favorite viewer-participation show *Candid Camera* has an online contest for the best counterintuitive real-life scenarios written by adolescents. Winners receive $100 and the possibility that their scenario will be broadcast. One winner had the following counterintuitive suggestion that was actually broadcast: "Why don't you measure people's height as they're entering a movie theater and seat them according to their height? The shorter people in the front and the taller people in the back, so no one's view would be obstructed. Some couples may have to sit apart from each other to make this work! Isn't it only fair that people sit according to their height?" (www.candidcamera.com/cc3/cc3n.html).

Selected Quotations Related to the Question-Finding Process

The following quotations refer to major characteristics of the question-finding process. These characteristics include recognizing cognitive incongruity, tolerating ambiguity, experiencing indeterminate learning, and supporting open-ended questioning.

It is better to ask some of the questions than to know all the answers.
(James Thurber, 1945, p. 249)

Often it is the realization of incongruity between our notion of the world and what it turns out to be that leads us to want to understand better. Sometimes we positively seek incongruities out, as if we liked having to deal with things we do not understand, things that challenge us intellectually.
(Margaret Donaldson, 1978, pp. 117–118)

Thinking begins...in a forked-road situation, a situation which is ambiguous, which presents a dilemma, which proposes alternatives.
(John Dewey, 1910/1991, p. 11)

A well-packed question carries its answer on its back as a snail carries its shell.
(James Stephens, 1920, p. 68)

By holding the tension of opposites [tolerating ambiguity], we [teachers] hold the gateway to inquiry open, inviting students into the territory in which we all can learn.
(Parker Palmer, 1998, p. 85)

While watching...children working on a geometric problem, a teacher said, "I guess for the first time clearly I saw children learning—the process of learning without the answers fully intact."
(Courtney Cazden, 2001, p. 170)

The unlearning of preconceptions might very well prove to be the most determinative single factor in the acquisition and retention of subject-matter knowledge.... When misconceptions are not uprooted, they may become more elaborated and stable as a result of instruction.
(David Paul Ausubel, Joseph Novak, & Helen Hanesian, 1968, p. 372–373)

Every new item of knowledge is the answer to a question and...is most readily ingested when the question is astir within the learner.

(Daniel Berlyne, 1965, p. 86)

Not only do [counterintuitive] instances...gain students' attention...but such examples also help students challenge habits of thought and practices, thus leading to their becoming better thinkers...[gaining] a greater appreciation of the need for exploration, reflection, and reasoning.

(Marshall Gordon, 1991, p. 511)

GLOSSARY

The following concepts and specialized terms are noted at the beginning of the chapters in this book, and they appear in boldface on first mention in the text. A number of definitions contain cross-references; these cross-references appear in italics.

academic motivation: State of interest and engagement in learning school subjects.

adolescent literacy: Multidimensional and multimedial mode of symbolic communication that impacts on the identity and social development of middle and high school learners. It denotes an expanded and generative notion of text including the use of everyday and popular culture sources (Alvermann, 2004; Stevens, 2002).

affective/cognitive synthesis: Combination of mental and emotional qualities that include a positive outlook and disposition and perceptive and meaningful thinking.

affective entrenchment: Tenacious belief in a topic supported by prior experiences and knowledge.

anomalous event: Unusual or unexpected occurrence that violates students' expectations and promotes a state of perplexity or bewilderment. Often used interchangeably with the term *discrepant event*.

augmented activation activity: Instructional strategy in which an unexpected situation or experiment is presented to refute students' preexisting notions about a topic. This strategy is employed to induce *conceptual change*.

catch facets: Stimuli that grab students' immediate attention, such as novel or surprising events.

code-switching: Literacy practice of shifting or alternating between home language practices and school language patterns.

cognitive-based literacy: Communication practices and abilities acquired through individual analytical reasoning and information processing.

cognitive closure: Students' mental process of prematurely closing off their minds to continued investigation of a topic.

cold conceptual change: Term used by critics of the original conceptual change model, who challenge the highly rationalistic and individualistic nature of the classic theory. Critics have revised the theory by stressing the importance of motivational and social factors in *conceptual change*.

competing narratives: Conflicting or divergent perspectives of the same event; term often used in *critical literacy* studies to denote ideological or world-view differences.

conceptual change: Students' process of altering and reconceptualizing their ideas. Some instructional strategies that attempt to foster conceptual change are conceptual conflict strategies; *question-finding* is one of these strategies.

conceptual conflict: Major element of Berlyne's (1965) curiosity theory that describes the mental state of perplexity that results from the introduction of unexpected ideas or surprising events.

conceptual conflict strategy: Presentation of a puzzling situation as a stimulus for students to question their preconceptions; second phase of the *question-driven conceptual change model*.

conceptual ecology: Nucleus or corpus of ideas, attitudes, and values that are formative in students' knowledge and beliefs; often used in *conceptual change* studies to note the difficulties inherent in conceptual change.

convergent thinking: Cognitive process of finding answers that explain and resolve problematic situations. In this book, convergent thinking processes are defined in terms of explaining or resolving states or conditions of *puzzlement* created by *discrepant events*. The question type associated with this thinking process is *puzzlement question (explanation type)* (e.g., Can you explain why the light object fell at the same rate as the heavy object?).

counterintuitive: Dissonant ideas and unexpected realities that challenge common sense; often used interchangeably with *discrepant events*.

covariation questions: Category of questions that address the causal relationship between variables. Often used in sciences to establish sets of experimental variables (e.g., How does acidity affect plant growth?).

critical awareness: Development of a consciousness that text represents realities that are socially and culturally constructed.

critical literacy: Communication acts and habits of thought that question the official knowledge by going beneath dominant discourse to understand the deep meaning, social context, and ideology of literate events. It is a practice of critical inquiry into self, society, and the very nature of content knowledge (Shor, 1987, 1992).

critical literacy practices: Literacy activities that help students develop critical abilities to interrogate the meaning of text (e.g., *examining multiple perspectives*).

critical literacy proficiencies: Compendium of literacy competencies that aid students in practicing literacy (e.g., developing *critical awareness*).

critical orientation to literacy: Disposition or stance that challenges the dominant position of mainstream text.

critical questions: Types of questions that challenge the subjectivities and ideological positions of text (e.g., How does this television advertisement make me feel about my body?).

cultural congruence: Synthesis of school and home practices that reflects a sharing of norms and values.

cultural constructions: Subjective versions of reality based on issues of gender, race, ethnicity, and social class.

cultural dissonance: Disjoint between home and school practices often leading to conflicting or antagonistic behavior.

culturally relevant pedagogy: Teaching methods that incorporate students' cultural and home practices into the curriculum.

culturally responsive classroom: Learning environment that recognizes different learning styles, encourages use of differential language patterns and dialects, and incorporates the norms and values of the home culture.

curiosity: Motivational construct that is defined by Berlyne (1954) as a state of arousal demonstrated by a "drive to know."

dialogic inquiry: Use of collaboration in exploring and investigating text.

dialogically organized classroom: Learning environment in which teachers and students work collaboratively to discuss and analyze texts.

discrepant event: Unexpected happening or situation that creates a mental state of perplexity or bewilderment.

divergent thinking: Cognitive process that generates alternate and open-ended responses. In this book, divergent thinking processes are defined in terms of creativity, wonder, and imagination. The specific question type associated with divergent thinking is *wonderment question* (e.g., Can you imagine the possibilities of life on another planet?).

driving question: A type of inquiry question initiated by personally relevant goals (e.g., How does the amount of sunlight in my house affect the growth of my plants?).

epistemic curiosity: Term used by Berlyne (1954) to describe behavior that shows that an individual seeks to acquire new knowledge in order to resolve conflict created by unexpected happenings or puzzling situations. This behavior is conducive to *question-finding*.

epistemic freezing: Term used by Kruglanski and Webster (1996) to describe the quick closing off of an individual's thinking on a topic; also described as a premature state of *cognitive closure*. This behavior is not conducive to *question-finding*.

examining multiple perspectives: Literacy practice that fosters the critical exploration of events by calling for students to juxtapose texts to be read against each other.

exposing preconceptions: Instructional strategy that attempts to bring to light or to surface students' preconceptions on a topic; the initial phase of the *question-driven conceptual change model.*

finding one's authentic voice: Acts of communication that provide opportunities for authentic, or personally relevant, self-expression by students in the face of dominant or hegemonic discourse patterns.

funds of knowledge: Literacy expression coined by Moll (1992), which refers to the practical intelligence and home-based wisdom that assists individuals in everyday living.

give talk: Haitian linguistic facility for argumentation typically used in scientific discussions.

guided inquiry approach: Instructional strategy in which students' authentic, or personally relevant, questions drive the investigation of target issues.

guided reciprocal peer questioning: Use of instructional aids (e.g., *question starters*) to encourage collaborative student questioning.

hold facets: Engaging materials of instruction that sustain and build student engagement and motivation for learning. Hold facets solidify the enticing features of *catch facets.*

immersion model of inquiry: Educational strategy that builds on students' knowledge base as a precondition for discovering and constructing new knowledge.

indeterminate learning situations: Concept expressed by Dewey (1938) to denote that inquiry learning begins through situations of uncertainty and perplexity.

intentional conceptual change: Students' purposeful and personal plan to change their initial conceptions on a topic.

intercultural social inquiry: Process of discovery learning involving collaboration between members of different cultural and social groups.

internalized oppression: Term describing the psychological process in which a marginalized group begins to believe and subconsciously accept the dominant group's rationale for discrimination. A major objective of *critical literacy* instruction is to help students recognize and oppose cultural practices that support internalized oppression.

interrogative mood: Predisposition toward questioning behavior or an eager need to ask questions.

intrinsic motivation: Condition of high interest or arousal that is inherent in the processing of information (Hunt, 1971). Berlyne (1965) stresses the point that intrinsically motivating activities are "satisfying in themselves" (p. 71). *Anomalous events* and puzzling situations are intrinsically motivating.

iterative nature of generating questions: Repeated action of questioning or the process of one question leading to another.

meaningful conflict: A perplexing situation that the student has a personal stake in resolving.

monologic talk: Teacher-dominated classroom discourse in which one voice predominates in class.

more knowledgeable other: Term used to describe a substitute mentor acting to assist the new learner in Vygotsky's (1978) zone of proximal development, which is the "distance between the actual developmental level as determined by independent problem solving and the level of potential development through problem solving under adult guidance" (p. 86).

motivation/domain synthesis: Description of the integration of motivational elements and academic disciplines–for example, *curiosity* and scientific discovery; *self-determination* and creative writing (language arts).

motivational construct: The fundamental building blocks of motivation (i.e., *self-efficacy*, *self-determination*, *curiosity*, and so forth).

multiple entry point teaching: Instructional strategy in which a unit of study is approached from different vantage points using varied resources.

naïve presuppositions: Premature ideas or first impressions often molded from childhood and strongly resistant to alteration. Some conceptual change scholars provide alternate terminology such as "unschooled theories" (Gardner, 2004, p. 61) or "preinstructional conceptions" (Chinn & Malhotra, 2002, p. 327).

open-inquiry lab environments: Science experiments conducted in a liberal setting without rigid prescriptions and fixed structure.

peripheral conceptual change: Students' superficial alteration or replacement of their preconceptions, which are not substantial enough to modify students' entrenched beliefs.

precognitive state of doubt: A mental state of perplexity or bewilderment in which the student becomes aware of and sensitive to gaps in his or her knowledge structures.

procedural prompts: Cues or scaffolds that guide strategy development (e.g., *question starters* or signal words).

project-based classroom: Inquiry learning environment often involving experiments and guided by students' authentic questions. In science classes, these authentic questions are sometimes referred to as *driving questions*.

puzzlement: Mental state of perplexity or bewilderment often caused by the unsettling effects of unexpected happenings or situations (i.e., *discrepant events*); a precondition of *question-finding*.

puzzlement questions (awareness type): Students' metacognitive questions, which express an awareness of gaps in their knowledge base when confronted with a puzzling situation (e.g., Do I know what is going on here?). These questions initiate the *question-finding* process and are convergent in nature.

puzzlement questions (explanation type): Students' convergent questions, which seek explanations or resolutions to puzzling situations (e.g., Can you explain why the man bit the dog?).

question-driven conceptual change model: Three-phase process of altering and reconceptualizing one's preconceptions through self-questioning.

question-finding: Process of generating questions induced by unexpected happenings and motivated by a compelling desire to offset a mental state of perplexity.

question starters: Interrogative word stems or prompts that guide students in the formation of different types of questions (e.g., What would happen if...? Can you explain...?).

radical conceptual change: Students' thorough reconceptualization of their presuppositions on a topic.

reciprocal questioning: Comprehension strategy in which the teacher and the students share in the process of generating questions and interpreting text.

recognizing social barriers and crossing borders of separation: Critical literacy practice that identifies and recommends social action to overcome patterns of segregation.

reconceptualizing prior knowledge: Process in which preconceptions and premature ideas have been restructured and reconceptualized to reflect academic learning. Occurs during the culminating phase of the *question-driven conceptual change model*.

refutational discussion: Instructional strategy in which an unexpected situation is introduced to challenge students' initial preconceptions elicited during classroom discussion; similar to *augmented activation activity* because both use situations of *conceptual conflict* to induce *conceptual change*.

refutational text: Materials or resources of instruction that expose a popular misconception on a topic and then immediately confront and refute it with the academic or scientific explanation.

regaining one's identity: Literacy practice focused on offsetting the dehumanizing effects of discursive text and reestablishing a positive sense of agency (e.g., adolescent girls challenge the media's patriarchal representation of the image of the female body); a major element of *critical literacy*.

resistant reading: Literacy act in which the reader reads "against the grain" of dominant discourse to challenge the ideological assumptions of text.

rival hypotheses: Generation of alternative ideas through collaborative inquiry.

second-guessing: Climate of inquiry that encourages tentative ideas, uncertainties, hunches, and preformulated thoughts.

self-determination: Psychological need for autonomy and identity development. In *critical literacy* terminology, this psychological need includes the quest for subjectively acceptable identities.

self-efficacy: An attitude and disposition of confidence held by students regarding their abilities to do a job or complete a performance; an important *motivational construct*.

self-monitoring questions: Metacognitive questions that relate to students' development of an awareness of their learning abilities and acquisition of knowledge. In this book, these questions are also known as *puzzlement questions (awareness type)*.

self-regulation: Metacognitive condition in which students monitor, control, and execute their actions and decisions; an important *motivational construct*.

sensation-seeking: Personality variable characterized by an inclination for sensation, novelty, complexity, and intriguing events.

sense-making: Process whereby students use their everyday language and cultural ways of knowing to construct new knowledge; used to express a sociocultural orientation to science literacy.

signifying: Genre of African American talk that stresses figurative language, body language, and speech rhythms.

situational interest: Type of motivation that uses exterior factors such as a stimulating learning environment and high-interest instructional materials to generate student engagement.

social construction of knowledge: Description of a cognitive developmental process in which students' knowledge is constructed through interaction and collaboration in social settings. For example, in chapter 4 (see pp. 87–88) when the teacher and students collaborate in discussing examples of racism in *The Adventures of Huckleberry Finn*, the students are participating in this process.

sociocognitive literacy: Learning theory that contends that literacy practices are constructed through interaction and collaboration with others. In this book, sociocognitive literacy is treated as a component of the broad-based social literacy dimension.

sociocultural literacy: Learning theory that contends that the meaning of text does not reside exclusively in text but is conceptualized within one's heritage, gender, and social conditions. In this book, sociocultural literacy is treated as a component of the broad-based social literacy dimension.

sociohistorical literacy: Learning theory that contends that the meaning of text is socially constructed by present realities and past circumstances and histories; often associated with *sociocultural literacy*. In this book, sociohistorical literacy is treated as a component of the broad-based social literacy dimension.

sociolinguistic literacy: Learning theory that conceives of social events and practices as major factors in language development and expression. In this book, sociolinguistic literacy is treated as a component of the broad-based social literacy dimension.

story-like participation structures: Communication patterns and genres of talk reflecting home responsibilities and cultural backgrounds; language that is conceptualized in real-world activities rather than school recitation patterns.

tentative exploratory behavior: Type of search activity in which the student demonstrates a willingness to travel uncharted territories for the purpose of finding preliminary or nurturing questions rather than obtaining immediate and final answers.

third space: Figurative language used to describe a part of classroom discourse in which students' authentic questions can be perused and genuine feelings can be expressed. First space refers to teacher's *monologic talk*. Second space refers to students' scripted responses to teacher's queries (Gutierrez, Rymes, & Larsen, 1995).

tolerance for ambiguity: Disposition that accepts the notion that two or more apparently contradictory ideas can be plausible at the same time.

whole-number bias: Erroneous application of whole-number principles to common and decimal fractions that has strong implications for question-finding and conceptual change in mathematical thinking.

wonderment questions: Questions that are open-ended, speculative, and imaginative; sometimes called divergent questions. These questions seek to elicit alternative responses to puzzling situations (e.g., Can you imagine what life could be like on another planet?).

REFERENCES

Adams, D.W. (1995). *Education for extinction: American Indians and the boarding school experience, 1875–1928*. Lawrence: University Press of Kansas.

Allington, R.L., & Weber, R. (1993). Questioning questions in teaching and learning from texts. In B.K. Britton, A. Woodward, & M. Binkley (Eds.), *Learning from textbooks: Theory and practice* (pp. 47–68). Hillsdale, NJ: Erlbaum.

Allison, A.W., & Shrigley, R. (1982). Teaching children to ask operational questions in science. *Science Education, 70*(1), 73–80.

Alvermann, D.E. (1991). The discussion web: A graphic aid for learning across the curriculum. *The Reading Teacher, 45*, 92–99.

Alvermann, D.E. (2002, September). *Science after school: Putting everyday literacies to work in the service of classroom learning*. Paper presented at the Conference on Philosophical, Psychological, and Linguistic Foundations for Language and Science Literacy Research: University of Victoria, BC.

Alvermann, D.E. (2003, November). *Seeing themselves as capable and engaged readers: Adolescents and re/mediated instruction*. Naperville, IL: Learning Point Associates. Retrieved May 5, 2005, from http://www.ncrel.org/litweb/readers

Alvermann, D.E. (2004). Multiliteracies and self-questioning in the service of science learning. In E.W. Saul (Ed.), *Crossing borders in literacy and science instruction: Perspectives on theory and practice* (pp. 226–238). Newark: DE: International Reading Association.

Alvermann, D.E., Commeyras, M., & Young, J.P. (1997). Interrupting gendered discursive practices in classroom talk about texts: Easy to think about, difficult to do. *Journal of Literacy Research, 29*(1), 73–104.

Alvermann, D.E., Moon, J.S., & Hagood, M.C. (1999). *Popular culture in the classroom: Teaching and researching critical media literacy*. Newark, DE: International Reading Association.

Ames, G.A., & Murray, F.B. (1982). When two wrongs make a right: Promoting cognitive change by social conflict. *Developmental Psychology, 18*(6), 894–897.

Ames, R., & Ames, C. (1989). Adolescent motivation and achievement. In J. Worell & F. Danner (Eds.), *The adolescent maker: Applications to development and education* (pp. 181–204). San Diego, CA: Academic.

Anand, B., Fine, M., Surrey, D., & Perkins, T. (2002). *Keeping the struggle alive: Studying desegregation in our town: A guide to doing oral history*. New York: Teachers College Press and National Middle School Association.

Anderman, E.M., Noar, S.M., Zimmerman, R.S., & Donohew, L. (2005). The need for sensation as a prerequisite for motivation to engage in academic tasks. In P.R. Pintrich & M.L. Maehr (Eds.), *Motivating students, improving schools: The legacy of Carol Midgley* (Vol. 13: Advances in Motivation and Achievement; pp. 1–26). Amsterdam: Elsevier JAI.

Anders, P.L., & Guzzetti, B.J. (1996). *Literacy instruction in the content areas*. Fort Worth, TX: Harcourt Brace College.

Antonacci, P., & Colasacco, J.M. (1995). Thinking apprenticeships: Cognitive learning environments. In C.N. Hedley, P. Antonacci, & M. Rabinowitz (Eds.), *Thinking and literacy: The mind at work* (pp. 259–274). Hillsdale, NJ: Erlbaum.

Au, K.H. (1993). *Literacy instruction in multicultural settings*. Forth Worth, TX: Harcourt Brace College.

Au, K.H. (1997a). Ownership, literacy achievement, and students of diverse cultural backgrounds. In J.T. Guthrie & A. Wigfield (Eds.), *Reading engagement: Motivating readers through integrated instruction* (pp. 168–182). Newark, DE: International Reading Association.

Au, K.H. (1997b). A socio-cultural model of reading instruction: The Kamehameha elementary education program. In S.A. Stahl & D.A. Hayes (Eds.), *Instructional models in reading* (pp. 181–202). Mahwah, NJ: Erlbaum.

Ausubel, D.P., Novak, J.D., & Hanesian, H. (1978). *Educational psychology: A cognitive view* (2nd ed.). New York: Holt, Rinehart and Winston.

Bakhtin, M. (1981). *The dialogic imagination*. Austin: University of Texas Press.

Ballenger, C. (1997). Social identities, moral narratives, scientific argumentation: Science talk in a bilingual classroom. *Languages and Education, 11*(1), 1–14.

Beach, R. (1992). Adopting multiple stances in conducting literacy research. In R. Beach, J.L. Green, M.L. Kamil, & T. Shanahan (Eds.), *Multidisciplinary perspectives on literacy research* (pp. 91–110). Urbana, IL: National Council of Teachers of English.

Bean, T.W. (2002). Making reading relevant for adolescents. *Educational Leadership, 60*(3), 34–37.

Bean, T.W., Bean, S.K., & Bean, K.F. (1999). The intergenerational conversations and two adolescents' multiple literacies: Implications for redefining content area literacy. *Journal of Adolescent & Adult Literacy, 42,* 438–448.

Beck, I.L., McKeown, M.G., Hamilton, R.L., & Kucan, L. (1997). *Questioning the author: An approach for enhancing student engagement with text.* Newark, DE: International Reading Association.

Bell, N., Grossen, M., & Perret-Clermont, A.N. (1985). Sociocognitive conflict and intellectual growth. In M.W. Berkowitz (Ed.), *Peer conflict and psychological growth* (pp. 41–54). San Francisco: Jossey-Bass.

Berlyne, D.E. (1954). A theory of human curiosity. *The British Journal of Psychology, 45,* 180–191.

Berlyne, D.E. (1960). *Conflict, arousal, and curiosity.* New York: McGraw-Hill.

Berlyne, D.E. (1965). Curiosity and education. In J.D. Krumboltz (Ed.), *Learning and the educational process* (pp. 67–89). Chicago: Rand-McNally.

Berlyne, D.E., & Frommer, F. (1966). Some determinants of the incidence and content of children's questions. *Child Development, 37,* 177–189.

Boggs, S.T. (1972). The meaning of questions and narratives of Hawaiian children. In C.B. Cazden, V.P. John, & D. Hymes (Eds.), *Functions of language in the classroom* (pp. 299–327). New York: Teachers College Press.

Brophy, J. (2004). *Motivating students to learn* (2nd ed.). Mahwah, NJ: Erlbaum.

Brown v. Board of Education, 347 U.S. 483 (1954).

Bruner, J. (1986). *Actual minds, possible worlds.* Cambridge, MA: Harvard University Press.

Buchs, C., Butera, F., Mugny, G., & Darnan, C. (2004). Conflict elaboration and cognitive outcomes. *Theory Into Practice, 43*(1), 23–30.

Busching, B.A., & Slesinger, B.A. (1995). Authentic questions: What do they look like? Where do they lead? *Language Arts, 72*(5), 341–351.

Busching, B.A., & Slesinger, B.A. (2002). *"It's our world too": Socially responsive learners in middle school language arts.* Urbana, IL: National Council of Teachers of English.

Byrnes, J.P. (2003). Cognitive development during adolescence. In G.R. Adams & M.D. Berzonsky (Eds.), *Blackwell's handbook on adolescence* (pp. 227–246). Malden, MA: Blackwell.

Campbell, P.B., & Sanders, J. (1997). Uninformed but interested: Findings of a national survey on gender equity in pre-service teacher education. *Journal of Teacher Education, 48*(1), 68–75.

Carlsen, W.S. (1991). Questioning in classrooms: A sociolinguistic perspective. *Review of Educational Research, 61*(2), 157–178.

Cazden, C.B. (2001). *Classroom discourse: The language and teaching of learning.* Portsmouth, NH: Heinemann.

Chin, C. (2001, April). *Student-generated questions: What they tell us about students' thinking.* Paper presented at the annual meeting of the American Educational Research Association, Seattle, WA.

Chin, C., Brown, D.E., & Bruce, B.C. (2002). Student-generated questions: A meaningful aspect of learning in science. *International Journal of Science Education, 24*(5), 521–549.

Chin, C., & Chia, L. (2004). Problem-based learning: Using students' questions to drive knowledge construction. *Science Teacher*, *88*(5), 707–729.

Chin, C., & Kayalvizhi, G. (2002). Posing problems for open investigations: What questions do pupils ask? *Research in Science & Technological Education*, *20*(2), 269–287.

Chinn, C.A., & Brewer, W.F. (1993). The role of anomalous data in knowledge acquisition: A theoretical framework and implications for science instruction. *Review of Educational Research*, *63*(1), 1–49.

Chinn, C.A., & Malhotra, B.A. (2002). Children's responses to anomalous scientific data: How is conceptual change impeded? *Journal of Educational Psychology*, *94*, 327–343.

Christensen, C.R. (1987). *Teaching and the case method*. Boston: Harvard Business School Press.

Ciardiello, A.V. (1990). *Effects of training models and prior knowledge on student question generation and processes in social studies*. Unpublished doctoral dissertation, Fordham University.

Ciardiello, A.V. (1993). Training students to ask reflective questions. *The Clearing House*, *66*(5), 312–314.

Ciardiello, A.V. (1998). Did you ask a good question today? Alternative cognitive and metacognitive strategies. *Journal of Adolescent & Adult Literacy*, *42*(3), 210–219.

Ciardiello, A.V. (2001). Tolerance and forgiveness: An interdisciplinary lesson on civic efficacy. *Social Studies and the Young Learner*, *14*(1), 26–29.

Ciardiello, A.V. (2003). "To wander and wonder": Pathways to literacy and inquiry through question-finding. *Journal of Adolescent & Adult Literacy*, *47*(3), 228–239.

Ciardiello, A.V. (2004). Democracy's young heroes: An instructional model of critical literacy practices. *The Reading Teacher*, *58*(2), 138–147.

Ciardiello, S. (2003). Meet them in The Lab: Using hip-hop music therapy groups with adolescents in residential settings. In N.E. Sullivan, E.S. Mesbur, N.C. Lang, D. Goodman, & L. Mitchell (Eds.), *Social work with groups: Social justice through personal, community, & societal change* (pp. 103–115). New York: Haworth.

Clement, J.J., & Steinberg, M.S. (2002). Step-wise evolution of mental models of electric circuits: A "learn-aloud" case study. *The Journal of the Learning Sciences*, *11*(4), 389–542.

Cobb, P. (2005). Where is the mind? A coordination of sociocultural and cognitive constructivist perspectives. In C.T. Fosnot (Ed.), *Constructivism: Theory, perspectives, and practices* (2nd ed., pp. 39–57). New York: Teachers College Press.

Cobb, P., & Hodge, L.L. (2002). A relational perspective on issues of cultural diversity and equity as they play out in the mathematics classroom. *Mathematical Thinking and Learning*, *4*(2/3), 249–284.

Cohen, R. (2002). *Dear Mrs. Roosevelt: Letters from children of the Great Depression*. Durham, NC: University of North Carolina Press.

Cole, M. (1996). *Cultural psychology: A once and future discipline*. Cambridge, MA: Belknap.

Cole, M., & Griffin, P. (1986). A sociohistorical approach to remediation. In S. de Castell, A. Luke, & K. Egan (Eds.), *Literacy, society, and schooling: A reader* (pp. 110–131). New York: Cambridge University Press.

Costa, J., Caldeira, H., Gallastegui, J., & Otero, J. (2000). An analysis of question-asking on scientific texts explaining natural phenomena. *Journal of Research in Science Teaching*, *37*(6), 602–614.

Csikszentmihalyi, M. (1990). *Flow: The psychology of optimal experience*. New York: Harper & Row.

Davey, B., & McBride, S. (1986). Effects of question-generation training on reading comprehension. *Journal of Educational Psychology*, *78*(4), 256–262.

Davis, J. (2001). Conceptual change. In M. Orey (Ed.), *Emerging perspectives on learning, teaching, and technology* [E-book]. Retrieved April 14, 2003, from http://www.coe.uga.edu/epltt/Conceptual Change.htm

Delpit, L. (1995). *Other people's children: Cultural conflict in the classroom*. New York: The New Press.

Dewey, J. (1913). *Interest and effort in education*. Boston: Houghton Mifflin.

Dewey, J. (1916). *Democracy and education*. New York: Macmillan.

Dewey, J. (1938). *Logic: The theory of inquiry*. New York: Henry Holt.

Dewey, J. (1991). *How we think*. Buffalo, NY: Prometheus. (Original work published 1910)

Dillon, D.R. (2000). *Kids insight: Reconsidering how to meet the literacy needs of all students*. Newark, DE: International Reading Association.

Dillon, D.R., & Moje, E.B. (1998). Listening to the talk of adolescent girls: Lessons about literacy, school, and life. In D.E. Alvermann, K.A. Hinchman, D.W. Moore, S.F. Phelps, & D.R. Waff (Eds.), *Re-conceptualizing the literacies in adolescents' lives* (pp. 193–233). Mahwah, NJ: Erlbaum.

Dillon, D.R., & O'Brien, D.G. (2002). *Motivation module: Minnesota Reading Excellence Act*. Retrieved October 8, 2004, from http://www.education.umn.edu/CI/MREA/Motivation?motivMOD.html

Dillon, D.R., O'Brien, D.G., & Volkmann, M. (2001). Reading, writing, and talking to get work done in biology. In E.B. Moje & D.G. O'Brien (Eds.), *Constructions of literacy: Studies of teaching and learning in and out of secondary schools* (pp. 51–75). Hillsdale, NJ: Erlbaum.

Dillon, J.T. (1982). The multidisciplinary study of questioning. *Journal of Educational Psychology, 74*(2), 147–165.

Dillon, J.T. (1988). The remedial status of student questioning. *Journal of Curriculum Studies, 20*(3), 197–210.

Dillon, J.T. (1998). Theory and practice of student questioning. In S.A. Karabenick (Ed.), *Strategic help seeking: Implications for learning and teaching* (pp. 171–193). Mahwah, NJ: Erlbaum.

Doise, W., & Mugny, G. (1984). *The social development of the intellect*. New York: Pergamon.

Dole, J. (2000). Readers, texts, and conceptual change learning. *Reading & Writing Quarterly, 16*(2), 99–118.

Dole, J.A., & Sinatra, G.H. (1998). Re-conceptualizing change in the cognitive construction of knowledge. *Educational Psychologist, 33*(2/3), 109–128.

Domizi, D.P. (2003). Lesson plan: History and conceptual change. Retrieved March 23, 2005, from http://itstudio.coe.uga.edu/ebook/LessonPlans/Spring02/domizi.html

Donaldson, M. (1978). *Children's minds*. New York: W.W. Norton.

Donovan, M., & Bransford, J. (2005). *How students learn: History, mathematics, and science in the classroom*. Washington, DC: National Academies Press.

Do our kids feel safe? One year after Columbine, thought-provoking questions and answers from students across America. (2000, April 16). *USA Weekend*. Retrieved July 4, 2006, from http://www.usaweekend.com/00_issues/000416/000416teens_index.html

Dreyfus, A., Jungwirth, E., & Eliovitch, R. (1990). Applying the "cognitive conflict" strategy for conceptual change—some implications, difficulties, and problems. *Science Education, 74*(5), 555–569.

Dudley-Marling, C. (1997). *Living with uncertainty: The messy reality of classroom practice*. Portsmouth, NH: Heinemann.

Eccles, J.S., & Roeser, R.W. (2003). School as developmental context. In G.R. Adams & M.D. Berzonsky (Eds.), *Blackwell's handbook on adolescence* (pp. 129–148). Malden, MA: Blackwell.

Edwards, B., & Davis, B. (1997). Learning from classroom questions and answers: Teachers' uncertainties about children's language. *Journal of Literacy Research, 29*(4), 471–505.

Egan, K. (1997). *The educated mind: How cognitive tools shape our understanding*. Chicago: University of Chicago Press.

Einstein, A., & Infeld, L. (1938). *The evolution of physics*. New York: Simon & Schuster.

Elkins, J., & Luke, A. (1999). Redefining adolescent literacies. *Journal of Adolescent & Adult Literacy, 43*, 212–215.

Fecho, B. (1998). Crossing boundaries of race in a critical literacy classroom. In D.E. Alvermann, K.A. Hinchman, D.W. Moore, S.F. Phelps, & D.R. Waff (Eds.), *Re-conceptualizing the literacies in adolescents' lives* (pp. 75–101). Mahwah, NJ: Erlbaum.

Fecho, B. (2000). Developing critical mass: Teacher education and critical inquiry pedagogy. *Journal of Teacher Education, 51*(3), 194–199.

Festinger, L. (1957). *A theory of cognitive dissonance*. Evanston, IL: Row, Peterson.

Fischbein, E. (1987). *Intuition in science and mathematics: An educational approach*. Dordrecht, Netherlands: Reidel.

Flower, L., Long, E., & Higgins, L. (2000). *Learning to rival: A literate practice for intercultural inquiry.* Mahwah, NJ: Erlbaum.

Flowerday, T., Schraw, G., & Stevens, J. (2004). The role of choice and interest in reader engagement. *Journal of Experimental Education, 72*(2), 93–114.

Freeman, J.G., McPhail, J.C., & Berndt, J.A. (2002). Sixth graders' views of activities that do and do not help them learn. *The Elementary School Journal, 102*(4), 335–347.

Freire, P. (1994). *Pedagogy of hope.* New York: Continuum.

Gardner, H. (1991). *The unschooled mind: How children think and how schools should teach.* New York: Basic.

Gardner, H. (2004). *Changing minds: The art and science of changing our own and other people's minds.* Boston: Harvard Business School Press.

Garner, R., Brown, R., Sanders, S., & Menke, D.J. (1992). "Seductive details" and learning from text. In K.A. Renninger, S. Hidi, & A. Krapp (Eds.), *The role of interest in learning and development* (pp. 239–253). Hillsdale, NJ: Erlbaum.

Gee, J.P. (1990). *Social linguistics and literacies: Ideology in discourses.* Bristol, PA: Falmer.

Gee, J.P. (2000–2001). Identity as an analytic lens for research in education. In W.G. Segato (Ed.), *Review of research in education* (pp. 99–125). Washington, DC: American Educational Research Association.

Gee, J.P. (2003). *What video games have to teach us about learning and literacy.* New York: Palgrave Macmillan.

Getzels, J.W. (1979). Problem-finding and research in educational administration. In G.L. Immelgart & W.L. Boyd (Eds.), *Problem-finding in educational administration* (pp. 1–22). Lexington, MA: D.C. Heath.

Glachan, M., & Light, P. (1982). Peer interaction and learning: Can two wrongs make a right? In G. Butterworth & P. Light (Eds.), *Social cognition: Studies of the development of understanding* (pp. 238–263). Chicago: University of Chicago Press.

Goody, E.N. (1978). Toward a theory of questions. In E.N. Goody (Ed.), *Questions and politeness: Strategies in social interaction* (pp. 17–43). New York: Cambridge University Press.

Goos, M. (2004). Learning mathematics in a classroom community of inquiry. *Journal for Research in Mathematics Education, 35*(4), 258–291.

Gordon, M. (1991). Counterintuitive instances encourage mathematical thinking. *Mathematics Teacher, 84*(7), 511–515.

Gottfried, A.E., Fleming, J.S., & Gottfried, A.W. (2001). Continuity of academic motivation from childhood through late adolescence. *Journal of Educational Psychology, 93*(1), 3–13.

Graeber, A.C., & Campbell, P.F. (1993). Misconceptions about multiplication and division. *The Arithmetic Teacher, 40*(7), 408–411.

Graesser, A.C., & McMahen, C.L. (1993). Anomalous information triggers questions when adults solve quantitative problems and comprehend stories. *Journal of Educational Psychology, 85*, 136–151.

Graesser, A.C., & Olde, B.A. (2003). How does one know whether a person understands a device? The quality of the questions the person asks when the device breaks down. *Journal of Educational Psychology, 95*(3), 524–536.

Greenleaf, C.L, Schoenbach, R., Csiko, C., & Mueller, F.L. (2001). Apprenticing adolescent readers to academic literacy. *Harvard Educational Review, 71*(1), 79–129.

Guthrie, J.T. (2001, March). Contexts for engagement and motivation in reading. *Reading Online, 4*(8). Retrieved October 29, 2003, from http://www.readingonline.org/articles/art_index.asp?HREF=/articles/handbook/guthrie/index.html

Guthrie, J.T., & Wigfield, A. (2000). Engagement and motivation in reading. In M.L. Kamil, P.B. Mosenthal, P.D. Pearson, & R. Barr (Eds.), *Handbook of reading research* (Vol. 3, pp. 403–422). Mahwah, NJ: Erlbaum.

Gutierrez, K., Rymes, B., & Larsen, J. (1995). Script, counterscript, and underlife in the classroom: James Brown versus Brown v. Board of Education. *Harvard Educational Review, 65*(3), 445–471.

Guzzetti, B.J. (2001). Texts and talk: The role of gender in learning physics. In E.B. Moje & D.G. O'Brien (Eds.), *Constructions of literacy: Studies of teaching and learning in and out of secondary schools* (pp. 125–146). Mahwah, NJ: Erlbaum.

Guzzetti, B.J., Snyder, T.E., Glass, G.V., & Gamas, W.S. (1993). Promoting conceptual change in science: A comparative meta-analysis of instructional interventions from reading education and science education. *Reading Research Quarterly, 28,* 116–159.

Guzzetti, B.J., & Williams, W.O. (1996). Gender, text, and discussion: Examining intellectual safety in the science classroom. *Journal of Research in Science Teaching, 33*(1), 5–20.

Hartnett, P., & Gelman, R. (1998). Early understanding of numbers: Paths or barriers to the construction of new understandings? *Learning and Instruction, 8*(4), 341–374.

Hatano, G., & Inagaki, K. (2003). When is conceptual change intended? A sociocultural view. In G.M. Sinatra & P.R. Pintrich (Eds.), *Intentional conceptual change* (pp. 407–427). Mahwah, NJ: Erlbaum.

Heath, S.B. (1982). Questioning at home and at school: A comparative study. In G. Spindler (Ed.), *Doing the ethnography of schooling: Educational anthropology in action* (pp. 102–131). New York: Holt, Rinehart and Winston.

Heath, S.B. (1991). The sense of being literate: Historical and cross-cultural features. In R. Barr, M.L. Kamil, P. Mosenthal, & P.D. Pearson (Eds.), *Handbook of reading research* (Vol. 2, pp. 3–25). White Plains, NY: Longman.

Herbeck, J., & Beier, C. (2003). A critical literacy curriculum: Helping pre-service teachers to understand reading and writing as emancipatory acts. *Thinking Classroom, 4*(4), 37–42.

Hidi, S., & Harackiewicz, J.M. (2000). Motivating the academically unmotivated: A critical issue for the 21st century. *Review of Educational Research, 70*(2), 151–179.

Hidi, S., Weiss, J., Berndorff, D., & Nolan, J. (1998). The role of gender, instruction, and a cooperative learning technique in science education across formal and informal settings. In L. Hoffmann, A. Krapp, K.A. Renninger, & J. Baumert (Eds.), *Interest and learning: Proceeding of the Seeon conference on interest and gender* (pp. 215–227). Kiel, Germany: IPN.

Hofstadter, R. (1973). *The American political tradition and the people who made it.* New York: Alfred A. Knopf.

Holton, G. (1978). *The scientific imagination: Case studies.* New York: Cambridge University Press.

Huber, R.A., & Moore, C.J. (2001). A model for extending hands-on science to be inquiry based. *School Science and Mathematics, 101*(1), 32–42.

Hudicourt-Barnes, J. (2003). The use of argumentation in Haitian Creole science classrooms. *Harvard Educational Review, 73*(1), 73–93.

Hunt, D.E. (1971). Toward a history of intrinsic motivation. In H.I. Day, D.E. Berlyne, & D.E. Hunt (Eds.), *Intrinsic motivation: A new direction in education* (pp. 1–31). Toronto: Holt, Rinehart and Winston of Canada.

Ivey, G., & Broaddus, K. (2001). "Just plain reading": A survey of what students want to read in middle school classrooms. *Reading Research Quarterly, 36,* 350–377.

James, W. (1900). *Talks to teachers on psychology and to students on some of life's ideals.* New York: Henry Holt.

Johnson, D.W., & Johnson, R.T. (1992). Encouraging thinking through constructive controversy. In N. Davidson & T. Worsham (Eds.), *Enhancing thinking through cooperative learning* (pp. 120–138). New York: Teachers College Press.

Johnson, S. (2005a). *Everything bad is good for you: How today's popular culture is actually making us smarter.* New York: Riverhead.

Johnson, S. (2005b, April 24). Watching TV makes you smarter. *New York Times Magazine,* 55–59.

John-Steiner, V., & Mahn, H. (1996). Sociocultural approaches to learning and development: A Vygotskian framework. *Educational Psychologist, 31*(3/4), 191–206.

Jones, D.C., Vigfusdottir, T.H., & Lee, Y. (2004). Body image and the appearance culture among adolescent girls and boys: An examination of friend conversations, peer criticism, appearance magazines, and the internalization of appearance ideals. *Journal of Adolescent Research, 19*(3), 323–339.

Kamil, M.L. (2003). *Adolescents and literacy: Reading for the 21st century.* Washington, DC: Alliance for Excellent Education.

King, A. (1992). Facilitating elaborative learning and guided student-generated questioning. *Educational Psychologist, 27*(1), 111–126.

King, A. (2002). Structuring peer interaction to promote high-level cognitive processing. *Theory Into Practice, 41*(1), 33–39.

King, A., & Rosenshine, B. (1993). Effects of guided cooperative questioning on children's knowledge construction. *Journal of Experimental Education, 61*(2), 127–148.

Kohl, H. (2003). *Stupidity and tears: Teaching and language in troubled times.* New York: The New Press.

Krajcik, J., Blumenfeld, P., Marx, R., & Soloway, E. (2000). In J. Minstrell & E.H. van Zee (Eds.), *Inquiry into inquiry learning and teaching science* (pp. 284–315). Washington, DC: American Association for the Advancement of Science.

Kruglanski, A.W., & Webster, D.M. (1996). Motivated closing of the mind: "Seizing" and "freezing." *Psychological Review, 103*(2), 263–283.

Labov, W. (1972). *Language in the inner city: Studies in the Black English vernacular.* Philadelphia: University of Pennsylvania Press.

Ladson-Billings, G. (1995). Making mathematics meaningful in multicultural contexts. In W. Secada, E. Fennema, & L.B. Adajian (Eds.), *New directions for equity in mathematics education* (pp. 126–145). New York: Cambridge University Press & National Council of Teachers of Mathematics.

Layman, J.W. (1996). *Inquiry and learning: Realizing science standards in the classroom.* New York: College Entrance Examination Board.

Lee, C.D. (1993). *Signifying as a scaffold for literary interpretation: The pedagogical implications of an African American discourse genre* (NCTE Research Report No. 26). Urbana: IL: National Council of Teachers of English.

Lee, C.D. (2000). Signifying in the zone of proximal development. In C.D. Lee & P. Smagorinsky (Eds.), *Vygotskian perspectives in literacy research* (pp. 191–221). New York: Cambridge University Press.

Leistyna, P., Woodrum, A., & Sherblom, S. (Eds.). (1996). *Breaking free: The transformative power of critical pedagogy.* Cambridge, MA: Harvard Educational Review.

Lemke, J.L. (1990). *Talking science: Language, learning, and values.* Norwood, NJ: Ablex.

Lewison, M., Flint, A.S., & Van Sluys, K. (2002). Taking on critical literacy: The journey of newcomers and novices. *Language Arts, 79*(5), 382–390.

Limon, M. (2002). Conceptual change in history. In M. Limon & L. Mason (Eds.), *Reconsidering conceptual change: Issues in theory and practice* (pp. 259–289). London: Kluwer Academic.

Limon, M., & Carretero, M. (1999). Conflicting data and conceptual change in history experts. In W. Schnotz, S. Vosniadou, & M. Carretero (Eds.), *New perspectives in conceptual change* (pp. 137–141). New York: Pergamon.

Lindfors, J.W. (1999). *Children's inquiry.* New York: Teachers College Press.

Lloyd, C.V. (2003). Song lyrics as texts to develop critical literacy. *Reading Online, 6*(10). Available: http://www.readingonline.org/articles/art_index.asp? HREF=lloyd/index.html

Loewenstein, G. (1994). The psychology of curiosity: A review and reinterpretation. *Psychological Bulletin, 116*(1), 75–98.

Long, E., Peck, W.C., & Baskins, J.A. (2002). STRUGGLE: A literate practice supporting life-project planning. In G. Hull & K. Schultz (Eds.), *School's out! Bridging out-of-school literacies with classroom practice* (pp. 131–160). New York: Teachers College Press.

Luke, A. (2000). Critical literacy in Australia: A matter of content and standpoint. *Journal of Adolescent & Adult Literacy, 43,* 448–461

Luke, A., & Freebody, P. (1997). Shaping the social practices of reading. In S. Muspratt, A. Luke, & P. Freebody (Eds.), *Constructing critical literacies: Teaching and learning textual practice* (pp. 185–225). Cresskill, NJ: Hampton.

Manguel, A. (1996). *A history of reading*. New York: Viking.

Manzo, A. (1969). The ReQuest procedure. *Journal of Reading, 13*(2), 123–127.

Martin, D.B. (2000). *Mathematics success and failure among African-American youth: The roles of sociohistorical context, community forces, school influence, and individual agency*. Mahwah, NJ: Erlbaum.

Martinello, M.L. (1998). Learning to question for inquiry. *The Educational Forum, 62*, 164–171.

Martlett, P.B., & Gordon, C.J. (2004). The use of alternative texts in physical education. *Journal of Adolescent & Adult Literacy, 48*, 226–237.

Maskill, R., & deJesus, H.P. (1997). Pupils' questions, alternative frameworks, and the design of science teaching. *International Journal of Science Education, 19*(7), 781–799.

Massialas, B.G., & Zevin, J. (1983). *Teaching creatively: Learning through discovery*. Malabar, FL: Robert E. Krieger Publishing.

McCarthy, T.L., & Watahomigie, L.J. (1998). Language and literacy in American Indian and Alaska Native communities. In B. Perez (Ed.), *Sociocultural contexts of language and literacy* (pp. 69–98). Mahwah, NJ: Erlbaum.

McLaughlin, M., & DeVoogd, G. (2004). Critical literacy as comprehension: Extending reader response. *Journal of Adolescent & Adult Literacy, 48*, 52–62.

McMahon, S.I. (1996). Book Club: The influence of a Vygotskian perspective on a literature-based reading program. In L. Dixon-Krauss (Ed.), *Vygotsky in the classroom: Mediated literacy instruction & assessment* (pp. 59–76). White Plains, NY: Longman.

Mehan, H. (1979). *Learning lessons: Social organization in the classroom*. Cambridge, MA: Harvard University Press.

Meltzer, J., Smith, N.C., & Clark, H. (2001). *Adolescent literacy resources: Linking research and practice*. Portsmouth, NH: The Center for Resource Management.

Merenluoto, K., & Lehtinen, E. (2002). Conceptual change in mathematics: Understanding the real numbers. In M. Limon & L. Mason (Eds.), *Reconsidering conceptual change: Issues in theory and practice* (pp. 233–258). Dordrecht, Netherlands: Kluwer Academic.

Mestre, J. (1994). Cognitive aspects of learning and teaching science. In S.J. Fitzsimmons & L.C. Kerpelman (Eds.), *Teacher enhancement for elementary and secondary science and mathematics: Status, issues, and problems*. Cambridge, MA: Abt Associates Center for Science & Technology Policy Studies.

Mishler, E.G. (1975). Studies in dialogue and discourse II: Types of discourse initiated by and sustained through questioning. *Journal of Psycholinguistic Research, 4*, 99–121.

Mishler, E.G. (1978). Studies in dialogue and discourse III: Utterance structure and utterance function in interrogative sequences. *Journal of Psycholinguistic Research, 7*(4), 279–305.

Mitchell, M. (1993). Situational interest: Its multifaceted structure in the secondary school mathematics classroom. *Journal of Educational Psychology, 85*(3), 424–436.

Moll, L. (1992). Literacy research in community and classrooms: A socio-cultural approach. In R. Beach, J.L. Green, M.L. Kamil, & T. Shanahan (Eds.), *Multidisciplinary perspectives in literacy research* (pp. 211–244). Urbana, IL: National Council of Teachers of English.

Monson, R.J., & Monson, M.P. (1994). Literacy as inquiry: An interview with Jerome Harste. *The Reading Teacher, 47*, 518–521.

Moore, D.W., Bean, T.W., Birdyshaw, D., & Rycik, J.A. (1999). *Adolescent literacy: A position statement for the Commission on Adolescent Literacy of the International Reading Association*. Newark, DE: International Reading Association.

Moses, R., & Cobb, C. (2001). *Radical equations: Math literacy and civil rights*. Boston: Beacon.

Moss, B., & Hendershot, J. (2002). Explaining sixth graders' selection of nonfiction trade books. *The Reading Teacher, 56*, 6–17.

Moss, J. (2004). Pipes, tubes, and breakers: New approaches to teaching the rational number system. In M.S. Donovan & J.D. Bransford (Eds.), *How students learn: History, mathematics, and science in the classroom* (pp. 309–349). Washington, DC: National Academies Press.

Napper-Owen, G.E., Kovar, S.K, Ermler, K.L., & Mehrhof, J.H. (1999). Curricula equity in required ninth-grade physical education. *Journal of Teaching in Physical Education, 19*(1), 2–21.

National Council for the Social Studies. (1994). *Expectations of excellence: Curriculum standards for the social studies.* Washington, DC: Author.

National Institute of Child Health and Human Development. (2000). *Report of the National Reading Panel. Teaching children to read: An evidence-based assessment of the scientific research literature on reading and its implications for reading instruction* (NIH Publication No. 00-4769). Washington, DC: U.S. Government Printing Office.

National Research Council. (1996). *National science education standards.* Washington, DC: National Academy Press.

National Research Council. (2000). *Inquiry and the national science education standards.* Washington, DC: National Academy Press.

Newman, D., Crowder, E., & Morrison, D. (1993). *Scientific sense-making in elementary classroom conversations.* (ERIC Document Reproduction Service No. ED 377 031)

Ni, Y., & Zhou, Y.-D. (2005). Teaching and learning fraction and rational numbers: The origins and implications of whole number bias. *Educational Psychologist, 40*(1), 27–52.

Norfleet, B. (2001). *When we liked Ike: Looking for postwar America.* New York: W.W. Norton.

Nussbaum, J., & Novick, S. (1982). Alternative frameworks, conceptual conflict and accommodation toward a principled teaching strategy. *Instructional Science, 11,* 183–200.

Nystrand, M., Gamoran, A., Kachur, R., & Prendergast, C. (1997). *Opening dialogue: Understanding the dynamics of language and learning in the English classroom.* New York: Teachers College Press.

Nystrand, M., Wu, L.L., Gamoran, A., Zeiser, S., & Long, D.A. (2003). Questions in time: Investigating the structure and dynamics of unfolding classroom discourse. *Discourse Processes, 35*(2), 135–198.

Oldfather, P., & Dahl, K. (1994). Toward a social constructivist reconceptualization of intrinsic motivation for literacy learning. *Journal of Reading Behavior, 26*(2), 139–157.

Oldfather, P., & Thomas, S. (1998). What does it mean when high school teachers participate in collaborative research with students on literacy motivations? *Teachers College Record, 99*(4), 647–691.

Oliver, K.I., & Lalik, R. (2000). *Bodily knowledge: Learning about equity and justice with adolescent girls.* New York: Peter Lang.

Oliver, K.I., & Lalik, R. (2004a). Critical inquiry on the body in girls' physical education classes: A critical poststructural perspective. *Journal of Teaching in Physical Education, 23*(2), 162–195.

Oliver, K.I., & Lalik, R. (2004b). "The Beauty Walk, this ain't my topic": Learning about critical inquiry with adolescent girls. *Journal of Curriculum Studies, 36*(5), 555–586.

Olsher, G., & Dreyfus, A. (1999). Biotechnologies as a context for enhancing junior high students' ability to ask meaningful questions about abstract biological processes. *International Journal of Science Education, 21*(2), 137–153.

Opdal, P.M. (2001). Curiosity, wonder, and education seen as perspective development. *Studies in Philosophy and Education, 20*(4), 331–344.

Palmer, P. (1998). *The courage to learn: Exploring the inner landscape of a teacher's life.* San Francisco: Jossey-Bass.

Perez, B., & Torres-Guzman, M. (1992). *Learning in two worlds: An integrated Spanish/English biliteracy approach.* New York: Longman.

Perret-Clermont, A.N. (1980). *Social interaction and cognitive development in children.* London: Academic.

Piaget, J. (1977). *The development of thought: Equilibration of cognitive structures.* New York: Viking.

Piaget, J. (1985). *The equilibration of cognitive structures: The central problem of intellectual development.* Chicago: University of Chicago Press.

Pintrich, P.R., Marx, R.W., & Boyle, R.A. (1993). Beyond cold conceptual change: The role of motivational beliefs and classroom contextual factors in the process of conceptual change. *Review of Educational Research, 63*(2), 167–199.

Pollan, M. (2001). *The botany of desire: A plant's eye view of the world.* New York: Random House.

Posner, G.J., Strike, K.A., Hewson, P.W., & Gertzog, W.A. (1982). Accommodation of a scientific conception: Toward a theory of conceptual change. *Science Education, 66,* 211–227.

Postman, N., & Weingartner, C. (1969). *Teaching as a subversive activity.* New York: Dell.

Pressley, M., Duke, N.K., & Boling, E.C. (2004). The educational science and scientifically-based instruction we need: Lessons from reading research and policy making. *Harvard Educational Review, 74*(1), 30–61.

Ramirez, A. (2006, July 5). Black collectors hate and buy them: Surprising popularity for Jim Crow items. *New York Times,* p. B3.

Resnick, L.B., Nesher, P., Leonard, F., Magone, M., Omanson, S., & Peled, I. (1989). Conceptual bases of arithmetic errors: The case for decimal fractions. *Journal of Research for Mathematics Education, 20*(1), 8–27.

Rex, L.A. (2001). The remaking of a high school reader. *Reading Research Quarterly, 36,* 288–316.

Risko, V.J., & Feldman, N. (1986). Teaching young remedial readers to generate questions as they read. *Reading Horizons, 27,* 54–64.

Rop, C.J. (2003). Spontaneous inquiry questions in high school chemistry classrooms: Perceptions of a group of motivated learners. *International Journal of Science Education, 25*(1), 13–33.

Rose, M. (1989). *Lives on the boundary: A moving account of the struggles and achievements of America's educationally underprepared.* New York: Penguin.

Rosenshine, B., Meister, C., & Chapman, S. (1996). Teaching students to generate questions: A review of the intervention studies. *Review of Educational Research, 66*(2), 181–221.

Roth, K. (2001, February). *Student-focused curriculum materials development: The "food for plants" story.* Retrieved April 6, 2005, from http:/www.project2061.org/cgi-bin/print.pl

Roth, W.M. (1995). *Authentic school science: Knowing and learning in open-inquiry science laboratories.* Dordrecht, Netherlands: Kluwer Academic.

Ryan, R.M., & Deci, E.R. (2000). Self-determination theory and the facilitation of intrinsic motivation, social development, and well-being. *American Psychologist, 55,* 68–78.

Sadker, M., & Sadker, D. (1994). *Failing at fairness: How America's schools cheat girls.* New York: Charles Scribner's Sons.

Scardamalia, M., & Bereiter, C. (1992). Text-based and knowledge-based questioning by children. *Cognition and Instruction, 9*(3), 177–199.

Schank, R.C. (1979). Interestingness: Controlling inferences. *Artificial Intelligence, 12*(3), 273–297.

Schank, R.C. (1988). *The creative attitude: Learning to ask and answer the right questions.* New York: Macmillan.

Schneps, M.H., & Sadler, P.M. (1988). *A private universe: An insightful lesson on how we learn* [Motion picture]. Santa Monica, CA: Pyramid Films.

Schraw, G., Flowerday, T., & Lehman, S. (2001). Increasing situational interest in the classroom. *Educational Psychology Review, 13*(3), 211–224.

Schunk, D.H., & Zimmerman, B.J. (1997). Developing self-efficacious readers and writers: The role of social and self-regulatory processes. In J.T. Guthrie & A. Wigfield (Eds.), *Reading engagement: Motivating readers through integrated instruction* (pp. 34–50). Newark, DE: International Reading Association.

Schwartz, B.B., Neuman, Y., & Biezuner, S. (2000). Two wrongs may make a right...if they argue together! *Cognition and Instruction, 18*(4), 461–494.

Scribner, S., & Cole, M. (1981). *The psychology of literacy.* Cambridge, MA: Harvard University Press.

Shanahan, C. (2004). Teaching science through literacy. In T.L. Jetton & J.A. Dole (Eds.), *Adolescent literacy and practice* (pp. 75–93). New York: Guilford.

Shepardson, D.P., & Moje, E.B. (1999). The role of anomalous data in restructuring fourth graders' frameworks for understanding electric circuits. *International Journal of Science Education, 21*(1), 77–94.

Shodell, M. (1995). The question-driven classroom: Student questions as course curriculum in biology. *American Biology Teacher, 57,* 278–281.

Shor, I. (1987). Educating the educators: A Freirean approach to the crisis in teacher education. In I. Shor (Ed.), *Freire in the classroom: A sourcebook for liberatory teaching* (pp. 7–32). Portsmouth, NH: Boynton/Cook.

Shor, I. (1992). *Empowering education: Critical teaching for social change.* Chicago: University of Chicago Press.

Shrigley, R. (1987). Discrepant events: Why they fascinate students. *Science and Children, 24,* 24–25.

Simpson, A. (1996). Critical questions: Whose questions? *The Reading Teacher, 50,* 118–127.

Sinatra, G.M., Southerland, S.A., McConaughy, F., & Demastes, J.W. (2003). Intentions and beliefs in students' understanding and acceptance of biological evolution. *Journal of Research in Science Teaching, 40*(5), 510–528.

Soltis, J.F. (1981). Education and the concept of knowledge. In J.F. Soltis (Ed.), *Philosophy and education: Eightieth yearbook of the National Society for the Study of Education* (pp. 95–113). Chicago: University of Chicago Press.

Stafylidou, S., & Vosniadou, S. (2004). The development of students' understanding of the numerical value of fractions. *Learning and Instruction, 14,* 503–518.

Stavy, R., Tsamir, P., & Tirosh, D. (2002). Intuitive rules: The case of "More A–More B." In M. Limon & L. Mason (Eds.), *Reconsidering conceptual change: Issues in theory and practice* (pp. 217–231). Dordrecht, Netherlands: Kluwer Academic.

Stephens, J. (1920). *Irish fairy tales.* New York: Macmillan.

Stevens, C. (1970). Where do the children play? On *Tea for the Tillerman* [CD]. San Francisco: A&M.

Stevens, L.P. (2002). Making the road by walking: The transition from content area literacy to adolescent literacy. *Reading Research and Instruction, 41*(3), 276–278.

Strickland, D.S., & Alvermann, D.E. (2004). Learning and teaching literacy in grades 4–12: Issues and challenges. In D.S. Strickland & D.E. Alvermann (Eds.), *Bridging the literacy achievement gap, grades 4–12* (pp. 1–14). New York: Teachers College Press.

Strike, K.A., & Posner, G.J. (1985). A conceptual change view of learning and understanding. In L.H. West & A.L. Pines (Eds.), *Cognitive structure and conceptual change* (pp. 211–231). Orlando, FL: Academic.

Strike, K.A., & Posner, G.J. (1992). A revisionist theory of conceptual change. In R.A. Duschl & R.J. Hamilton (Eds.), *Philosophy of science, cognitive psychology, and educational theory and practice* (pp. 147–176). Albany: State University of New York Press.

Suchman, J.R. (1969). *Developing inquiry.* Chicago: Science Research Associates.

Swafford, J., & Bryan, J.K. (2000). Instructional strategies for promoting conceptual change: Supporting middle school students. *Reading and Writing Quarterly, 16*(2), 139–161.

Taboada, A., & Guthrie, J.T. (2006). Contributions of student questioning and prior knowledge to construction of knowledge from reading information texts. *Journal of Literacy Research, 38*(1), 1–35.

Torney-Purta, J. (1994). Dimensions of adolescents' reasoning about political and historical issues: Ontological switches, developmental processes, and situated learning. In M. Carretero & J.F. Voss (Eds.), *Cognitive and instructional processes in history and the social sciences* (pp. 103–122). Hillsdale, NJ: Erlbaum.

Truss, L. (2003). *Eats, shoots & leaves: The zero tolerance approach to punctuation.* New York: Gotham.

Tsai, C.C. (2000). Enhancing science instruction: The use of "conflict maps." *International Journal of Science Education, 22*(3), 285–302.

Vacca, R.T., & Alvermann, D.E. (1998). The crisis in adolescent literacy: Is it real or imagined? *National Association of Secondary School Principals Bulletin, 82,* 4–9.

Vamvakoussi, X., & Vosniadou, S. (2004). Understanding the structure of the set of rational numbers: A conceptual change approach. *Learning and Instruction*, *14*, 453–467.

van der Meij, H. (1998). The great divide between teacher and student questioning. In S.A. Karabenick (Ed.), *Strategic help seeking: Implications for teaching and learning* (pp. 195–218). Mahwah, NJ: Erlbaum.

van der Meij, H., & Dillon, J.T. (1994). Adaptive student questioning and students' verbal ability. *Journal of Experimental Education*, *62*(4), 277–290.

Vosniadou, S., & Verschaffel, L. (2004). Extending the conceptual change approach to mathematics learning and teaching. *Learning and Instruction*, *14*, 445–451.

Vygotsky, L.S. (1978). *Mind in society: The development of higher psychological processes* (M. Cole, V. John-Steiner, S. Scribner, & E. Souberman, Eds. & Trans.). Cambridge, MA: Harvard University Press. (Original work published 1934)

Wade, R.C. (1994). Conceptual change in elementary social studies: A case study of fourth graders' understanding of human rights. *Theory and Research in Social Education*, *22*(1), 74–95.

Warren, B., Ballenger, C., Ogonowski, M., Rosebery, A.S., & Hudicourt-Barnes, J. (2001). Rethinking diversity in learning science: The logic of everyday sense-making. *Journal of Research in Science Teaching*, *38*(5), 529–552.

Warren, B., & Rosebery, A.S. (1996). "This question is just too, too easy!": Students' perspectives on accountability in science. In L. Schauble & R. Glaser (Eds.), *Innovations in learning: New environments for education* (pp. 97–126). Mahwah, NJ: Erlbaum.

Watts, M., Alsop, S., Gould, G., & Walsh, A. (1997). Promoting teachers' constructive reflection: Pupils' questions as critical incidents. *International Journal of Science Education*, *19*, 1025–1037.

Watts, M., Gould, G., & Alsop, S. (1997). Questions of understanding: Categorizing pupils' questions in science. *School Science Review*, *79*(286), 57–63.

Webb, D. (2004). Scooters, skates, and dolls: Toys against delinquency in Milwaukee. *Wisconsin Magazine of History*, *87*, 4–13.

Wells, G. (2000). Dialogic inquiry in education: Building on the legacy of Vygotsky. In B.D. Lee & P. Smagorinsky (Eds.), *Vygotskian perspectives on literacy research: Constructing meaning through collaborative inquiry* (pp. 51–85). New York: Cambridge University Press.

Wells, M.C. (1996). *Literacies lost: When students move from progressive middle schools to a traditional high school*. New York: Teachers College Press.

Wertsch, J.V., & Toma, C. (1995). Discourse and learning in the classroom: A sociocultural approach. In L.P. Steffe & J. Gale (Eds.), *Constructivism in education* (pp. 159–183). Hillsdale, NJ: Erlbaum.

West, L., & Pines, L. (1984). An interpretation of research in "conceptual understanding" within a sources-of-knowledge framework. *Research in Science Education*, *14*, 47–56.

Wigfield, A., Guthrie, J.T., Tonks, S., & Perencevich, K.C. (2004). Children's motivation for reading: Domain specificity and instructional influences. *Journal of Educational Research*, *97*(6), 299–309.

Wigfield, A., & Tonks, S. (2002). Adolescents' expectancies for success and achievement of task values during the middle and high school years. In F. Pajares & T. Urdan (Eds.), *Academic motivation of adolescents* (pp. 53–82). Greenwich, CO: Information Age.

Willis, A.I. (2002). Dissin' and disremembering: Motivation and culturally and linguistically diverse students' literacy learning. *Reading & Writing Quarterly*, *18*(4), 293–319.

Wills, G. (2005). *The rosary: Prayer comes round*. New York: Viking.

Wineburg, S., & Fournier, J. (1994). Contextualized thinking in history. In M. Carretero & J. Voss (Eds.), *Cognitive and instructional processes in history and the social sciences* (pp. 285–308). Hillsdale, NJ: Erlbaum.

Young, J.P. (2001). Displaying practices of masculinity: Critical literacy and social contexts. *Journal of Adolescent & Adult Literacy*, *45*, 4–14.

Zittleman, K., & Sadker, D. (2002–2003). *Teacher education textbooks: The unfinished revolution*. Retrieved September 23, 2004, from http://www.sadker.org/textbooks.htm

Literature Cited

Babbitt, N. (1975). *Tuck everlasting*. New York: Farrar, Straus and Giroux.

Beattle, O., & Geiger, J. (1992). *Buried in ice*. Toronto, ON: Scholastic/Madison.

Browne, A. (2001). *Voices in the park*. New York: Dorling Kendersley.

Chaucer, G. (1978). *The Canterbury tales*. New York: Penguin.

Faulkner, W. (1948). *Intruder in the dust*. New York: Random House.

Frank, O. (1952). *Anne Frank: Diary of a young girl*. New York: Doubleday.

Hoose, P. (2001). *We were there, too! Young people in American history*. New York: Farrar, Straus and Giroux.

Innocenti, R., & Gallez, C. (1990). *Rose Blanche*. New York: Stewart, Tabori & Chang.

Kaufman, B. (1964). *Up the down staircase*. Englewood Cliffs, NJ: Prentice Hall.

Kidd, S.M. (2002). *The secret life of bees*. New York: Penguin.

King, C., & Osborne, L.B. (1997). *Oh, freedom! Kids talk about the civil rights movement with the people who made it happen*. New York: Knopf.

Klass, D. (1994). *California blue*. New York: Scholastic.

Levin, M. (1937). *The old bunch*. New York: Viking.

Lionni, L. (1970). *Fish is fish*. New York: Dragonfly.

Lowry, L. (1993). *The giver*. Boston: Houghton Mifflin.

McCourt, F. (2005). *Teacher man: A memoir*. New York: Scribner.

Miles, M. (1971). *Annie and the old one*. Boston: Atlantic Monthly Press.

Nafisi, A. (2003). *Reading Lolita in Tehran: A memoir in books*. New York: Random House.

Reiss, J. (1972). *The upstairs room*. New York: Crowell.

Rich, A. (2004). *The school among the ruins: Poems 2000–2004*. New York: W.W. Norton.

Rilke, R.M. (1954). *Letters to a young poet* (Trans. M.D. Herder). New York: Norton.

Roth, S. (2001). *Happy Birthday Mr. Kang*. Washington DC: National Geographic Children's Books.

Salinger, J.D. (1951). *The catcher in the rye*. Boston: Little, Brown.

Say, A. (1993). *Grandfather's journey*. Boston: Houghton Mifflin.

Smith, B. (1943). *A tree grows in Brooklyn*. New York: Harper Perennial Modern Classics.

Spinelli, J. (1997). *Wringer*. New York: HarperCollins.

Taylor, M. (1976). *Roll of thunder, hear my cry*. New York: Dial.

Taylor, M. (1987). *The gold Cadillac*. New York: Dial.

Thurber, J. (1945). The Scotty who knew too much. In *The Thurber Carnival*. New York: Harper & Brothers.

Twain, M. (1931). *The adventures of Huckleberry Finn*. New York: International Collectors Library.

Walker, A. (1982). *The color purple*. New York: Washington Square.

Walker, A. (1983). *In search of our mothers' gardens: Womanist prose*. San Diego, CA: Harcourt Brace Jovanovich.

Wiesel, E. (1982). *Night*. New York: Bantam.

Yolen, J. (1990). *The devil's arithmetic*. New York: Puffin.

Photographs and Documents

Bubley, E. (1943). A rest stop for Greyhound bus passengers on the way from Louisville, Kentucky, to Nashville, Tennessee, with separate accommodations for colored passengers. Farm Security Administration, Office of War Information Collection, U.S. Library of Congress, Washington, DC. LC-USZ62-62919. Retrieved July 5, 2006, from http://www.loc.gov/rr/print/list/085_disc.html

Lange, D. (1936). Migrant Mother collection. Prints and Photographs Division, Farm Security Administration, Office of War Information Collection, U.S. Library of Congress, Washington, DC. Retrieved July 17, 2006, from http://www.loc.gov/rr/print/list/128_migm.html

Letter from Elvis Presley fans to President Dwight Eisenhower. Dwight Eisenhower Library, U.S. National Archives, Washington, DC. Retrieved September 3, 2006, from http://www.archives.gov/publications/prologue/images/spring-2004-elvis-letter.jpg

Letter from Elvis Presley to President Richard Nixon. Nixon Presidential Materials holdings, U.S. National Archives, Washington, DC. Retrieved July 4, 2006, from http://www.gwu.edu/~nsarchiv/nsa/elvis/docs/doc1.pdf

Letter to President Reagan, U.S. National Archives, Washington, DC. Retrieved July 4, 2006, from http://www.archives.gov/publications/prologue/spring_2004_childrens.letters.html

Palmer, J.A. (1876). Aunt Betsy's cabin in Aiken, South Carolina. Collection of the New-York Historical Society, New York. Negative number 48099.

Rothstein, A. (1937). World's highest standard of living...There's no way like the American way. Birmingham, AL. Farm Security Administration, Office of War Information Collection, U.S. Library of Congress, Washington, DC. LC-USF3301-002393-M2. Retrieved July 4, 2006, from http://historyproject.ucdavis.edu

Toy lending project in Jackson, Mississippi. Mississippi Department of Archives and History, Mississippi Historical Society, Jackson, Mississippi. Retrieved July 24, 2006, from http://www.mshistory.k12.us/features/feature49/feb6.htm

Vachon, J. (1939). Sign in a beer parlor window. Sisseton, SD. Farm Security Administration, Office of War Information Collection, U.S. Library of Congress, Washington, DC. LC-USF33-1661-M3. Retrieved July 5, 2006, from http://www.loc.gov/rr/print/list/085_disc.html

Westgard, A.L. (1912). Covered wagon with jackrabbit mules encounters an automobile on the trail near Big Springs, Nebraska. U.S. National Archives, Washington, DC. Retrieved July 17, 2006, from http://www.archives.gov/research/american-west/images/042.jpg

INDEX

Note: Page numbers followed by *f* and *t* indicate figures and tables, respectively.

INAGAKI, K., 108
INDETERMINATE LEARNING SITUATIONS, 87
INDIVIDUAL INTEREST, 27
INFELD, L., 98
INITIATION–RESPONSE–EVALUATION, 72, 87
INNER-CITY STUDENTS, 95
INNOCENTI, R., 36, 58
INTELLIGIBILITY, 103–104
INTENTIONAL CONCEPTUAL CHANGE, 109
INTERCULTURAL SOCIAL INQUIRY, 100
INTEREST, STUDENT, 27–31
INTERNALIZED OPPRESSION, 59–61
INTERNATIONAL READING ASSOCIATION (IRA), xiii, xiv, 1–2, 26
INTERROGATIVE MOOD, 8
INTERVIEWS, 37, 58
INTRINSIC MOTIVATION, 6–7, 27
INTRUDER IN THE DUST (FAULKNER), 65
INTUITIONS, 121–124, 126–127
ISLAMIC GOVERNMENT, 57
ITERATIVE NATURE OF GENERATING QUESTIONS, 84
IVEY, G., 27

J

JAMES, W., 27
JOHNSON, D.W., 108
JOHNSON, R.T., 108
JOHNSON, S., 124
JOHN-STEINER, V., 70, 104
JONES, A.B., ix
JONES, D.C., 37
JOURNALS, 19
JUNGWIRTH, E., 106

K

KACHUR, R., 87
KAMIL, M.L., xiv
KAUFMAN, B., 1
KAYALVIZHI, G., 127
KIDD, S.M., 65
KING, A., xii–xiii, 71, 72, 75, 89, 90
KING, C., 65
KLASS, D., 62
KNOWLEDGE: funds of, 70–71; and question-finding implementation, 17; search for, 6; situational nature of, 76; social construction of, 31
KOHL, H., 81
KOVAR, S.K., 62
KRAJCIK, J., 97
KRUGLANSKI, A.W., 109, 110
KUCAN, L., 64

L

THE LAB WORK PROGRAM, 42
LABOV, W., 72
LADSON-BILLINGS, G., 95
LALIK, R., 16, 18, 37, 38, 59, 62, 66
LANGUAGE: and cultural dissonance, 78–79, 80; definition of, 72; effects of history on, 77; and questioning, 72; research on, 72–74
LANGUAGE ARTS: cultural congruence in, 82–84; motivating instruction in, 34–37; regained identity unit of study for, 62–63; skepticism resources in, 128t; social barriers recognition unit in, 58–59
LARSEN, J., 80
LAYMAN, J.W., 34
LEARNING ENVIRONMENT, 18
LEE, C.D., 82, 83
LEE, Y., 37
LEHMAN, S., 29
LEHTINENE, E., 123
LEISTYNA, P., 59
LEMKE, J.L., 84
LEONARD, F., 76, 122
LESSON PLANS, 144–147
LEVIN, M., 90, 154
LEWISON, M., 50
LIBERATION, 56–57
LIGHT, P., 76
LIMON, M., 117, 120
LINCOLN, A., 118–121
LINDFORS, J.W., 11
LIONNI, L., 129
LITERACY: changing nature of, 71; crisis in, xiv; factors affecting, 26; and language functions, 72; liberating process of, 56–57; and motivation, 26–31; resources on, 28t; of slaves, 66; sociocognitive dimensions of, 74–76;

sociocultural dimensions of, 77–78; traditional educational views of, xiv. *See also specific types*
LLOYD, C.V., 42–43
LOEWENSTEIN, G., 5
LONG, D.A., 87
LONG, E., 11, 100
LOWER ACHIEVING STUDENTS, 52–53
LOWRY, L., 62
LUKE, A., 18, 46, 49, 53

M

MAGONE, M., 76, 122
MAHN, H., 70, 104
MANGUEL, A., 66
MANZO, A., 74
MALHOTRA, B.A., 165
MARGINALIZED PEOPLE, 51, 53
MARTIN, D.B., 96, 97
MARTINELLO, M.L., 72
MARTLETT, P.B., 62
MARX, R., 97
MARX, R.W., 104
MASCULINITY, 62
MASKILL, R., 111
MASSIALAS, B.G., 18
MATH: in culturally responsive classrooms, 95–96; in dialogically organized classrooms, 91–92; question-driven conceptual change model for, 121–127; skepticism resources in, 128t
MCBRIDE, S., xii
MCCARTHY, T.L., 82
MCCONAUGHY, F., 109
MCCOURT, F., 36–37
MCKEOWN, M.G., 64
MCLAUGHLIN, M., 55
MCMAHEN, C.L., ix, 6, 10, 16
MCMAHON, S.I., 88, 89, 104
MCPHAIL, J.C., 27
MEANINGFUL CONFLICT, 106
MEHAN, H., 72
MEHRHOF, J.H., 62
MEISTER, C., xii–xiii, 71, 72
MELTZER, J., xiv
MEMOIRS, 137–138
MENKE, D.J., 32

MENTORS, 90–91
MERENLUOTO, K., 123
MESTRE, J., 123
MILES, M., 94
MINORITY STUDENTS: and cultural congruence, 82–86; and cultural dissonance, 78–82
MISHLER, E.G., 73, 74
MITCHELL, M., 29
MODELING, 55
MOJE, E.B., 17, 53, 55, 70
MOLL, L., 70, 73
MONOLOGIC TALK, 80
MONSON, M.P., 49
MONSON, R.J., 49
MONTCLAIR HIGH SCHOOL, 101
MOON, J.S., 124
MOORE, C.J., 29
MOORE, D.W., 1–2, xiii, 26, 27, 68, 70
MORE KNOWLEDGEABLE OTHER, 84
MORRISON, D., 113, 115, 116
MOSES, R., 96
MOSS, B., 25
MOSS, J., 123
MOTIVATION: and adolescent development, 25–26; and adolescent literacy, 26–31; and benefits of question-finding, xv; and conceptual change, 109–110; and content areas, 33–40; content-specific nature of, 33; and curiosity, 25; and epistemic curiosity, 6; influences on, 41–42; in language arts instruction, 34–37; and link to discrepant information and questioning behavior, 6–7; loss of, 29; and question-finding, 33; in question-finding process, 8; resources on, 28t; and situational interest, 27–31, 32
MOTIVATIONAL CONSTRUCT, 25
MOTIVATION/DOMAIN SYNTHESIS, 38
MUELLER, F.L., 18
MUGNY, G., 93, 108
MULTIPLE ENTRY POINT TEACHING, 107–108
MULTIPLE INTELLIGENCES, 108
MURRAY, F.B., 76
MUSIC, 42–43

VOLKMANN, M., 18
VOSNIADOU, S., 123
VYGOTSKY, L.S., 68, 76, 93, 104, 113

W

WADE, R.C., 117
WALKER, A., 82, 134
WALSH, A., 127
WARREN, B., 84, 85, 86
WATAHOMIGIE, L.J., 82
WATTS, M., 111, 127
WE WERE THERE, TOO! (HOOSE), 41
WEB RESOURCES, 141–142
WEBB, D., 99
WEBER, R., 75
WEBSTER, D.M., 109, 110
WEINGARTNER, C., 52
WEISS, J., 29
WELLS, G., 87
WELLS, M.C., 2
WERTSCH, J.V., 89
WEST, L., 110
WHOLE-NUMBER BIAS, 122, 123
WIESEL, E., 135
WIGFIELD, A., 25, 33, 38
WILLIAMS, W., 39, 54, 55
WILLIS, A.I., 41

WILLS, G., 67
WINEBURG, S., 120
WONDER, 133–134
WONDERMENT QUESTIONS: characteristics of, 10*t*; examples of, 16*t*; in multiple perspectives examination, 51; in question-finding process, 9–14; and sociocognitive dimension of literacy, 76
WOODRUM, A., 59
WORLD WAR II, 3–4, 58–59
WRINGER (SPINELLI), 62
WU, L.L., 87

Y

YOLEN, J., 58
YOUNG ADULT LITERATURE, 142–143, 154
YOUNG, J.P., 54, 59, 62

Z

ZEISER, S., 87
ZEVIN, J., 18
ZHOU, Y.-D., 122
ZIMMERMAN, B.J., 25
ZIMMERMAN, R.S., 29
ZITTLEMAN, K., 55
ZONE OF PROXIMAL DEVELOPMENT, 68